Explanation of the Three Fundamental Principles of Islaam

by **Shaykh Muhammad ibn Saalih al-'Uthaymeen**

Prepared by Fahd ibn Naasir ibn Ibraaheem as-Sulaymaan

Translated by Aboo Talhah Daawood ibn Ronald Burbank

ISBN 1 898649 24 3 (paperback)

ISBN 1 898649 25 1 (hardback)

British Library Cataloguing in Publication Data.

A catalogue record for this book is available from the British Library.

First Edition, 1418 AH/1997 CE

Cover design: Abu Yahya

Typeset by: Al-Hidaayah Publishing and Distribution
Printed in Malta by Progress Press Co. Ltd.
Published by: Al-Hidaayah Publishing and Distribution

P.O. Box 3332

Birmingham

United Kingdom

B10 9AW

Tel: 0121 753 1889

Fax: 0121 753 2422

E-mail: ahpd@hidaayah.demon.co.uk

Publisher's Note

All praise is for Allaah, Lord of the worlds. Peace and prayers be upon Muhammad, his family his Companions and all those who follow in their footsteps until the Last Day.

Before you is the English translation of *Sharh Thalaathatul-Usool* by Shaykh Muhammad bin Saalih al-Uthaymeen. This is an explanation of the booklet *Thalaathatul-Usool* ("The Three Principles") by Shaykh Muhammad bin 'Abdul-Wahhaab, *rahimahullaah*, who wrote this in order to convey to every Muslim that which is obligatory upon him to know - infact the "three principles" are based on the three questions that we will all be asked in our graves. As such this book will be beneficial for everyone *inshaallaah*.

The author of the book in hand, Shaykh Muhammad bin Saalih al-Uthaymeen is one of the leading scholars of the Muslim world today. He is actively involved in *da'wah*, both through his lectures and his writings, some of which have been translated into English. Not only is he well known for his vast knowledge but also his ability to teach and convey that knowledge - may Allaah reward him with good.

The following have been added to increase the usefulness of this book:
•For those who wish to memorise the orignal Arabic text of *Thalaathatul-Usool* ("The Three Principles"), the has been included to facilitate that.
• An explanatory translation of the *Aayaat* based on the classical books of *tafseer*.
• A glossary of Arabic terms used in the text.

May Allaah reward all those who helped in the preparation and publication of this work.

Al-Hidaayah Publishing and Distribution

Contents

Transliteration Table

Consonants

ء	'		ض	<u>d</u>
ب	b		ط	<u>t</u>
ت	t		ظ	<u>dh</u>
ث	th		ع	'
ج	j		غ	gh
ح	<u>h</u>		ف	f
خ	kh		ق	q
د	d		ك	k
ذ	dh		ل	l
ر	r		م	m
ز	z		ن	n
س	s		ه	h
ش	sh		و	w
ص	<u>s</u>		ي	y

Vowels

◌َ	a		اَ	aa
◌ُ	u		وُ	oo
◌ِ	i		يِ	ee

5

In the name of Allaah, the Most Merciful, the Bestower of Mercy.

Biography of Shaykh Muḥammad ibn 'Abdul-Wahhaab

He was the *Imaam*, the *Shaykh*, Muḥammad ibn 'Abdul-Wahhaab ibn Sulaymaan ibn 'Alee ibn Muḥammad ibn Aḥmad ibn Raashid ibn Burayd ibn Muḥammad ibn Mushrif ibn 'Umar, from a branch of the tribe of Banoo Tameem.

This scholar was born in the town of 'Unayzah in the year 1115 H in a household known for knowledge, nobility and attachment to the religion. His father was an eminent scholar, and his grandfather was the scholar of Najd in his time. He himself memorized the Qur'aan before reaching the age of ten, and studied *fiqh* (details of Islamic law and practice) of which he learned a great deal. Indeed his father was greatly pleased at the strength of his memory. He devoted a great deal of time to studying the books of *tafseer* (explanation of the Qur'aan) and *hadeeth* (the sayings and actions of the Prophet (ﷺ)). He sought knowledge day and night and he used to memorise the books of the various branches of Islamic knowledge. He also travelled throughout Najd and to Makkah and studied the books of knowledge with the scholars. Then he travelled to al-Madeenah and studied under the scholars there. From them was the great scholar Shaykh 'Abdullah ibn Ibraaheem ash-Shammaree. He also studied under his son who was well versed in the laws of inheritance, Ibraaheem ash-Shammaree, the author of *al-'Adhbul-Faa'id fee Sharḥ Alfiyyatil Faraa'iḍ*. It was they who introduced him to the famous scholar of *hadeeth* Muḥammad Ḥayaat as-Sindee. With him he studied the sciences of *hadeeth* and sciences related to its narrators. He also granted him permission (*ijaazah*) to narrate the source books of *hadeeth*. Shaykh Muḥammad ibn 'Abdul-Wahhaab, may Allaah, the Most High, have mercy upon him, was granted deep understanding and a very high degree of intelligence by Allaah, and he devoted his time to research, study and writing. He used to record and remember whatever points of benefit he came across whilst reading and researching and he never grew tired of writing. Indeed he transcribed many of the works of Ibn Taymiyyah and Ibnul-Qayyim, *raḥimahumullaah*, and many valuable manuscripts written in his own handwriting are preserved in various museums. After the death of his father he himself openly called to the *Salafee da'wah,* to singling out Allaah with all worship and all that is His due, to the rejection of all evil, and he opposed the innovators who directed worship to the graves. He was aided, strengthened and his call to the truth was made widespread through the help of the Aal Sa'ood.

He also published many beneficial works, from them: The outstanding and valuable work entitled: *Kitaabut-tawheed*, which has been printed many times; every time an edition is sold out it is reprinted. Also *Kashfush-Shubuhaat, al-Kabaa'ir, Mukhtasarul-Insaaf, ash-Sharhul-Kabeer, Mukhtasar Zaadil-Ma'aad*, and he has a large number of *Fataawaa* (religious rulings) and treatises, which have been collected under the title: *Majmoo'ah Muallafaat al-Imaam Muhammad ibn 'Abdil-Wahhaab*, under the supervision of Imaam Muhammad ibn Sa'ud University.

He died in the year 1206 H. May Allaah cover him in mercy and reward him well for his services to Islaam and the Muslims. Indeed Allaah is the One who hears and responds to supplications. All praise and thanks are for Allaah - and may Allaah send praises and blessings of peace upon our Prophet Muhammad, upon his family, true followers, and upon all his Companions.

Fahd ibn Naasir as-Sulaymaan

Biography of Shaykh Muḥammad ibn Ṣaaliḥ Al-'Uthaymeen

• His lineage: He is Aboo 'Abdullaah, Muḥammad ibn Ṣaaliḥ ibn Muḥammad ibn 'Uthaymeen al-Wuhaybee at-Tameemee.
• His birth: He was born in the town of 'Unayzah on the 27th of the blessed month of Ramaḍaan in the year 1347 H.
• His early life: He recited the Noble Qur'aan with his maternal grandfather 'Abdur-Raḥmaan ibn Sulaymaan Aal Daamigh, *rahimahullaah*. He first memorised the entire Qur'aan, and then continued to seek knowledge. He learned writing, arithmetic and other disciplines. Also two students of Shaykh 'Abdur-Raḥmaan as-Sa'dee, *rahimahullaah*, took up the task of teaching small children; one of them was Shaykh 'Alee aṣ-Ṣaaliḥee, and the other was Shaykh Muḥammad ibn 'Abdul-'Azeez al-Mutawwa', *rahimahumullaah* under whom Shaykh Ibn 'Uthaymeen studied the abridgement of *al-'Aqeedatul-Waasitiyyah* of Shaykh 'Abdur-Raḥmaan as-Sa'dee, and *Minhaajus-Saalikeen* in *Fiqh*, also by Shaykh 'Abdur-Raḥmaan and *al-Ajroomiyyah* and *al-Alfiyyah*.

He studied *fiqh* and the laws of inheritance with Shaykh 'Abdur-Raḥmaan ibn 'Alee ibn 'Awdaan. With Shaykh 'Abdur-Raḥmaan ibn Naaṣir as-Sa'dee, who is considered his first Shaykh, since he remained with him for some time, he studied *tawḥeed, tafseer, ḥadeeth, fiqh*, the principles of *fiqh* (*uṣoolul-fiqh*), laws of inheritance, sciences of *ḥadeeth*, Arabic Grammar (*naḥw*) and morphology (*ṣarf*).

Indeed the noble Shaykh was highly regarded by Shaykh 'Abdur-Raḥmaan, *rahimahullaah*, and when Shaykh Muḥammad's father moved to Riyadh he initially expressed a desire that his son should do likewise. However Shaykh 'Abdur-Raḥmaan as-Sa'dee, *rahimahullaah*, wrote to him: "This is not possible, rather we hope that Muḥammad will remain with us and benefit." Shaykh Muḥammad, *hafidhahullaah*, himself said: "I was greatly influenced by him in his manner of teaching and presenting knowledge and making it understandable to the students by use of examples and explanations. I was also greatly influenced by his good manners. Indeed Shaykh 'Abdur-Raḥmaan, *rahimahullaah*, had excellent manners and character along with a great deal of knowledge and worship. He would joke pleasantly with the young and laugh with the elders, and he was the most excellent person in manners that I have seen."

He also studied under the eminent and noble Shaykh 'Abdul-'Azeez ibn Baaz who is considered his second Shaykh. He began studying under him by studying *Saheeh al-Bukhaaree*, some of the works of Shaykh-ul-Islaam Ibn Taymiyyah and some of the books of *fiqh*. Shaykh Muhammad says: "I was influenced by Shaykh 'Abdul-'Azeez ibn Baaz, *hafidhahullaah*, with regard to the great attention he gave to *hadeeth*, and I was also influenced by his manners and the way in which he makes himself available to and puts himself at the service of the people."

In the year 1371 H he began teaching in the congregational mosque, and when the educational institutes were opened in Riyadh he joined them in the year 1372 H. The Shaykh, *hafidhahullaah*, says: "I entered the educational institute in the second year and took up the studies upon the advice of Shaykh 'Alee as-Saalihee and having been given permission for that by Shaykh 'Abdur-Rahmaan as-Sa'dee. The institute at that time had two sections: a general section and a higher level. I joined the higher level and it was also the case that anyone who wanted to complete their studies more quickly could do so by studying the following years work in the holiday period, and then take the exams at the start of the following year. If he passed the exam he could then pass on to the next year after that. So by this means I studied in a shorter time period."

After two years he qualified and was given a teaching position in the educational institute of 'Unayzah, whilst continuing his own studies in affiliation with the College of *Sharee'ah*, and continuing his studies under Shaykh 'Abdur-Rahmaan as-Sa'dee.

When the noble Shaykh 'Abdur-Rahmaan as-Sa'dee, *rahimahullaah*, died, Shaykh Muhammad was made *imaam* of the main congregational mosque of 'Unayzah, and took up teaching in the national library of 'Unayzah, in addition to teaching in the educational institute. He later moved to teaching in the College of *Sharee'ah* and the College of *Usoolud-Deen* (the Fundamentals and Principles of the Religion) in the Qaseem branch of Imaam Muhammad ibn Sa'ud Islamic University, which he continues to this day. He is also a member of the council of eminent scholars of the Kingdom of Saudi Arabia, and the Shaykh, *hafidhahullaah*, is very active in calling to Allaah, the Mighty and Majestic, and in enlightening the callers in every place. He has made great efforts in this field.

It is also worthy of mention that the noble Shaykh Muḥammad ibn Ibraaheem, *rahimahullaah*, offered him and encouraged him to take the position of judge. Indeed he even sent out the decision that he had been given the position as head of the *Sharee'ah* court in Aḥsaa, but he requested that he should be excused from taking the position. After a number of requests and personally speaking to him, the Shaykh, *rahimahullaah*, granted him his wish not to take up the post.

His works: He has written around forty different works, some larger books and some treatises. These will, if Allaah wills, be combined in a single collection of his verdicts and treatises.

The Arabic Text of *Thalaathatul-Usool*

بِسْمِ اللَّهِ الرَّحْمَنِ الرَّحِيمِ اِعْلَمْ رَحِمَكَ اللَّهُ ، أَنَّهُ يَجِبُ عَلَيْنَا تَعَلُّمُ أَرْبَعِ مَسَائِلَ ، الأُولَى: العِلْمُ وَهُوَ مَعْرِفَةُ اللَّهِ و مَعْرِفَةُ نَبِيِّهِ و مَعْرِفَةُ دِينِ الإِسْلَامِ بِالأَدِلَّةِ. الثَّانِيَةُ: العَمَلُ بِهِ. الثَّالِثَةُ: الدَّعْوَةُ إِلَيْهِ. الرَّابِعَةُ: الصَّبْرُ عَلَى الأَذَى فِيهِ. وَالدَّلِيلُ قَوْلُهُ تَعَالَى: ﴿ **وَالعَصْرِ إِنَّ الإِنْسَانَ لَفِي خُسْرٍ إِلَّا الَّذِينَ آمَنُوا وَعَمِلُوا الصَّالِحَاتِ وَتَوَاصَوْا بِالحَقِّ وَتَوَاصَوْا بِالصَّبْرِ** ﴾. قَالَ الشَّافِعِيُّ رَحِمَهُ اللَّهُ تَعَالَى: « لَوْ مَا أَنْزَلَ اللَّهُ حُجَّةً عَلَى خَلْقِهِ إِلَّا هَذِهِ السُّورَةَ لَكَفَتْهُمْ ». و قَالَ البُخَارِيُّ رَحِمَهُ اللَّهُ: « بَابٌ العِلْمُ قَبْلَ القَوْلِ وَالعَمَلِ ». وَالدَّلِيلُ قَوْلُهُ تَعَالَى: ﴿ **فَاعْلَمْ أَنَّهُ لَا إِلَهَ إِلَّا اللَّهُ وَاسْتَغْفِرْ لِذَنْبِكَ** ﴾ فَبَدَأَ بِالعِلْمِ قَبْلَ القَوْلِ وَالعَمَلِ. اِعْلَمْ رَحِمَكَ اللَّهُ ، أَنَّهُ يَجِبُ عَلَى كُلِّ مُسْلِمٍ و مُسْلِمَةٍ تَعَلُّمُ ثَلَاثِ هَذِهِ المَسَائِلِ وَالعَمَلُ بِهِنَّ ، الأُولَى: أَنَّ اللَّهَ خَلَقَنَا وَرَزَقَنَا وَلَمْ يَتْرُكْنَا هَمَلاً ، بَلْ أَرْسَلَ إِلَيْنَا رَسُولاً فَمَنْ أَطَاعَهُ دَخَلَ الجَنَّةَ وَمَنْ عَصَاهُ دَخَلَ النَّارَ ، وَالدَّلِيلُ قَوْلُهُ تَعَالَى: ﴿ **إِنَّا أَرْسَلْنَا إِلَيْكُمْ رَسُولاً شَاهِدًا عَلَيْكُمْ كَمَا أَرْسَلْنَا إِلَى فِرْعَوْنَ رَسُولاً فَعَصَى فِرْعَوْنُ الرَّسُولَ فَأَخَذْنَاهُ أَخْذًا وَبِيلاً** ﴾. الثَّانِيَةُ: أَنَّ اللَّهَ لَا يَرْضَى أَنْ يُشْرَكَ مَعَهُ أَحَدٌ فِي عِبَادَتِهِ لَا مَلَكٌ مُقَرَّبٌ ، وَلَا نَبِيٌّ مُرْسَلٌ ، وَالدَّلِيلُ قَوْلُهُ تَعَالَى: ﴿ **وَأَنَّ المَسَاجِدَ لِلَّهِ فَلَا تَدْعُوا مَعَ اللَّهِ أَحَدًا** ﴾. الثَّالِثَةُ: أَنَّ مَنْ أَطَاعَ الرَّسُولَ وَوَحَّدَ اللَّهَ لَا يَجُوزُ لَهُ مُوَالَاةُ مَنْ حَادَّ اللَّهَ وَرَسُولَهُ وَ لَوْ كَانَ أَقْرَبَ قَرِيبٍ وَالدَّلِيلُ قَوْلُهُ

11

تَعَالَى: ﴿ لَا تَجِدُ قَوْمًا يُؤْمِنُونَ بِاللَّهِ وَالْيَوْمِ الْآخِرِ يُوَادُّونَ مَنْ حَادَّ اللَّهَ وَرَسُولَهُ وَلَوْ كَانُوا آبَاءَهُمْ أَوْ أَبْنَاءَهُمْ أَوْ إِخْوَانَهُمْ أَوْ عَشِيرَتَهُمْ أُولَئِكَ كَتَبَ فِي قُلُوبِهِمُ الْإِيمَانَ وَأَيَّدَهُمْ بِرُوحٍ مِنْهُ وَيُدْخِلُهُمْ جَنَّاتٍ تَجْرِي مِنْ تَحْتِهَا الْأَنْهَارُ خَالِدِينَ فِيهَا رَضِيَ اللَّهُ عَنْهُمْ وَرَضُوا عَنْهُ أُولَئِكَ حِزْبُ اللَّهِ أَلَا إِنَّ حِزْبَ اللَّهِ هُمُ الْمُفْلِحُونَ ﴾. اِعْلَمْ أَرْشَدَكَ اللَّهُ لِطَاعَتِهِ أَنَّ الْحَنِيفِيَّةَ مِلَّةَ إِبْرَاهِيمَ أَنْ تَعْبُدَ اللَّهَ وَحْدَهُ مُخْلِصًا لَهُ الدِّينَ ، وَبِذَلِكَ أَمَرَ اللَّهُ جَمِيعَ النَّاسِ وَخَلَقَهُمْ لَهَا كَمَا قَالَ اللَّهُ تَعَالَى: ﴿ وَمَا خَلَقْتُ الْجِنَّ وَالْإِنْسَ إِلَّا لِيَعْبُدُونَ ﴾ وَمَعْنَى يَعْبُدُونَ يُوَحِّدُونَ. وَأَعْظَمُ مَا أَمَرَ اللَّهُ بِهِ التَّوْحِيدُ وَهُوَ إِفْرَادُ اللَّهِ بِالْعِبَادَةِ ، وَأَعْظَمُ مَا نَهَى عَنْهُ الشِّرْكُ وَهُوَ دَعْوَةُ غَيْرِهِ مَعَهُ وَالدَّلِيلُ قَوْلُهُ تَعَالَى: ﴿ وَاعْبُدُوا اللَّهَ وَلَا تُشْرِكُوا بِهِ شَيْئًا ﴾. فَإِذَا قِيلَ لَكَ مَا الْأُصُولُ الثَّلَاثَةُ الَّتِي يَجِبُ عَلَى الْإِنْسَانِ مَعْرِفَتُهَا فَقُلْ مَعْرِفَةُ الْعَبْدِ رَبَّهُ وَدِينَهُ وَنَبِيَّهُ مُحَمَّدًا ﷺ . فَإِذَا قِيلَ لَكَ مَنْ رَبُّكَ فَقُلْ رَبِّيَ اللَّهُ الَّذِي رَبَّانِي وَرَبَّى جَمِيعَ الْعَالَمِينَ بِنِعَمِهِ وَهُوَ مَعْبُودِي لَيْسَ لِي مَعْبُودٌ سِوَاهُ ، وَالدَّلِيلُ قَوْلُهُ تَعَالَى: ﴿ الْحَمْدُ لِلَّهِ رَبِّ الْعَالَمِينَ ﴾ وَكُلُّ مَا سِوَى اللَّهِ عَالَمٌ وَأَنَا وَاحِدٌ مِنْ ذَلِكَ الْعَالَمِ فَإِذَا قِيلَ لَكَ بِمَ عَرَفْتَ رَبَّكَ؟ فَقُلْ: بِآيَاتِهِ وَمَخْلُوقَاتِهِ وَمِنْ آيَاتِهِ اللَّيْلُ وَالنَّهَارُ وَالشَّمْسُ وَالْقَمَرُ ، وَمِنْ مَخْلُوقَاتِهِ السَّمَوَاتُ السَّبْعُ وَالْأَرَضُونَ السَّبْعُ وَمَنْ فِيهِنَّ وَمَا بَيْنَهُمَا وَالدَّلِيلُ قَوْلُهُ تَعَالَى:

﴿ وَمِنْ آيَاتِهِ اللَّيْلُ وَالنَّهَارُ وَالشَّمْسُ وَالْقَمَرُ لَا تَسْجُدُوا لِلشَّمْسِ وَلَا لِلْقَمَرِ وَاسْجُدُوا لِلَّهِ الَّذِي خَلَقَهُنَّ إِنْ كُنْتُمْ إِيَّاهُ تَعْبُدُونَ ﴾ وَقَوْلُهُ تَعَالَى: ﴿ إِنَّ رَبَّكُمُ اللَّهُ الَّذِي خَلَقَ السَّمَاوَاتِ وَالْأَرْضَ فِي سِتَّةِ أَيَّامٍ ثُمَّ اسْتَوَى عَلَى الْعَرْشِ يُغْشِي اللَّيْلَ النَّهَارَ يَطْلُبُهُ حَثِيثًا وَالشَّمْسَ وَالْقَمَرَ وَالنُّجُومَ مُسَخَّرَاتٍ بِأَمْرِهِ أَلَا لَهُ الْخَلْقُ وَالْأَمْرُ تَبَارَكَ اللَّهُ رَبُّ الْعَالَمِينَ ﴾. وَالرَّبُّ هُوَ الْمَعْبُودُ وَالدَّلِيلُ قَوْلُهُ تَعَالَى: ﴿ يَا أَيُّهَا النَّاسُ اعْبُدُوا رَبَّكُمُ الَّذِي خَلَقَكُمْ وَالَّذِينَ مِنْ قَبْلِكُمْ لَعَلَّكُمْ تَتَّقُونَ الَّذِي جَعَلَ لَكُمُ الْأَرْضَ فِرَاشًا وَالسَّمَاءَ بِنَاءً وَأَنْزَلَ مِنَ السَّمَاءِ مَاءً فَأَخْرَجَ بِهِ مِنَ الثَّمَرَاتِ رِزْقًا لَكُمْ فَلَا تَجْعَلُوا لِلَّهِ أَنْدَادًا وَأَنْتُمْ تَعْلَمُونَ ﴾. قَالَ ابْنُ كَثِيرٍ رَحِمَهُ اللَّهُ تَعَالَى » الْخَالِقُ لِهَذِهِ الْأَشْيَاءِ هُوَ الْمُسْتَحِقُّ لِلْعِبَادَةِ «.

وَأَنْوَاعُ الْعِبَادَةِ الَّتِي أَمَرَ اللَّهُ بِهَا مِثْلُ الْإِسْلَامِ ، وَالْإِيمَانِ ، وَالْإِحْسَانِ ، وَمِنْهُ الدُّعَاءُ وَالْخَوْفُ ، وَالرَّجَاءُ ، وَالتَّوَكُّلُ ، وَالرَّغْبَةُ ، وَالرَّهْبَةُ ، وَالْخُشُوعُ ، وَالْخَشْيَةُ وَالْإِنَابَةُ ، وَالِاسْتِعَانَةُ ، وَالِاسْتِعَاذَةُ ، وَالِاسْتِغَاثَةُ ، وَالذَّبْحُ ، وَالنَّذْرُ وَغَيْرُ ذَلِكَ مِنْ أَنْوَاعِ الْعِبَادَةِ الَّتِي أَمَرَ اللَّهُ بِهَا كُلِّهَا لِلَّهِ تَعَالَى وَالدَّلِيلُ قَوْلُهُ تَعَالَى: ﴿ وَأَنَّ الْمَسَاجِدَ لِلَّهِ فَلَا تَدْعُوا مَعَ اللَّهِ أَحَدًا ﴾ فَمَنْ صَرَفَ مِنْهَا شَيْئًا لِغَيْرِ اللَّهِ فَهُوَ مُشْرِكٌ كَافِرٌ وَالدَّلِيلُ قَوْلُهُ تَعَالَى: ﴿ وَمَنْ يَدْعُ مَعَ اللَّهِ إِلَهًا آخَرَ لَا بُرْهَانَ لَهُ بِهِ فَإِنَّمَا حِسَابُهُ عِنْدَ رَبِّهِ إِنَّهُ لَا يُفْلِحُ الْكَافِرُونَ ﴾ وَفِي

الحَدِيثِ « الدُّعَاءُ مُخُّ العِبَادَةِ » وَالدَّلِيلُ قَوْلُهُ تَعَالَى: ﴿ وَقَالَ رَبُّكُمُ ادْعُونِي أَسْتَجِبْ لَكُمْ إِنَّ الَّذِينَ يَسْتَكْبِرُونَ عَنْ عِبَادَتِي سَيَدْخُلُونَ جَهَنَّمَ دَاخِرِينَ ﴾. وَدَلِيلُ الخَوْفِ قَوْلُهُ تَعَالَى: ﴿ فَلاَ تَخَافُوهُمْ وَخَافُونِ إِنْ كُنْتُمْ مُؤْمِنِينَ ﴾ وَدَلِيلُ الرَّجَاءِ قَوْلُهُ تَعَالَى: ﴿ فَمَنْ كَانَ يَرْجُو لِقَاءَ رَبِّهِ فَلْيَعْمَلْ عَمَلاً صَالِحًا وَلاَيُشْرِكْ بِعِبَادَةِ رَبِّهِ أَحَدًا ﴾ وَدَلِيلُ التَّوَكُّلِ قَوْلُهُ تَعَالَى: ﴿ وَعَلَى اللَّهِ فَتَوَكَّلُوا إِنْ كُنْتُمْ مُؤْمِنِينَ ﴾ وَقال: ﴿ وَمَنْ يَتَوَكَّلْ عَلَى اللَّهِ فَهُوَ حَسْبُهُ ﴾ وَدَلِيلُ الرَّغْبَةِ وَالرَّهْبَةِ وَالخُشُوعِ قَوْلُهُ تَعَالَى: ﴿ إِنَّهُمْ كَانُوا يُسَارِعُونَ فِي الخَيْرَاتِ وَيَدْعُونَنَا رَغَبًا وَرَهَبًا وَكَانُوا لَنَا خَاشِعِينَ ﴾ وَدَلِيلُ الخَشْيَةِ قَوْلُهُ تَعَالَى: ﴿ فَلاَ تَخْشَوْهُمْ وَاخْشَوْنِ ﴾ وَدَلِيلُ الإِنَابَةِ قَوْلُهُ تَعَالَى: ﴿ وَأَنِيبُوا إِلَى رَبِّكُمْ وَأَسْلِمُوا لَهُ ﴾ وَدَلِيلُ الاسْتِعَانَةِ قَوْلُهُ تَعَالَى: ﴿ إِيَّاكَ نَعْبُدُ وَإِيَّاكَ نَسْتَعِينُ ﴾ وَفِي الحَدِيثِ « إِذَا اسْتَعَنْتَ فَاسْتَعِنْ بِاللَّهِ » وَدَلِيلُ الاسْتِعَاذَةِ قَوْلُهُ تَعَالَى: ﴿ قُلْ أَعُوذُ بِرَبِّ الفَلَقِ ﴾ و ﴿ قُلْ أَعُوذُ بِرَبِّ النَّاسِ ﴾ وَدَلِيلُ الاسْتِغَاثَةِ قَوْلُهُ تَعَالَى: ﴿ إِذْ تَسْتَغِيثُونَ رَبَّكُمْ فَاسْتَجَابَ لَكُمْ ﴾ وَدَلِيلُ الذَّبْحِ قَوْلُهُ تَعَالَى: ﴿ قُلْ إِنَّ صَلاَتِي وَنُسُكِي وَمَحْيَايَ وَمَمَاتِي لِلَّهِ رَبِّ العَالَمِينَ لاَ شَرِيكَ لَهُ ﴾ الآيَةُ، وَمِنَ السُّنَّةِ « لَعَنَ اللَّهُ مَنْ ذَبَحَ لِغَيْرِ اللَّهِ ». وَدَلِيلُ النَّذْرِ قَوْلُهُ تَعَالَى: ﴿ يُوفُونَ بِالنَّذْرِ

وَيَخَافُونَ يَوْمًا كَانَ شَرُّهُ مُسْتَطِيرًا ﴾ الأَصْلُ الثَّانِي: مَعْرِفَةُ دِينِ الإِسْلَامِ بِالأَدِلَّةِ وَهُوَ الاسْتِسْلَامُ لِلَّهِ بِالتَّوْحِيدِ وَالانْقِيَادُ لَهُ بِالطَّاعَةِ وَالبَرَاءَةُ مِنَ الشِّرْكِ وَأَهْلِهِ. وَهُوَ ثَلَاثُ مَرَاتِبَ: الإِسْلَامُ، وَالإِيمَانُ، وَالإِحْسَانُ، وَكُلُّ مَرْتَبَةٍ لَهَا أَرْكَانٌ فَأَرْكَانُ الإِسْلَامِ خَمْسَةٌ شَهَادَةُ أَنْ لَا إِلَهَ إِلَّا اللَّهُ وَأَنَّ مُحَمَّدًا رَسُولُ اللَّهِ وَإِقَامُ الصَّلَاةِ، وَإِيتَاءُ الزَّكَاةِ، وَصَوْمُ رَمَضَانَ وَحَجُّ بَيْتِ اللَّهِ الحَرَامِ. فَدَلِيلُ الشَّهَادَةِ قَوْلُهُ تَعَالَى: ﴿ **شَهِدَ اللَّهُ أَنَّهُ لَا إِلَهَ إِلَّا هُوَ وَالمَلَائِكَةُ وَأُوْلُوا العِلْمِ قَائِمًا بِالقِسْطِ لَا إِلَهَ إِلَّا هُوَ العَزِيزُ الحَكِيمُ** ﴾ وَمَعْنَاهَا لَا مَعْبُودَ بِحَقٍّ إِلَّا اللَّهُ «لَا إِلَهَ» نَافِيًا جَمِيعَ مَا يُعْبَدُ مِنْ دُونِ اللَّهِ «إِلَّا اللَّهُ» مُثْبِتًا العِبَادَةَ لِلَّهِ وَحْدَهُ لَا شَرِيكَ لَهُ فِي عِبَادَتِهِ كَمَا أَنَّهُ لَا شَرِيكَ لَهُ فِي مُلْكِهِ. وَتَفْسِيرُهَا الَّذِي يُوَضِّحُهَا قَوْلُهُ تَعَالَى: ﴿ **وَإِذْ قَالَ إِبْرَاهِيمُ لِأَبِيهِ وَقَوْمِهِ إِنَّنِي بَرَاءٌ مِمَّا تَعْبُدُونَ إِلَّا الَّذِي فَطَرَنِي فَإِنَّهُ سَيَهْدِينِ وَجَعَلَهَا كَلِمَةً بَاقِيَةً فِي عَقِبِهِ لَعَلَّهُمْ يَرْجِعُونَ** ﴾ وَقَوْلُهُ: ﴿ **قُلْ يَا أَهْلَ الكِتَابِ تَعَالَوْا إِلَى كَلِمَةٍ سَوَاءٍ بَيْنَنَا وَبَيْنَكُمْ أَلَّا نَعْبُدَ إِلَّا اللَّهَ وَلَا نُشْرِكَ بِهِ شَيْئًا وَلَا يَتَّخِذَ بَعْضُنَا بَعْضًا أَرْبَابًا مِنْ دُونِ اللَّهِ فَإِنْ تَوَلَّوْا فَقُولُوا اشْهَدُوا بِأَنَّا مُسْلِمُونَ** ﴾ وَدَلِيلُ شَهَادَةِ أَنَّ مُحَمَّدًا رَسُولُ اللَّهِ قَوْلُهُ تَعَالَى: ﴿ **لَقَدْ جَاءَكُمْ رَسُولٌ مِنْ أَنْفُسِكُمْ عَزِيزٌ عَلَيْهِ مَاعَنِتُّمْ حَرِيصٌ عَلَيْكُمْ بِالمُؤْمِنِينَ رَؤُوفٌ رَحِيمٌ** ﴾ وَمَعْنَى شَهَادَةِ أَنَّ مُحَمَّدًا رَسُولُ اللَّهِ: طَاعَتُهُ فِيمَا أَمَرَ وَتَصْدِيقُهُ فِيمَا أَخْبَرَ

، وَاجْتِنَابُ مَا نَهَى عَنْهُ وَزَجَرَ ، وَأَلَّا يُعْبَدَ اللَّهُ إِلَّا بِمَا شَرَعَ. وَدَلِيلُ الصَّلَاةِ وَالزَّكَاةِ وَتَفْسِيرِ التَّوْحِيدِ قَوْلُهُ تَعَالَى: ﴿ وَمَا أُمِرُوا إِلَّا لِيَعْبُدُوا اللَّهَ مُخْلِصِينَ لَهُ الدِّينَ حُنَفَاءَ وَيُقِيمُوا الصَّلَاةَ وَيُؤْتُوا الزَّكَاةَ وَذَلِكَ دِينُ الْقَيِّمَةِ ﴾ وَدَلِيلُ الصِّيَامِ قَوْلُهُ تَعَالَى: ﴿ يَا أَيُّهَا الَّذِينَ آمَنُوا كُتِبَ عَلَيْكُمُ الصِّيَامُ كَمَا كُتِبَ عَلَى الَّذِينَ مِنْ قَبْلِكُمْ لَعَلَّكُمْ تَتَّقُونَ ﴾ وَدَلِيلُ الْحَجِّ قَوْلُهُ تَعَالَى: ﴿ وَلِلَّهِ عَلَى النَّاسِ حِجُّ الْبَيْتِ مَنِ اسْتَطَاعَ إِلَيْهِ سَبِيلًا وَمَنْ كَفَرَ فَإِنَّ اللَّهَ غَنِيٌّ عَنِ الْعَالَمِينَ ﴾ الْمَرْتَبَةُ الثَّانِيَةُ: الْإِيمَانُ وَهُوَ بِضْعٌ وَسَبْعُونَ شُعْبَةً فَأَعْلَاهَا قَوْلُ لَا إِلَهَ إِلَّا اللَّهُ وَأَدْنَاهَا إِمَاطَةُ الْأَذَى عَنِ الطَّرِيقِ ، وَالْحَيَاءُ شُعْبَةٌ مِنَ الْإِيمَانِ وَأَرْكَانُهُ سِتَّةٌ أَنْ تُؤْمِنَ بِاللَّهِ وَمَلَائِكَتِهِ وَكُتُبِهِ وَرُسُلِهِ وَالْيَوْمِ الْآخِرِ وَ تُؤْمِنَ بِالْقَدَرِ خَيْرِهِ وَشَرِّهِ وَالدَّلِيلُ عَلَى هَذِهِ الْأَرْكَانِ السِّتَّةِ قَوْلُهُ تَعَالَى: ﴿ لَيْسَ الْبِرَّ أَنْ تُوَلُّوا وُجُوهَكُمْ قِبَلَ الْمَشْرِقِ وَالْمَغْرِبِ وَلَكِنَّ الْبِرَّ مَنْ آمَنَ بِاللَّهِ وَالْيَوْمِ الْآخِرِ وَالْمَلَائِكَةِ وَالْكِتَابِ وَالنَّبِيِّينَ ﴾ وَدَلِيلُ الْقَدَرِ قَوْلُهُ تَعَالَى: ﴿ إِنَّا كُلَّ شَيْءٍ خَلَقْنَاهُ بِقَدَرٍ ﴾ الْمَرْتَبَةُ الثَّالِثَةُ الْإِحْسَانُ رُكْنٌ وَاحِدٌ وَهُوَ أَنْ تَعْبُدَ اللَّهَ كَأَنَّكَ تَرَاهُ فَإِنْ لَمْ تَكُنْ تَرَاهُ فَإِنَّهُ يَرَاكَ وَالدَّلِيلُ قَوْلُهُ تَعَالَى: ﴿ إِنَّ اللَّهَ مَعَ الَّذِينَ اتَّقَوْا وَالَّذِينَ هُمْ مُحْسِنُونَ ﴾ وَقَوْلُهُ: ﴿ وَتَوَكَّلْ عَلَى الْعَزِيزِ الرَّحِيمِ الَّذِي يَرَاكَ حِينَ تَقُومُ وَتَقَلُّبَكَ فِي السَّاجِدِينَ إِنَّهُ هُوَ السَّمِيعُ الْعَلِيمُ ﴾ وَقَوْلُهُ:

16

وَمَاتَكُوْنُ فِي شَأْنٍ وَمَاتَتْلُوْ مِنْهُ مِنْ قُرْآنٍ وَلَا تَعْمَلُوْنَ مِنْ عَمَلٍ إِلَّا كُنَّا عَلَيْكُمْ شُهُوْدًا إِذْ تُفِيْضُوْنَ فِيْهِ ﴿ الآيَةُ. وَالدَّلِيْلُ مِنَ السُّنَّةِ حَدِيْثُ جِبْرَائِيْلَ الْمَشْهُوْرُ عَنْ عُمَرَ رَضِيَ اللَّهُ عَنْهُ قَالَ: بَيْنَمَا نَحْنُ جُلُوْسٌ عِنْدَ رَسُوْلِ اللَّهِ صَلَّى اللَّهُ عَلَيْهِ وَسَلَّمَ ذَاتَ يَوْمٍ إِذْ طَلَعَ عَلَيْنَا رَجُلٌ شَدِيْدُ بَيَاضِ الثِّيَابِ شَدِيْدُ سَوَادِ الشَّعْرِ لَا يُرَى عَلَيْهِ أَثَرُ السَّفَرِ وَلَا يَعْرِفُهُ مِنَّا أَحَدٌ ، حَتَّى جَلَسَ إِلَى النَّبِيِّ صَلَّى اللَّهُ عَلَيْهِ وَسَلَّمَ فَأَسْنَدَ رُكْبَتَيْهِ إِلَى رُكْبَتَيْهِ وَوَضَعَ كَفَّيْهِ عَلَى فَخِذَيْهِ وَقَالَ: يَا مُحَمَّدُ أَخْبِرْنِي عَنِ الإِسْلَامِ ، فَقَالَ رَسُوْلُ اللَّهِ صَلَّى اللَّهُ عَلَيْهِ وَسَلَّمَ: "الإِسْلَامُ أَنْ تَشْهَدَ أَنْ لَا إِلَهَ إِلَّا اللَّهُ وَأَنَّ مُحَمَّدًا رَسُوْلُ اللَّهِ ، وَتُقِيْمَ الصَّلَاةَ ، وَتُؤْتِيَ الزَّكَاةَ ، وَتَصُوْمَ رَمَضَانَ ، وَتَحُجَّ الْبَيْتَ إِنِ اسْتَطَعْتَ إِلَيْهِ سَبِيْلًا" قَالَ: صَدَقْتَ ، فَعَجِبْنَا لَهُ يَسْأَلُهُ وَيُصَدِّقُهُ. قَالَ: فَأَخْبِرْنِي عَنِ الإِيْمَانِ ، قَالَ: "أَنْ تُؤْمِنَ بِاللَّهِ وَمَلَائِكَتِهِ وَكُتُبِهِ وَرُسُلِهِ وَالْيَوْمِ الآخِرِ ، وَ تُؤْمِنَ بِالْقَدَرِ خَيْرِهِ وَشَرِّهِ ، قَالَ: صَدَقْتَ ، قَالَ: فَأَخْبِرْنِي عَنِ الإِحْسَانِ ، قَالَ: "أَنْ تَعْبُدَ اللَّهَ كَأَنَّكَ تَرَاهُ ، فَإِنْ لَمْ تَكُنْ تَرَاهُ فَإِنَّهُ يَرَاكَ ، قَالَ: فَأَخْبِرْنِي عَنِ السَّاعَةِ ، قَالَ: "مَا الْمَسْؤُوْلُ عَنْهَا بِأَعْلَمَ مِنَ السَّائِلِ ، قَالَ: فَأَخْبِرْنِي عَنْ أَمَارَاتِهَا ، قَالَ: "أَنْ تَلِدَ الأَمَةُ رَبَّتَهَا ، وَأَنْ تَرَى الْحُفَاةَ الْعُرَاةَ الْعَالَةَ رِعَاءَ الشَّاءِ يَتَطَاوَلُوْنَ فِي الْبُنْيَانِ" قَالَ: فَمَضَى فَلَبِثْنَا مَلِيًّا فَقَالَ: "يَا عُمَرُ أَتَدْرِي مَنِ السَّائِلُ"؟ قُلْتُ: اللَّهُ وَرَسُوْلُهُ أَعْلَمُ ،

قَالَ: "هَذَا جِبْرِيلُ أَتَاكُمْ يُعَلِّمُكُمْ أَمْرَ دِينِكُمْ". الأَصْلُ الثَّالِثُ: مَعْرِفَةُ نَبِيِّكُمْ مُحَمَّدٍ ﷺ وَهُوَ مُحَمَّدُ بْنُ عَبْدِ اللَّهِ بْنِ عَبْدِ المُطَّلِبِ بْنِ هَاشِمٍ وَهَاشِمٌ مِنْ قُرَيْشٍ وَقُرَيْشٌ مِنَ العَرَبِ وَالعَرَبُ مِنْ ذُرِّيَّةِ إِسْمَاعِيلَ بْنِ إِبْرَاهِيمَ الخَلِيلِ عَلَيْهِ وَعَلَى نَبِيِّنَا أَفْضَلُ الصَّلاةِ وَالسَّلامِ. وَلَهُ مِنَ العُمْرِ ثَلاثٌ وَسِتُّونَ سَنَةً أَرْبَعُونَ قَبْلَ النُّبُوَّةِ وَثَلاثٌ وَعِشْرُونَ نَبِيًّا وَرَسُولاً، نُبِّئَ بِاقْرَأْ وَأُرْسِلَ بِالمُدَّثِّرِ وَبَلَدُهُ مَكَّةُ وَهَاجَرَ إِلَى المَدِينَةِ. بَعَثَهُ اللَّهُ بِالنَّذَارَةِ عَنِ الشِّرْكِ وَيَدْعُو إِلَى التَّوْحِيدِ وَالدَّلِيلُ قَوْلُهُ تَعَالَى: ﴿ يَا أَيُّهَا المُدَّثِّرُ قُمْ فَأَنْذِرْ وَرَبَّكَ فَكَبِّرْ وَثِيَابَكَ فَطَهِّرْ وَالرُّجْزَ فَاهْجُرْ وَلا تَمْنُنْ تَسْتَكْثِرْ وَلِرَبِّكَ فَاصْبِرْ ﴾ وَمَعْنَى ﴿ قُمْ فَأَنْذِرْ ﴾ يُنْذِرُ عَنِ الشِّرْكِ وَيَدْعُو إِلَى التَّوْحِيدِ ﴿ وَرَبَّكَ فَكَبِّرْ ﴾ أَيْ عَظِّمْهُ بِالتَّوْحِيدِ ﴿ وَثِيَابَكَ فَطَهِّرْ ﴾ أَيْ طَهِّرْ أَعْمَالَكَ عَنِ الشِّرْكِ ﴿ وَالرُّجْزَ فَاهْجُرْ ﴾ الرُّجْزُ الأَصْنَامُ وَهَجْرُهَا – تَرْكُهَا وَالبَرَاءَةُ مِنْهَا وَأَهْلِهَا. أَخَذَ عَلَى هَذَا عَشَرَ سِنِينَ يَدْعُو إِلَى التَّوْحِيدِ وَبَعْدَ العَشْرِ عُرِجَ بِهِ إِلَى السَّمَاءِ. وَ فُرِضَتْ عَلَيْهِ الصَّلَوَاتُ الخَمْسُ وَصَلَّى فِي مَكَّةَ ثَلاثَ سِنِينَ وَبَعْدَهَا أُمِرَ بِالهِجْرَةِ إِلَى المَدِينَةِ. وَالهِجْرَةُ: الانْتِقَالُ مِنْ بَلَدِ الشِّرْكِ إِلَى بَلَدِ الإِسْلامِ وَالهِجْرَةُ فَرِيضَةٌ عَلَى هَذِهِ الأُمَّةِ مِنْ بَلَدِ الشِّرْكِ إِلَى بَلَدِ الإِسْلامِ وَهِيَ بَاقِيَةٌ إِلَى أَنْ تَقُومَ السَّاعَةُ وَالدَّلِيلُ قَوْلُهُ تَعَالَى: ﴿ إِنَّ الَّذِينَ تَوَفَّاهُمُ المَلائِكَةُ ظَالِمِي أَنْفُسِهِمْ قَالُوا فِيمَ كُنْتُمْ قَالُوا كُنَّا مُسْتَضْعَفِينَ فِي الأَرْضِ

18

قَالُوا أَلَمْ تَكُنْ أَرْضُ اللَّهِ وَاسِعَةً فَتُهَاجِرُوا فِيهَا فَأُولَٰئِكَ مَأْوَاهُمْ جَهَنَّمُ وَسَاءَتْ مَصِيرًا إِلَّا الْمُسْتَضْعَفِينَ مِنَ الرِّجَالِ وَالنِّسَاءِ وَالْوِلْدَانِ لَا يَسْتَطِيعُونَ حِيلَةً وَلَا يَهْتَدُونَ سَبِيلًا فَأُولَٰئِكَ عَسَى اللَّهُ أَنْ يَعْفُوَ عَنْهُمْ وَكَانَ اللَّهُ عَفُوًّا غَفُورًا ﴾ وَقَوْلُهُ تَعَالَى: ﴿ يَاعِبَادِيَ الَّذِينَ آمَنُوا إِنَّ أَرْضِي وَاسِعَةٌ فَإِيَّايَ فَاعْبُدُونِ ﴾ قَالَ الْبَغَوِيُّ رَحِمَهُ اللَّهُ تَعَالَى: سَبَبُ نُزُولِ هَذِهِ الْآيَةِ فِي الْمُسْلِمِينَ الَّذِينَ بِمَكَّةَ لَمْ يُهَاجِرُوا نَادَاهُمُ اللَّهُ بِاسْمِ الْإِيمَانِ وَالدَّلِيلُ عَلَى الْهِجْرَةِ مِنَ السُّنَّةِ قَوْلُهُ ﷺ: " لَا تَنْقَطِعُ الْهِجْرَةُ حَتَّى تَنْقَطِعَ التَّوْبَةُ وَلَا تَنْقَطِعُ التَّوْبَةُ حَتَّى تَطْلُعَ الشَّمْسُ مِنْ مَغْرِبِهَا " فَلَمَّا اسْتَقَرَّ بِالْمَدِينَةِ أُمِرَ بِبَقِيَّةِ شَرَائِعِ الْإِسْلَامِ مِثْلُ الصَّلَاةِ وَالزَّكَاةِ، وَالْحَجِّ، وَالْجِهَادِ، وَالْأَذَانِ، وَالْأَمْرِ بِالْمَعْرُوفِ وَالنَّهْيِ عَنِ الْمُنْكَرِ وَغَيْرِ ذَلِكَ مِنْ شَرَائِعِ الْإِسْلَامِ أَخَذَ عَلَى هَذَا عَشَرَ سِنِينَ وَبَعْدَهَا تُوُفِّيَ صَلَوَاتُ اللَّهِ وَسَلَامُهُ عَلَيْهِ وَدِينُهُ بَاقٍ، وَهَذَا دِينُهُ لَا خَيْرَ إِلَّا دَلَّ الْأُمَّةَ عَلَيْهِ وَلَا شَرَّ إِلَّا حَذَّرَهَا مِنْهُ وَالْخَيْرُ الَّذِي دَلَّ عَلَيْهِ: التَّوْحِيدُ وَجَمِيعُ مَا يُحِبُّهُ اللَّهُ وَيَرْضَاهُ، وَالشَّرُّ الَّذِي حَذَّرَ مِنْهُ: الشِّرْكُ وَجَمِيعُ مَا يَكْرَهُهُ اللَّهُ وَيَأْبَاهُ، بَعَثَهُ اللَّهُ إِلَى النَّاسِ كَافَّةً وَافْتَرَضَ اللَّهُ طَاعَتَهُ عَلَى جَمِيعِ الثَّقَلَيْنِ: الْجِنِّ وَالْإِنْسِ وَالدَّلِيلُ قَوْلُهُ تَعَالَى: ﴿ قُلْ يَا أَيُّهَا النَّاسُ إِنِّي رَسُولُ اللَّهِ إِلَيْكُمْ جَمِيعًا ﴾. وَأَكْمَلَ اللَّهُ بِهِ الدِّينَ وَالدَّلِيلُ قَوْلُهُ تَعَالَى: ﴿ الْيَوْمَ أَكْمَلْتُ لَكُمْ دِينَكُمْ وَأَتْمَمْتُ عَلَيْكُمْ نِعْمَتِي وَرَضِيتُ لَكُمْ

الإِسْلَامَ دِينًا ۞ وَالدَّلِيلُ عَلَى مَوْتِهِ ﷺ قَوْلُهُ تَعَالَى: ﴿ إِنَّكَ مَيِّتٌ وَإِنَّهُمْ مَيِّتُونَ ثُمَّ إِنَّكُمْ يَوْمَ الْقِيَامَةِ عِنْدَ رَبِّكُمْ تَخْتَصِمُونَ ﴾ وَالنَّاسُ إِذَا مَاتُوا يُبْعَثُونَ وَالدَّلِيلُ قَوْلُهُ تَعَالَى: ﴿ مِنْهَا خَلَقْنَاكُمْ وَفِيهَا نُعِيدُكُمْ وَمِنْهَا نُخْرِجُكُمْ تَارَةً أُخْرَى ﴾ وَقَوْلُهُ تَعَالَى: ﴿ وَاللَّهُ أَنْبَتَكُمْ مِنَ الْأَرْضِ نَبَاتًا ثُمَّ يُعِيدُكُمْ فِيهَا وَيُخْرِجُكُمْ إِخْرَاجًا ﴾ وَبَعْدَ الْبَعْثِ مُحَاسَبُونَ وَمُجْزِيُّونَ بِأَعْمَالِهِمْ وَالدَّلِيلُ قَوْلُهُ تَعَالَى: ﴿ لِيَجْزِيَ الَّذِينَ أَسَاؤُوا بِمَا عَمِلُوا وَيَجْزِيَ الَّذِينَ أَحْسَنُوا بِالْحُسْنَى ﴾ وَمَنْ كَذَّبَ بِالْبَعْثِ كَفَرَ وَالدَّلِيلُ قَوْلُهُ تَعَالَى: ﴿ زَعَمَ الَّذِينَ كَفَرُوا أَنْ لَنْ يُبْعَثُوا قُلْ بَلَى وَرَبِّي لَتُبْعَثُنَّ ثُمَّ لَتُنَبَّؤُنَّ بِمَا عَمِلْتُمْ وَذَلِكَ عَلَى اللهِ يَسِيرٌ ﴾ وَأَرْسَلَ اللهُ جَمِيعَ الرُّسُلِ مُبَشِّرِينَ وَمُنْذِرِينَ وَالدَّلِيلُ قَوْلُهُ تَعَالَى: ﴿ رُسُلًا مُبَشِّرِينَ وَمُنْذِرِينَ لِئَلَّا يَكُونَ لِلنَّاسِ عَلَى اللهِ حُجَّةٌ بَعْدَ الرُّسُلِ ﴾ وَأَوَّلُهُمْ نُوحٌ عَلَيْهِ السَّلَامُ وَآخِرُهُمْ مُحَمَّدٌ ﷺ وَالدَّلِيلُ عَلَى أَنَّ أَوَّلَهُمْ نُوحٌ عَلَيْهِ السَّلَامُ قَوْلُهُ تَعَالَى: ﴿ إِنَّا أَوْحَيْنَا إِلَيْكَ كَمَا أَوْحَيْنَا إِلَى نُوحٍ وَالنَّبِيِّينَ مِنْ بَعْدِهِ ﴾ وَكُلُّ أُمَّةٍ بَعَثَ اللهُ إِلَيْهَا رَسُولًا مِنْ نُوحٍ إِلَى مُحَمَّدٍ يَأْمُرُهُمْ بِعِبَادَةِ اللهِ وَحْدَهُ وَيَنْهَاهُمْ عَنْ عِبَادَةِ الطَّاغُوتِ وَالدَّلِيلُ قَوْلُهُ تَعَالَى: ﴿ وَلَقَدْ بَعَثْنَا فِي كُلِّ أُمَّةٍ رَسُولًا أَنِ اعْبُدُوا اللَّهَ وَاجْتَنِبُوا الطَّاغُوتَ ﴾ وَافْتَرَضَ اللهُ عَلَى جَمِيعِ الْعِبَادِ الْكُفْرَ بِالطَّاغُوتِ وَالْإِيمَانَ بِاللهِ قَالَ ابْنُ الْقَيِّمِ رَحِمَهُ اللَّهُ تَعَالَى: الطَّاغُوتُ

مَا تَجَاوَزَ بِهِ الْعَبْدُ حَدَّهُ مِنْ مَعْبُودٍ أَوْ مَتْبُوعٍ أَوْ مُطَاعٍ وَالطَّوَاغِيتُ كَثِيرَةٌ وَرُؤُوسُهُمْ خَمْسَةٌ: إِبْلِيسُ لَعَنَهُ اللهُ وَمَنْ عُبِدَ وَهُوَ رَاضٍ، وَمَنْ دَعَا النَّاسَ إِلَى عِبَادَةِ نَفْسِهِ وَمَنِ ادَّعَى شَيْئاً مِنْ عِلْمِ الْغَيْبِ وَمَنْ حَكَمَ بِغَيْرِ مَا أَنْزَلَ اللهُ: وَالدَّلِيْلُ قَوْلُهُ تَعَالَى: ﴿ لَا إِكْرَاهَ فِي الدِّين قَدْ تَبَيَّنَ الرُّشْدُ مِنَ الغَيِّ فَمَنْ يَكْفُرْ بِالطَّاغُوتِ وَيُؤْمِنْ بِاللَّه فقد اسْتَمْسَكَ بِالْعُرْوَةِ الوُثْقَى ﴾ وَهَذَا مَعْنَى لَا إِلَهَ إِلَّا اللهُ. وَفِي الْحَدِيْثِ: " رَأْسُ الأَمْرِ الإِسْلَامُ وَعَمُودُهُ الصَّلَاةُ وَذِرْوَةُ سَنَامِهِ الجِهَادُ فِي سَبِيلِ اللَّهِ " وَاللَّهُ أَعْلَمُ وَصَلَّى اللَّهُ عَلَى مُحَمَّدٍ وَآلِهِ وَصَحْبِهِ وَسَلَّمَ.

The English Translation of *Thalaathatul-Usool*

In the name of Allaah, the Most-Merciful, the Bestower of Mercy.

Know, may Allaah have mercy upon you, that it is obligatory upon you to have knowledge of four matters:
> (i) Knowledge (*al-'Ilm*), which is knowledge and awareness of Allaah, and knowledge of His Prophet,
> and knowledge of the religion of Islaam with the proofs.
> (ii) Action upon that.
> (iii) Calling to that.
> (iv) Patiently persevering and bearing any harm encountered upon that way.

The proof is the saying of Allaah, the Most High: **"By time, mankind is in loss, except for those who truly believe and worship Allaah alone, and do right-eous deeds, performing that which is obligatory upon them and avoiding that which they are forbidden, and enjoin one another with patient perseverance upon obedience to Allaah and in facing harm and trials."** [Soorah al-'Asr (103)]

Ash-Shaafi'ee, may Allaah, the Most High, have mercy upon him, said: "If Allaah had sent down to His creation no other proof besides this *Soorah*, it would have been sufficient for them."

Al-Bukhaaree may Allaah have mercy upon him, said:"Chapter: Knowledge precedes speech and action' and the proof is the saying of Allaah, the Most High, **"*Know* that none has the right to be worshipped except Allaah, and ask forgiveness of your Lord for your sins."** [Soorah Muhammad (47):19]. So He began by mentioning knowledge before speech or action.'

Know, may Allaah have mercy upon you, that it is obligatory upon every Muslim, male and female, to learn and act upon the following three matters:

THE FIRST: That Allaah created us and provided sustenance for us, and He did not leave us without a purpose rather He sent Messengers to us. So whoever obeys him will enter Paradise, and whoever rejects and disobeys him will enter the Fire, and the proof is the Saying of the Most High: **"We sent a Messenger to you, O people, as a witness in favour of you or against you on the Day of Resurrection, just as We sent a Messenger to the Pharaoh. But the Pharaoh denied**

and rejected the Messenger, so We seized him with a severe punishment."
[Soorah al-Muzzammil (73):16]

THE SECOND: Allaah is not pleased that anyone should be made a sharer in worship along with Him, neither any angel brought near, nor any prophet sent as a messenger, and the proof is the Saying of Allaah, the Most High, **"And the places of worship are for Allaah alone, so do not invoke anyone along with Allaah."** [Soorah al-Jinn (72):18]

THE THIRD: That whoever is obedient to the Messenger and singles out Allaah with all worship, upon *tawheed*, then it is not permissible for him to have friend-ship and alliance with those who oppose Allaah and His Messenger, even if they are those most closely related to him, and the proof is the Saying of Allaah, the Most High: **"You will not find a people who believe in Allaah and the Last Day loving those who oppose Allaah and His Messenger, even if they are their fathers, or their sons, or their brothers, or their kinsfolk. Rather Allaah has decreed true Faith for their hearts, and strengthened them with proof, light and guidance from Him; and He will enter them into the gardens of Paradise beneath whose trees rivers will flow, and they will dwell therein forever. Allaah is pleased with them and they with Him. They are the party of Allaah. Indeed the party of Allaah are the successful."** [Soorah al-Mujaadilah (58):22]

Know, may Allaah direct you to obedience to Him, that the true and straight Reli-gion, the way of Ibraaheem is that you worship Allaah alone making the Religion purely and sincerely for Him. This is what Allaah commanded all of the people with, and it was for this that He created them. Allaah, the Most High, says: **"I did not create *jinn* and mankind except that they should worship Me"** [Soorah adh-Dhaariyaat (51):56] and the meaning of *worship* (*'ibaadah*) here is to single Allaah out with all worship (*tawheed*). And the greatest of all that Allaah has commanded is *tawheed* which is to single out Allaah with all worship. The most serious thing that He forbade is *shirk*, which is to invoke others besides Him, along with Him. The proof is His Saying, the Most High: **"Worship Allaah alone, making all worship purely for Him, and do not associate anything in worship along with Him."** [Soorah an-Nisaa (4):36]

So if it is said to you: What are the three principles which a person must know? then say the servants knowledge of His Lord and His Religion (*Deen*), and his Prophet Muhammad (ﷺ).

[THE FIRST PRINCIPLE]

So if it is said to you: 'Who is your Lord?' Then say: 'My Lord is Allaah, who has nurtured me and all of creation with His favours and blessings, He is the one whom I worship, and there is no other whom I worship besides Him.' The proof is the Saying of Allaah, the Most High: **"All praise is for Allaah, the Lord of all creation"** [Soorah al-Faatihah (1):1]. Everything besides Allaah is a created being and I am one of the creation.

So if it is said to you: 'How did you arrive at this knowledge of your Lord?' Then say: 'Through His signs and those things which He has created; and from his signs are the night and the day, the sun and the moon; and from that which He has created are the seven heavens, and the seven earths, and all those within them, and whatever is between them.' The proof is the Saying of Allaah, the Most High: **"And from His signs are the night and the day, and the sun and the moon. Do not prostrate to the sun, nor to the moon, but prostrate to Allaah who created them, if you truly worship Him"** [Soorah Fussilat (41):37] and His, the Most High's Saying: **"Your Lord is Allaah who created the heavens and the earth in six days, then ascended upon the Throne. He causes the night to cover the day which it follows with haste; and the sun, the moon and the stars are subservient and subject to His command. Certainly creation and commandment are His alone. Exalted is Allaah the Lord of all creation."** [Soorah al-A'raaf (7):54]

The Lord is the one who is worshipped, and the proof is the Saying of Allaah, the Most High, **"O mankind, single out your Lord with all worship; He who created you and all those who came before you, so that you may be of those who seek to avoid Allaah's anger and punishment, those whom Allaah is pleased with. He who has made the earth a resting place for you and has made the sky a canopy, and sent down rain from the sky, and brought out with it crops and fruits from the earth as provision for you. So do not set up rivals with Allaah in your worship whilst you know that you have no Lord besides Him."** [Soorah al-Baqarah (2):21-22]

Ibn Katheer, *rahimahullaah,* said: "The creator of these things is the One Who deserves to be worshipped." All the types of worship which Allaah commanded - like Islaam (submission and obedience to Allaah), *eemaan* (true Faith comprising belief of the heart, speech of the tongue and action of the limbs), and *ihsaan* (perfection of worship), and from that is invocation/supplication (*du'aa*), reverential fear (*khawf*), hope and longing (*rajaa*), trust and reliance (*tawakkul*), fervent desire (*raghbah*), dread (*rahbah*), reverence and humility (*khushoo'*), awe (*khashyah*), turning repentantly (*inaabah*), appealing for aid and assistance (*isti'aanah*), seeking refuge (*isti'aadhah*), seeking deliverance and rescue (*istighaathah*), sacrificing (*dhabh*), vows (*nadhr*) and the rest of the types of worship commanded by Allaah, all of them are to be done exclusively for Allaah, the Most High. The proof for this is the Saying of Him, the Most High: **"And the places of Prayer are for Allaah alone, so do not invoke anyone along with Allaah"** [Soorah al-Jinn (72):18].

Anyone who directs any part of that to anything besides Allaah, then he is a *mushrik* (associationist), an unbeliever (*kaafir*), and the proof is the Saying of Him, the Most High, **"And whoever worships along with Allaah any other object of worship has no proof for that; his reckoning will be with his Lord. Indeed the unbelievers will never prosper"** [Soorah al-Mu'minoon (23):117]. In the *hadeeth* there occurs: *"Invocation is the core of worship."* And the evidence for this is the Saying of Allaah, the Most High: **"Your Lord says: O people, invoke Me and supplicate to Me making your worship sincerely for Me alone, and I will answer you, and pardon you and have mercy upon you. Indeed those who disdain to worship Me alone will enter Hell-Fire in disgrace"** [Soorah Ghaafir (40):60].

The evidence for reverential fear (*khawf*) is the Saying of Allaah, the Most High: **"So do not fear them, but fear Me and beware of disobeying Me, if you are truly Believers"** [Soorah Aal-'Imraan (3):175].

The evidence for hope and longing (*ar-rajaa*) is the Saying of Allaah the Most High: **"So whoever hopes to see His Lord and be rewarded by Him, then let him make his worship correct and make it purely and sincerely for Him; and let him not make any share of it for anyone other than Him"** [Soorah al-Kahf (18):110].

The evidence for trust and reliance (*at-tawakkul*) is the Saying of Allaah, the Most High, **"And place your reliance and trust in Allaah if you are true Believers"** [Soorah al-Maa'idah (5):23] and He said: **"And whoever places his reliance and trust in Allaah then He will suffice him"** [Soorah at-Talaaq (65):3].

The evidence for the fervent desire (*ar-raghbah*), dread (*ar-rahbah*) and reverence and humility (*al-khushoo'*) is the Saying of Allaah, the Most High: **"They used to hasten to acts of devotion and obedience to Allaah, and they used to worship Allaah upon love and desire, and upon fear, and were reverent and humble before Allaah"** [Soorah al-Ambiyaa (21):90].

The evidence for awe/dread (*al-khashyah*) is the Saying of Allaah, the Most High: **"So do not have awe of them, but have awe of Me"** [Soorah al-Maa'idah (5):3].

The evidence for turning repentantly (*al-inaabah*) is the Saying of Allaah, the Most High: **"So turn, O you people, repentantly and obediently to your Lord, and submit obediently to Him"** [Soorah az-Zumar (39):54].

The evidence for appealing for aid and assistance (*al-isti'aanah*) is the Saying of Allaah, the Most High: **"O Allaah You alone we worship, and to You alone we appeal for aid"** [Soorah al-Faatihah (1):5] and in the *hadeeth* there occurs: *"If you seek help, then seek the help of Allaah."* [Reported by at-Tirmidhee and declared *Saheeh* by Shaykh al-Albaanee in *al-Mishkaat* (no.5302)]

The evidence for seeking refuge (*al-isti'aadhah*) is the Saying of Allaah, the Most High: **"Say: I seek refuge with the Lord of the dawn"** [Soorah al-Falaq (113):1] and: **"Say: I seek refuge with the Lord of mankind"** [Soorah an-Naas (114):1].

The evidence for seeking deliverance and rescue (*al-istighaathah*) is the Saying of Allaah, the Most High: **"When you sought aid and deliverance of your Lord and He responded to you"** [Soorah al-Anfaal (8):9].

The evidence for sacrificing (*adh-dhabh*) is the Saying of Allaah, the Most High: **"Say, O Muhammad (ﷺ), indeed my Prayer, my sacrifice, my living and my dying are all purely and solely for Allaah, Lord of all creation. There is no share of any of that for other than him"** [Soorah al-An'aam (6):162-3]. Also the Prophet (ﷺ) said: *"Allaah has cursed anyone who sacrifices for other than Allaah."* [Reported by Muslim (Eng. transl. 3/1093-1094/no.4876)]

The evidence for vows (*an-nadhr*) is the Saying of Allaah, the Most High: **"They fulfil their vows and they fear a day whose evil is widespread"** [Soorah al-Insaan (76):7].

THE SECOND PRINCIPLE

Knowledge of the Religion (*Deen*) of Islaam with the proofs. It is to submit to Allaah with *tawheed*, and to yield obediently to Him, and to free and disassociate oneself from *shirk* and its people. And it is of three levels: Islaam (submission and obedience to Allaah), *eemaan* (true faith comprising belief of the heart, speech of the tongue and action of the limbs), and *ihsaan* (perfection of worship). Each level has its pillars.

[**The first level**] The pillars of Islaam are five: The testification that none has the right to be worshipped except Allaah, and that Muhammad is the Messenger of Allaah; to establish the Prayer; to pay the *zakaat*; to fast Ramadaan; and to make *hajj* to the sacred House of Allaah.

So the proof for the testification (*shahaadah*) is the Saying of Allaah, the Most High, **"Allaah bears witness that none has the right to be worshipped but Him; and likewise the angels and the people of knowledge bear witness: He Who maintains justice, none has the right to be worshipped but Him, the All-Mighty, the All-Wise."** [Soorah Aal-'Imraan (3):18]. Its meaning is that none has the right to be worshipped except Allaah: *"laa ilaaha"* (Nothing has the right to be worshipped besides Allaah), and *"illallaah"* (except Allaah) affirms worship for Allaah alone, and that there is to be no one given any share of His Dominion and Sovereignty.

The explanation which will make it clear is the Saying of Allaah, the Most High, **"And remember when Ibraaheem said to his father and his people: 'I am totally free from everything that you worship except for the one who created me, He will guide me upon the true Religion and the way of right-guidance.' And Allaah made this saying, that none has the right to be worshipped except Allaah, to persist amongst Ibraaheem's progeny, so that they might remember and return to obedience to their Lord, and to worshipping Him alone, and repent from their unbelief and their sins"** [Soorah az-Zukhruf (43):26-28]. And His Saying, **"Say: O People of the Book, come to a word of justice between us, that we will single Allaah out with all worship and will not worship anything besides Him, and will disassociate ourselves from everything that is worshipped besides Him. Nor will we take one another as Lords besides Allaah by obeying one another in that which involves disobedience to Allaah. So if they turn away, then say: 'Bear witness that we are Muslims, submitting to**

Allaah and making our worship purely and sincerely for Him, and not worshipping anything else besides Him'" [Soorah Aal-'Imraan (3):64].

The proof for the testification that Mu<u>h</u>ammad is the Messenger of Allaah, is the Saying of Allaah, the Most High, **"There has indeed come to you Allaah's Messenger, from amongst yourselves and known to you. It grieves him that you should suffer. He is eager and anxious for the guidance of those of you who are astray, and that they should repent and return to the truth, and he is full of compassion and mercy for the Believers"** [Soorah at-Tawbah (9):128]. The meaning of the testification that Mu<u>h</u>ammad is the Messenger of Allaah is: to obey him in whatever he commands; to believe and testify to the truth of everything he informs of; to avoid whatever he forbade and prohibited; and that you worship Allaah only with that which he prescribed.

The evidence for the Prayer (a<u>s</u>-<u>s</u>alaat) and the zakaat, and the explanation of taw<u>h</u>eed is the Saying of Allaah, the Most High, **"And they were not commanded except that they should worship Allaah alone, making their worship and obedience purely for Him, upon the true Religion and free from shirk; and that they should establish the Prayer, and pay the zakaat - and that is the straight and true Religion"** [Soorah al-Bayyinah (98):5].

The evidence for Fasting (<u>s</u>iyaam) is the Saying of Allaah, the Most High, **"O you who believe Fasting is prescribed as an obligation for you as it was prescribed as an obligation for those who came before you, so that you may attain taqwaa (obedience to Allaah and avoidance of whatever He has forbidden)"** [Soorah al-Baqarah (2):183].

The evidence for <u>h</u>ajj is the Saying of Allaah, the Most High, **"And <u>h</u>ajj to Allaah's sacred House is an obligation upon those able to perform it; and whoever refuses and rejects the obligation of <u>h</u>ajj to Allaah's House, then Allaah has no need of him or of any of the creation"** [Soorah Aal-'Imraan (3):97].

The second level: Eemaan - and it has seventy and odd branches, the highest of them is the saying that 'none has the right to be worshipped except Allaah' (laa ilaaha illallaah), the lowest of them is removal of that which is harmful from the path, and a sense of shame (al-<u>h</u>ayaa) is a branch of eemaan. Its pillars are six: to truly believe in Allaah; His angels; His Books; His Messengers; the Last Day; and that you truly believe in pre-decree (al-qadar) its good and its evil. The proof for these six pillars is the Saying of Allaah, the Most High, **"It is not righteousness that you turn your faces to the east or the west, but rather righteousness is the righteousness of those who truly believe in Allaah, and the Last Day, and the Angels, and the Books, and the Prophets."** [Soorah al-Baqarah (2):177]

The proof for pre-decree is the Saying of Allaah, the Most High, **"We have created all things in accordance with a pre-decreed measure."** [Soorah al-Qamar (54):49]

The third level is *al-ihsaan* [lit. to do well or perfectly], it is a single pillar which is: that you worship Allaah as if you were seeing Him, and even though you do not see Him then He certainly sees you. The proof is the Saying of Allaah, the Most High, **"Allaah is with those who fear Him and keep away from what He has forbidden, and those who are people of *ihsaan* - those who do well in carrying out whatever He has obligated, taking care of His rights and being constant in obedience to Him, He aids, guides and assists them"** [Soorah an-Nahl (16):128], and His Saying, **"And place your reliance O Muhammad in the All-Mighty, the Bestower of Mercy. He Who sees you when you stand to pray, and sees your movements along with those who follow you in the Prayer - in your standing, bowing, prostration and sitting. Your Lord is the One who hears whatever you recite and mention in your Prayer, and Who knows whatever you and those following you do in your Prayer - so recite the Qur'aan in it, and correctly perform it, since your Lord sees and hears you"** [Soorah ash-Shooraa (26):217-220], and His Saying, **"You are not involved in any matter, O Muhammad, nor do you recite the Book of Allaah, nor do you do any action - O people - whether it is good or evil, except that We are witnessing your deeds when you do them..."** [Soorah Yoonus (10):61]

The proof from the *sunnah* is the well-known *hadeeth* of Jibraa'eel, reported from 'Umar, *radiyallaahu 'anhu*, that he said, *"Whilst we were sitting in the presence of Allaah's Messenger (ﷺ) one day a man came to us having very white clothes and very black hair. No trace of having travelled was to be seen upon him, nor did any of us know him. So he came and sat down with the Prophet (ﷺ) and put his knees against his knees, and placed his palms upon his thighs and said: "O Muhammad, inform me about Islaam." So Allaah's Messenger (ﷺ) said: "Islaam is that you testify that none has the right to be worshipped except Allaah, and that Muhammad is the Messenger of Allaah; establish the Prayer; pay the zakaat; fast Ramadaan; and perform pilgrimage (hajj) to the House if you are able to do so."*

29

He said: "You have spoken the truth." So we were amazed at him asking him a question and then saying that he had spoken the truth. He said: "Then inform me about eemaan." He said: "It is that you truly believe in Allaah, His angels, His Books, His Messengers, the Last Day; and that you truly believe in pre-decree - its good and its bad." He said: "You have spoken the truth." He said: "Then inform me about al-ihsaan." He said: "It is that you worship Allaah as if you were seeing Him, and though you do not see Him then He certainly sees you." He said: "Then inform me of the (Last) Hour." He said: "The one who is asked about it knows no better than the one who is asking." He said: "Then inform me about its signs." He said: "That the slave-girl will give birth to her mistress; and that you will see the barefooted, unclothed and destitute shepherds competing in the building of tall buildings." He said: so he left, and we remained for some time, then he (ﷺ) asked: "O 'Umar, do you know who the questioner was? I replied: "Allaah and His Messenger know best." He said: "That was Jibreel, he came to you to teach you your Religion (Deen)."

THE THIRD PRINCIPLE

Knowledge of your Prophet Muhammad (ﷺ), and he was: Muhammad ibn 'Abdullaah ibn 'Abdul-Muttalib ibn Haashim; and Haashim was from (the tribe of) Quraysh; Quraysh were from the Arabs; and the Arabs have descended from Ismaa'eel, the son of Ibraaheem - the chosen beloved (*khaleel*) - may the most excellent blessings and peace be upon him and upon our Prophet. He lived for sixty-three years: forty years before prophethood, and twenty-three years as a prophet and a messenger. He was sent as a prophet with '*iqra*' [i.e. the beginning of *Soorah al-'Alaq*], and as a messenger with [*Soorah*] *Muddaththir*. His land was Makkah and he performed *hijrah* (prescribed migration) to al-Madeenah. Allaah sent him to warn against *shirk* and to call to *tawheed*.

The proof is the Saying of Allaah, the Most High, **"O you (Muhammad (ﷺ) wrapped in garments! Arise and warn your people; and venerate and worship your Lord, and purify your self, your garments and your deeds; and shun the idols; and do not give anything in order to receive something more in return; and patiently persevere for the sake of your Lord in the face of any harm you encounter"** [Soorah al-Mudaththir (74):1-7].

The meaning of **"Arise and warn your people"** is that he was to warn against *shirk* and to call to *tawheed*. **"Venerate and worship your Lord"** means honour and venerate Him with *tawheed*. **"Purify yourself, your garments, and your** deeds" means purify your actions from any *shirk*. "**Shun the idols**", *ar-rujz* means the idols, and *hajr* of them means shunning them, and freeing and disassociating oneself from them and their people.

He carried out this duty for ten years, calling to *tawheed*, and after ten years he was taken up through the heavens [i.e. the *mi'raaj*]; and the five Prayers were obligated upon him, and he prayed in Makkah for three years, and then he was commanded to perform *hijrah* (prescribed migration) to al-Madeenah.

Hijrah is migrating from the land of *shirk* to the land of Islaam. *Hijrah* from the land of *shirk* to the land of Islaam is an obligation upon this *ummah* and it continues until the Last Hour, and the proof is the Saying of Allaah, the Most High, "**As for those whose souls the angels take in a state of having earned Allaah's Anger, then the angels will say to them: 'In what condition were you regarding your Religion?' They will say: 'We were weakened by the great numbers and strength of the people of *shirk* in our land who prevented us from *eemaan* and from following the Messenger.' They will reply: 'Was not Allaah's earth spacious so that you could leave your land and homes where the people of *shirk* dominate and go to a land where you could worship Allaah alone and follow His Prophet?!' So these people will find their abode in Hell, and what an evil destination that is. Except for the weak ones from the men, women and children who were unable to migrate or find a way to do so. As for such, it may be that Allaah will pardon them, and Allaah is ever One who pardons and forgives the sins of His servants**" [Soorah an-Nisaa' (4):97-99].

Also the Saying of Allaah, the Most High, "**O My servants who believe in Me and My Messenger Muhammad (ﷺ), indeed My earth is spacious, so flee away from whoever prevents you from obedience to Me, and make your worship and obedience purely and sincerely for Me, and do not obey anyone in disobedience to Me**" [Soorah al-'Ankaboot (29):56]. Al-Baghawee, *rahimahullaah*, said: "This *Aayah* was sent down with regard to the Muslims who were in Makkah who did not migrate; Allaah addressed them with the title of *eemaan*.

The proof for the *hijrah* found in the *sunnah* is his (ﷺ) saying: "*Hijrah will not be discontinued until repentance is discontinued, and repentance will not be discontinued until the sun rises from its place of setting.*"

31

So when he (ﷺ) settled in al-Madeenah he ordered the rest of the prescribed duties of Islaam, such as: the *zakaat*, the Prayer, the *hajj*, *jihaad*, the *adhaan*, and commanding good and forbidding evil, and the rest of the prescribed duties of Islaam. He spent ten years establishing that, after which he passed away, may Allaah extol and send blessings of peace upon him and his Religion remains, and this is his Religion: There is no good except that he guided his *ummah* to it, and no evil except that he warned them against it. So the good that he called them to was *at-tawheed*, and all that Allaah loves and is pleased with; and the evil that he warned against was *ash-shirk* and all that Allaah hates and rejects. Allaah sent him as a Messenger to all of the people, and Allaah made it obligatory upon all of the *jinn* and mankind to obey him. The proof is the Saying of Allaah, the Most High, **"Say, O Muhammad, to all of the people: 'I am the Messenger of Allaah to you all'"** [Soorah al-A'raaf (7)158].

Through him Allaah completed the Religion, and the proof is the Saying of Allaah, the Most High, **"This day have I completed your Religion for you, and perfected My blessings upon you, and am pleased with Islaam as your Religion"** [Soorah al-Maa'idah (5):3].

The proof that he (ﷺ) died is the Saying of Allaah, the Most High, **"O Muhammad (ﷺ), you will soon die, and your people - those who deny you and those who believe will die. Then on the Day of Resurrection you will all dispute before your Lord until everyone oppressed receives their right from the oppressor, and Judgement is established between them in truth"** [Soorah az-Zumar (39):30-31].

After death the people will be resurrected, and the proof is the Saying of Allaah, the Most High, **"From the earth We created you, O mankind, and to it We shall return you after death, and from it We shall raise you to life yet again"** [Soorah Taa Haa (20):55]. Also the Saying of Allaah, the Most High, **"And Allaah created you from the dust of the earth, then He will cause you to return to being dust within the earth, then He will bring you forth and restore you to life"** [Soorah Nooh (71):17-18].

After the Resurrection the people will be brought to account and will be rewarded or punished for their actions. The proof is the Saying of Allaah, the Most High, **"That He may requite those who did evil and disobeyed Him, and punish them in the Fire for what they did; and that He may reward those who did** good and were obedient to Him, with what is best (Paradise)" [Soorah an-Najm (53):3]. Furthermore, whoever denies the Resurrection is an unbeliever, and the proof is the Saying of Allaah, the Most High, **"The unbelievers claim that Allaah will not resurrect them after death. Say to them, O Muhammad, 'By my Lord you will certainly be resurrected from you graves, and then you will be informed of the deeds which you did in the world. That is easy for Allaah'"** [Soorah at-Taghaabun (64):7].

Allaah sent all of the messengers as bringers of good tidings and as warners, and the proof is the Saying of Allaah, the Most High, **"Messengers who were sent with the good news of Allaah's reward for those who obey Allaah and believe in His messengers, and as warner's of Allaah's punishment for those who disobey Allaah and disbelieve in His messengers: so that those who disbelieve in Allaah and worship others besides Him may have no excuse to avoid punishment after the sending of the messengers"** [Soorah an-Nisaa' (4):165]. The first of them was Nooh, 'alayhis-salaam, and the last of them was Muhammad (ﷺ); and the proof that the first of them was Nooh, 'alayhis-salaam, is the Saying of Allaah, the Most High, **"We have sent you, O Muhammad, as a Messenger with Revelation, just as We sent Revelation to Nooh and the Messengers after him"** [Soorah an-Nisaa' (4):163].

Allaah sent a Messenger to every nation, from Nooh until Muhammad, commanding them to worship Allaah alone, and forbidding them from the worship of *at-taaghoot* [i.e. everything that is worshipped besides Allaah], and the proof is the Saying of Allaah, the Most High, **"We sent a Messenger to every nation ordering them that they should worship Allaah alone, obey Him and make their worship purely for Him, and that they should shun everything worshipped besides Allaah"** [Soorah an-Nahl (16):36].

Allaah made it obligatory upon all of the servants to reject and disbelieve in *at-taaghoot*, and to have *eemaan* in Allaah. Ibnul-Qayyim, *rahimahullaah*, said: "*At-taaghoot* is anyone regarding whom the servant goes beyond the due bounds, whether it is someone worshipped, obeyed, or followed."

The *taaghoot* are many, and their heads are five:
(i) Iblees - may Allaah's curse be upon him;
(ii) whoever is worshipped and is pleased with that;
(iii) whoever calls the people to the worship of himself;

(iv) whoever claims to possess anything from the knowledge of the affairs of the hidden and unseen (*al-Ghayb*); and

(v) whoever judges by other than what Allaah sent down.

The proof is the Saying of Allaah, the Most High, **"No one is to be compelled to enter the Religion, true guidance has been made clear and distinct from false-hood. So whoever rejects *at-taaghoot* (all that is worshipped besides Allaah) - and truly believes and worships Allaah alone, then he has grasped the firmest handhold that will never break"** [Soorah al-Baqarah (2):256] and this is the meaning of *laa ilaaha illallaah* (None has the right to be worshipped except Allaah).

And in the *hadeeth*: *The head of the affair is al-Islaam, and its supporting pillar is the Prayer, and its highest part is jihaad in Allaah's cause.*

And Allaah knows best, and may Allaah extol and send blessings of peace upon Muhammad, his true followers and his Companions.

Explanation of the Three Fundamental Principles
of Islaam

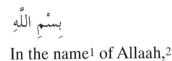

In the name[1] of Allaah,[2]

---

[1] The author, may Allaah have mercy upon him, begins his book with the *Basmalah* (In the name of Allaah, the Most Merciful, the Bestower of Mercy) following the example set by the Book of Allaah, the Mighty and Majestic, which begins with it, and also in accordance with the *hadeeth*: *"Every important matter which is not begun with 'In the name of Allaah' is deprived of good."* (Translator's note: This *hadeeth* is declared to be *da'eef jiddan* (very weak) by Shaykh al-Albaanee in his *Irwaa ul-Ghaleel* (no 1)] It is also in accordance with the way of the Messenger (ﷺ) since he used to begin his letters with it. This sentence has an unspoken part, essential to the completion of the meaning, and its full meaning is: 'In the name of Allaah I write.' The unspoken word is taken to be a verb (i.e. 'I write', in this case) since verbs are necessary for actions, and we understand that it is to come after 'In the name of Allaah' and not before it due to two points: (i) To seek blessing by beginning with the name of Allaah, the one free of all imperfections and the Most High, and (ii) That this is a way of expressing the fact that this is the only cause for writing. So by taking this sentence to be what is meant we find that it makes full sense, as opposed to the case, for example, if we were about to read a book and just said: "In the name of Allaah I begin" since what you are starting would not be clear. But "In the name of Allaah I begin to read" leaves no room for doubt, so what we have understood the unspoken words to be makes full and complete sense.

[2] **Allaah** is the title of the sole Lord who created and fashioned everything, He the Majestic and Most High. This is the name of His which all of His other names follow on from. As occurs in His Saying:

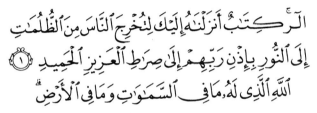

"Alif Laam Raa. This is a Book which we sent down to you in

35

الرَّحْمَنِ الرَّحِيمِ

the Most-Merciful,3 the Bestower of Mercy,4

"*Alif Laam Raa*. This is a Book which we sent down to you in order that you might lead mankind out of darkness into light by the permission of their Lord, to the Path of the All-Mighty, the one worthy of all Praise: Allaah, to whom belongs everything that is in the heavens and the earth."

[Soorah Ibraaheem (14):1-2]

So in this saying of Allaah, the Most High, the noun which is the name of the Majestic Lord 'Allaah' is not a descriptive attribute, rather we say that it is a word which follows as an explanation and clarification of what has preceded.

3 *Ar-Rahmaan* (The Most Merciful) is one of the names which are particular to Allaah, the Mighty and Majestic, and cannot be applied to other than Him. *Ar-Rahmaan* means the one who has as His attribute very great and extensive Mercy.

4 *Ar-Raheem* (The Bestower of Mercy) is a name which is applied to Allaah, the Mighty and Majestic, and the term may be restrictedly applied to others also. Its meaning is the one who is merciful to others. *Ar-Rahmaan* is the one who possesses very great and extensive mercy, and *ar-Raheem* is the one who bestows that Mercy upon others (i.e. He has mercy upon them). So when these two names of Allaah come together, then what is meant by *ar-Raheem* is the one who has mercy upon whomever He wishes from His servants. As Allaah, the Most High, says:

يُعَذِّبُ مَن يَشَآءُ وَيَرْحَمُ مَن يَشَآءُۖ وَإِلَيْهِ تُقْلَبُونَ ﴿٢١﴾

"He justly punishes whomever He wills (i.e. the disobedient) and shows mercy to whomever He wills, and to Him you will be returned."

[Soorah al-'Ankaboot (29):21]

اِعْلَمْ رَحِمَكَ اللَّهُ

Know,5 may Allaah have mercy upon you,6

---

5 Knowledge (*'Ilm*) is to comprehend the reality of something as it truly is, with certainty. The levels of comprehension are six:

(i) Knowledge (*al-'Ilm*): which is to comprehend the reality of something as it truly is, with certainty.

(ii) Slight ignorance (*al-Jahlul-Baseet*): which is absence of full comprehension.

(iii) Aggravated/compounded ignorance (*al-Jahlul-Murakkab*): which is to comprehend something in a way contrary to its true reality.

(iv) Delusion (*al-Wahm*): which is to think that one comprehends something despite the presence of that which should cause you to realise that you are incorrect.

(v) Doubt (*ash-Shakk*): which is to think that you comprehend something, yet you are aware of something contrary to it which you think has the same possibility of being the truth.

(vi) Preponderant belief (*Dhann*): which is comprehension of something, despite the presence of something which is contrary to it, but which is less likely to be true.

Knowledge (*'Ilm*) is of two categories: Inevitable (*durooree*) and speculative (*nadharee*). Inevitable knowledge is that which is known inevitably without any need to investigate or prove with the evidence, for example the fact that fire is hot. Whereas speculative knowledge is that which requires investigation and proof, for example the knowledge that it is obligatory to have intention (*niyyah*) when making ablution (*wudoo*).

6 "*Rahimakallaah*" May Allaah shower his Mercy upon you such as will enable you to reach what you seek for, and escape what you fear. So the full meaning is: May Allaah forgive your previous sins, and guide you to what is good and correct in future, and protect you from sins in future, this is the case if the term *rahmah* (mercy) is used on its own. If however the term *maghfirah* (forgiveness) is used along with it, then *maghfirah* means forgiveness of ones previous sins, whereas *rahmah* (mercy) will refer to the granting of what is good and protection from sins in future. So the words of the author, *rahimahullaah*, show the care and concern which he has for the reader, and that he intends and desires good for him.

أَنَّهُ يَجِبُ عَلَيْنَا تَعَلُّمُ أَرْبَعِ مَسَائِلَ ، الأُوْلَى: العِلْمُ وَهُوَ مَعْرِفَةُ اللَّهِ و مَعْرِفَةُ نَبِيِّهِ

that it is obligatory upon you to have knowledge of four matters:[7]
(i) Knowledge (al-'Ilm), which is knowledge and awareness of Allaah,[8]
and knowledge of His Prophet,[9]

---

[7] These matters which the author, *rahimahullaah*, mentions comprise the whole of the religion, and should be given great attention due to their tremendous benefit.

[8] *"Ma'rifatullaah"* - Knowledge and awareness of Allaah, the Mighty and Majestic, with the heart, with such knowledge and awareness that it makes the person accept whatever He has prescribed and laid down, and causes him to submit to that, and to judge by the Prescribed Laws (*Sharee'ah*) which His Messenger Muhammad (ﷺ) came with. The servant increases in knowledge and awareness of His Lord by considering the clear signs pertaining to the religion found in the book of Allaah, the Mighty and Majestic, and in the *Sunnah* of His Messenger (ﷺ), and also by considering the signs which Allaah has provided for us in the creation. So whenever a person examines and considers these signs he will increase in his knowledge and awareness of His creator and His God, who alone has the right to all his worship. Allaah, the Mighty and Majestic, says:

وَفِى ٱلْأَرْضِ ءَايَتٌ لِّلْمُوقِنِينَ ۝ وَفِىٓ أَنفُسِكُمْ أَفَلَا تُبْصِرُونَ ۝

**"And on the earth there are signs for those with certain Faith,
and also in your ownselves. Will you not then consider."**
[Soorah adh-Dhaariyaat (51):20-21]

[9] Knowledge about His Messenger Muhammad (ﷺ) which is such that it makes the person accept whatever he brought - the guidance and the religion of truth - and such that he affirms and attests to the truth of whatever he informed us of; complies with whatever orders he gave; avoids whatever he forbade; judges by the revealed laws (*Sharee'ah*) which he came with; and is fully pleased with his judgement. Allaah, the Mighty and Majestic, says,

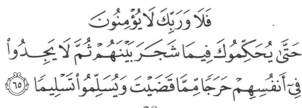

فَلَا وَرَبِّكَ لَا يُؤْمِنُونَ
حَتَّىٰ يُحَكِّمُوكَ فِيمَا شَجَرَ بَيْنَهُمْ ثُمَّ لَا يَجِدُوا۟
فِىٓ أَنفُسِهِمْ حَرَجًا مِّمَّا قَضَيْتَ وَيُسَلِّمُوا۟ تَسْلِيمًا ۝

"But no, by your Lord, they do not have Faith until they make you, O Muḥammad (ﷺ) judge in all matters of dispute between them, and they find no resistance in themselves against your decisions, and accept them with full submission."

[Soorah an-Nisaa' (4):65]

إِنَّمَا كَانَ قَوْلَ ٱلْمُؤْمِنِينَ إِذَا دُعُوٓاْ إِلَى ٱللَّهِ وَرَسُولِهِ لِيَحْكُمَ بَيْنَهُمْ أَن يَقُولُواْ سَمِعْنَا وَأَطَعْنَا وَأُوْلَٰٓئِكَ هُمُ ٱلْمُفْلِحُونَ ﴿٥١﴾

"The only saying of the true believers when they are called to the judgement of His Messenger in matters of dispute, is that they say: We hear and we obey. They are the successful who will dwell forever in Paradise."

[Soorah an-Noor (24):51]

يَٰٓأَيُّهَا ٱلَّذِينَ ءَامَنُوٓاْ أَطِيعُواْ ٱللَّهَ وَأَطِيعُواْ ٱلرَّسُولَ وَأُوْلِى ٱلْأَمْرِ مِنكُمْ فَإِن تَنَٰزَعْتُمْ فِى شَىْءٍ فَرُدُّوهُ إِلَى ٱللَّهِ وَٱلرَّسُولِ إِن كُنتُمْ تُؤْمِنُونَ بِٱللَّهِ وَٱلْيَوْمِ ٱلْأَخِرِ ذَٰلِكَ خَيْرٌ وَأَحْسَنُ تَأْوِيلًا ﴿٥٩﴾

"And if you differ with regard to any of the affairs of your Religion, then refer it back to the Book of Allaah and the *Sunnah* of His Messenger, if you are truly Believers in Allaah and the Last Day, that is what is good and better in its final outcome."

[Soorah an-Nisaa' (4):59]

فَلْيَحْذَرِ ٱلَّذِينَ يُخَالِفُونَ عَنْ أَمْرِهِ أَن تُصِيبَهُمْ فِتْنَةٌ أَوْ يُصِيبَهُمْ عَذَابٌ أَلِيمٌ ﴿٦٣﴾

"Let those who oppose the command of the Messenger in any of their affairs fear and beware that a trial (unbelief, hypocrisy or heresy) should befall them, or a severe punishment."

[Soorah an-Noor (24):63]

وَ مَعْرِفَةُ دِيْنِ الإِسْلاَمِ

and knowledge of the religion of Islaam[10]

Imaam Ahmad, *rahimahullaah*, said: "Do you know what the trial is? The trial is *shirk*, (polytheism) since if he rejects anything from his (ﷺ) sayings, then some form of heresy may be cast into his heart and cause him to be destroyed."

[10] 'Knowledge of the religion of Islaam' - Islaam in its general sense is the worship of Allaah in the way in which He prescribed through the messengers that He sent as has been mentioned by Allaah, the Mighty and Majestic, in many *Aayaat* which show that the previous revealed laws were all submission (Islaam) to Allaah, the Mighty and Majestic, Allaah, the Most High, says concerning Ibraaheem:

رَبَّنَا وَٱجْعَلْنَا مُسْلِمَيْنِ لَكَ وَمِن ذُرِّيَّتِنَا أُمَّةً مُّسْلِمَةً لَّكَ

"O Our Lord, make us Muslims, submitting, obeying and worshipping You alone, and from our progeny those who are Muslims, submitting to You."

[Soorah al-Baqarah (2):128]

Islaam in its particular sense, after the sending of the Prophet (ﷺ) refers to that which Muhammad (ﷺ) was sent with. This is because that which the Prophet (ﷺ) was sent with abrogates all of the previous religions so that whoever follows him is a Muslim, and whoever declines to follow him is not a Muslim. So the followers of the Prophets in the time of their prophets were Muslims; the Jews in the time of Moosaa (ﷺ) were Muslims, and the Christians in the time of 'Eesaa (ﷺ) were Muslims, but since the Prophet Muhammad (ﷺ) was sent and they disbelieved in him they are not Muslims. Furthermore this Religion of Islaam is the only religion acceptable to Allaah and the only one which will benefit a person. Allaah, the Mighty and Majestic, says,

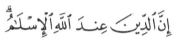

"The only Religion acceptable to Allaah is Islaam."

[Soorah Aal-'Imraan (3):19]

بِالأَدِلَّةِ.

with the proofs.[11]

وَمَن يَبْتَغِ غَيْرَ ٱلْإِسْلَٰمِ دِينًا فَلَن يُقْبَلَ مِنْهُ وَهُوَ فِى ٱلْأَخِرَةِ مِنَ ٱلْخَٰسِرِينَ ﴿٨٥﴾

"And whoever seeks to follow a religion other than Islaam then Allaah will not accept that from him, and in the Hereafter he will be one of the losers."

[Soorah Aal-'Imraan (3):85]

This Islaam is the Islaam with which Allaah favoured Muhammad (ﷺ) and his nation, Allaah, the Most High, says:

ٱلْيَوْمَ أَكْمَلْتُ لَكُمْ دِينَكُمْ وَأَتْمَمْتُ عَلَيْكُمْ نِعْمَتِى وَرَضِيتُ لَكُمُ ٱلْإِسْلَٰمَ دِينًا

"This day have I perfected your Religion for you, and completed My favour upon you, and am pleased with Islaam (complete submission and obedience to Allaah) as your Religion."

[Soorah al-Maa'idah (5):3]

11 The proof being that which leads to that which is sought; and the proofs for this matter are both textual and intellectual. Textual proof is whatever is affirmed by Revelation (*wahy*) which is the Book and the *Sunnah*, and intellectual proof is that which is established through observation and consideration; Allaah, the Mighty and Majestic, has frequently mentioned this type of proof in His Book, and there are many *Aayaat* where Allaah tells us that "from His signs are" such and such, and in this way intellectual proofs by Allaah, the Most High, are quoted.

As regards knowledge of the Prophet (ﷺ) through textual proofs, then examples of these are the Sayings of Allaah, the Most High,

الثَّانِيَةُ: الْعَمَلُ بِهِ. الثَّالِثَةُ: الدَّعْوَةُ إِلَيْهِ

(ii) Action upon that.12

(iii) Calling to that.13

"Muḥammad is the Messenger of Allaah..."

[Soorah al-Fatḥ (48):29]

وَمَا مُحَمَّدٌ إِلَّا رَسُولٌ قَدْ خَلَتْ مِن قَبْلِهِ ٱلرُّسُلُ

"And Muḥammad is but a messenger, just like the messengers who passed away before him."

[Soorah Aal-'Imraan (3):144]

The intellectual proofs are by examining and considering the clear signs which he came with: the greatest of them being the Book of Allaah, the Mighty and Majestic, which comprehends true and beneficial narrations of events, and just rulings which ensure that wellbeing is achieved. In addition to the miracles which occurred at his hands, and the affairs of the hidden and unseen which he informed of and foretold, and could only be known by means of Revelation - and which occurred just as he had said.

12 This means acting in accordance with what this knowledge demands, with regard to *eemaan* (true Islamic Faith comprising correct belief of the heart, speech of the tongue and action of the body parts) in Allaah, establishment of obedience to Him by doing what He has commanded and avoiding what He has forbidden, by performing those actions of worship which benefit each individual, such as: the Prayer, fasting and the pilgrimage (*ḥajj*), and those actions of worship which benefit the whole community, such as ordering the good and forbidding evil, and *jihaad* in Allaah's path and the like.

Action is, in reality, the fruit of knowledge, so whoever acts without knowledge has resembled the Christians, and whoever knows but does not act has resembled the Jews.

13 Calling to the prescribed way laid down by Allaah, the Most High, which the Messenger (ﷺ) came with, in it are three of four stages which Allaah, the Mighty and Majestic, mentioned in his saying:

$$\text{اَدْعُ إِلَىٰ سَبِيلِ رَبِّكَ بِالْحِكْمَةِ}$$

$$\text{وَالْمَوْعِظَةِ الْحَسَنَةِ وَجَادِلْهُم بِالَّتِي هِيَ أَحْسَنُ}$$

"Call to the way prescribed by your Lord with wisdom (as contained in the Book and the *Sunnah*), and with fine admonition, and debate with them in the best manner."

[Soorah an-Nahl (16):125]

And the fourth is contained in His saying:

$$\text{وَلَا تُجَادِلُوٓا أَهْلَ الْكِتَٰبِ إِلَّا بِالَّتِي هِيَ أَحْسَنُ إِلَّا}$$

$$\text{الَّذِينَ ظَلَمُوا مِنْهُمْ}$$

"And do not debate with the People of the Book except with the best words (calling to Allaah by means of His signs and by drawing attention to the proofs He has provided), except for those who remain obstinately upon unbelief and would rather wage war."

[Soorah al-'Ankaboot (29):46]

An essential requirement for this call is knowledge of the Prescribed Way laid down by Allaah, the Mighty and Majestic, so that the call is based upon knowledge and clear evidence, as Allaah, the Most High, says:

$$\text{قُلْ هَٰذِهِۦ}$$

$$\text{سَبِيلِيٓ أَدْعُوٓا إِلَى اللَّهِ عَلَىٰ بَصِيرَةٍ أَنَا۠ وَمَنِ اتَّبَعَنِي وَسُبْحَٰنَ}$$

$$\text{اللَّهِ وَمَآ أَنَا۠ مِنَ الْمُشْرِكِينَ ١٠٨}$$

"Say, O Muhammad, this (call to the *tawheed* of Allaah and that all worship should be made purely for Allaah alone) is my way: I call to Allaah (alone, ascribing no partner to Him), upon cerain knowledge (*baseerah*) myself and those who follow me, and Allaah is free from all imperfections and partners, and I am free from those who associate anything in worship along with Him."

[Soorah Yoosuf (12):108]

The certain knowledge (*baṣeerah*) is with regard to that which he calls to; and means that the caller has knowledge of the *Sharee'ah* rulings, and how the call is to be made, and knows about the condition of those to whom the call is made.

The fields of *da'wah* are many: Calling to Allaah, the Most High, by giving speeches and lectures; calling to Allaah through writing articles; calling to Allaah by means of circles of knowledge; calling to Allaah by writing books propagating the Religion; and calling to Allaah in gatherings established for particular purposes. If a person sits in a gathering where he has come due to an invitation to a meal, for example, then this is an opportunity to call to Allaah, the Mighty and Majestic. However it should be done in such a way as will not bore or irritate the people. This may be achieved by putting forward some matter of knowledge to those present so that a discussion may begin, and it is well known that discussions and questions and answers are of great benefit in understanding what Allaah sent down to His Messenger (ﷺ) and in causing others to understand it. It may be more effective than giving an uninterrupted speech or lecture.

Calling to Allah, the Mighty and Majestic, was the duty of the messengers, and was the way of those who followed them ι͵ n good. So when a person knows the one whom he has to worship, and knows his Prophet, and his Religion, and Allaah has favoured him with that and guided him to it, then he should strive to save his brothers by calling them to Allaah, the Mighty and Majestic, and should be glad to hear of the good tidings which the Prophet (ﷺ) gave to 'Alee ibn Abee Ṯaalib, *radiyallaahu'anhu*, on the day of Khaybar: *"Proceed without hurrying until you reach their territory. Then call them to Islaam, and inform them of the rights of Allaah, the Most High, binding upon them; for by Allaah, it is better for you that Allaah should guide a single man through you than red camels."* [*Saḥeeḥ al-Bukhaaree* (Eng. transl. vol. 5, p. 368-369, no. 521)]. He (ﷺ) said in a narration reported by Muslim: *"Whoever calls to guidance then there is for him a reward like the rewards of those who follow him and that will reduce nothing from their rewards, and whoever calls to misguidance will have sin upon him like the sins of those who follow him, and that will reduce nothing from their sins"* [*Saḥeeḥ Muslim* (Eng. transl. vol. 4, p. 1406 no. 6470)]. He (ﷺ) said also in a narration: *"Whoever guides to some good deed then he receives a reward like that of its doer"* [(*Saḥeeḥ Muslim* (Eng. transl. vol. 3, p. 1050, no. 4665)].

الرَّابِعَةُ: الصَّبْرُ عَلَى الأَذَى فِيْهِ.

(iv) Patiently persevering and bearing any harm encountered upon that way.14

---

14 *As-Sabr* (Patient perseverance) is to confine oneself to obedience to Allaah; and to withhold oneself from disobedience to Allaah, and from being angry with what Allaah has decreed. So one should withhold ones soul from annoyance, resentment and exasperation. Rather one should always be eager and energetic in calling to Allaah's Religion, even if faced with ill-treatment. This is because causing harm to those who call to good is a trait found in mankind, except for those whom Allaah has guided. Allaah, the Most High, said to His Prophet (ﷺ):

وَلَقَدْ كُذِّبَتْ
رُسُلٌ مِّن قَبْلِكَ فَصَبَرُوا۟ عَلَىٰ مَا كُذِّبُوا۟ وَأُوذُوا۟ حَتَّىٰٓ أَتَىٰهُمْ نَصْرُنَا

"Indeed messengers before you, O Muhammad, were denied and rejected but they patiently bore the denial, rejection and harm of their people until our aid came to them."

[Soorah al-An'aam (6):34]

The more severe the harm becomes the nearer is Allaah's aid. It is not the case that Allaah's aid is only that a person is aided in his lifetime and sees that his *da'wah* has produced positive results, rather this aid may come after his death such that Allaah causes the peoples hearts to accept what he called to, so that they follow it and adhere to it. This is also counted as being help and a grant of victory from Allaah, even though it is after his death. So the caller should patiently persevere in his call and continue upon it; patiently persevering upon the Religion of Allaah, the Mighty and Majestic, which he calls to; having patience in facing whatever harm he encounters. Indeed the messengers faced harm and hurt from the words and actions of the people. Allaah, the Most High, says,

كَذَٰلِكَ مَآ أَتَى الَّذِينَ مِن قَبْلِهِم مِّن رَّسُولٍ إِلَّا قَالُوا۟ سَاحِرٌ أَوْ مَجْنُونٌ

"Likewise no messenger came to the previous people except that they said: 'He is a sorcerer, a madman.'"

[Soorah adh-Dhaariyaat (51):52]

"And for each of the prophets We have made an enemy from the idol worshippers."

[Soorah al-Furqaan (25):31]

But the caller should face this with patient perseverance. See the saying of Allaah, the Mighty and Majestic, to His Messenger (ﷺ),

"Indeed it is We who have sent down this Qur'aan to you, O Muhammad, gradually."

[Soorah al-Insaan (76):23]

It might be expected for this *Aayah* to be followed by an order to give thanks for the favours of your Lord, but rather Allaah, the Mighty and Majestic, said after it,

"And be patient with what your Lord has decreed."

[Soorah al-Insaan (76):24]

This contains an indication that everyone who stands with this Qur'aan must certainly face that which requires him to have patience and perseverance. Also consider the example of the Prophet (ﷺ) when his people struck him and caused blood to flow from him. As he was wiping away the blood from his face he was saying: *"O Allaah, forgive my people for they do not know"* [Reported by al-Bukhaaree (Eng. transl. 4/454/no.683)].

The caller should have patience and persevere hoping for Allaah's reward. Patience (*sabr*) is of three kinds:
(i) Patience upon obedience to Allaah;
(ii) Patience upon avoiding that which Allaah has forbidden;
(iii) Patience with regard to the decrees of Allaah which He puts into effect; both those which the servants have no control over at all, and also those pertaining to the harm and attacks which Allaah brings about by the hands of some of the people.

46

وَالدَّلِيْلُ قَوْلُهُ تَعَالَى: ﴿ وَالعَصْرِ إِنَّ الإِنْسَانَ لَفِي خُسْرٍ إِلاَّ الَّذِيْنَ آمَنُوْا وَعَمِلُوْا الصَّالِحَاتِ وَتَوَاصَوْا بِالْحَقِّ وَتَوَاصَوْا بِالصَّبْرِ ﴾.

The proof is the saying of Allaah, the Most High: **"By time, mankind is in loss, except for those who truly believe and worship Allaah alone, and do righteous deeds, performing that which is obligatory upon them and avoiding that which they are forbidden, and enjoin one another with patient perseverance upon obedience to Allaah and in facing harm and trials."**[15] [Soorah al-'Asr (103)]

---

15 His saying, "The proof..." means the proof for these four stages. As for the Saying of Allaah, the Most High, then Allaah, the Mighty and Majestic swears in this *Soorah* by time; time in which the events, both good and evil, occur. Allaah, the Mighty and Majestic, swears by it that all of mankind are in loss, except for those having these four characteristics:

  (i) True Faith (*eeman*),
  (ii) Righteous actions,
  (iii) Enjoining one another with the truth commanded by Allaah,
  (iv) Enjoining one another with patient perseverance.

Ibn al-Qayyim said: "Striving against ones own self (*Jihaadun-Nafs*) is four levels:

  (i) That he strives upon learning the guidance and the true Religion, which is such that there can be no success or bliss for the soul in this life or in the Hereafter except through it;
  (ii) That he strives to act upon what he has learned;
  (iii) That he strives to call to it, and to teach it to those who do not know it;
  (iv) That he accustoms his soul to having patience and perseverance upon the hardships involved in calling to Allaah and the harm caused by the people, and he patiently bears this for Allaah's sake.

So if a person completes these four stages then he becomes one of the rightly-guided and wise scholars and teachers (*ar-Rabbaaniyyoon*)."

Allaah, the Mighty and Majestic, swears in this *Soorah* by time that everyone from mankind is in loss, no matter how great his wealth is and how numerous his offspring are, despite his position and status, except for those who gather these four characteristics:

(i) True Faith which comprises everything which draws a person closer to Allaah, the Most High, both correct creed and belief (*'aqeedah*) and beneficial knowledge.

(ii) Righteous action: which is every saying or action which draws a person closer to Allaah, i.e. that which is done purely and sincerely for Allaah and is done in accordance with the way of Muhammad (ﷺ).

(iii) Enjoining one another upon good, which is to motivate, encourage and urge one another to do that which is good.

(iv) Enjoining one another with patient perseverance, and to have patience and to persevere upon carrying out whatever Allaah, the Most High, has ordered, and in avoiding whatever Allaah has forbidden, and to have patience with whatever Allaah decrees.

Mutual enjoinment of good and of patience comprises ordering the good and forbidding the evil, which is the support of this *Ummah* and upon which depends its well being, victory and attainment of honour and excellence:

$$كُنتُمْ خَيْرَ أُمَّةٍ أُخْرِجَتْ لِلنَّاسِ تَأْمُرُونَ بِالْمَعْرُوفِ$$

$$وَتَنْهَوْنَ عَنِ الْمُنكَرِ وَتُؤْمِنُونَ بِاللَّهِ$$

"You are the best of the people raised up for mankind: ordering true Faith in Allaah and His Messenger and action according to what Allaah ordained; and forbidding association of others in worship along with Allaah, denial of His Messenger and doing that which He has forbidden; and you believe truly in Allaah and single Him out, making all worship purely and sincerely for Him."
[Soorah Aal-'Imraan (3):110]

قَالَ الشَّافِعِيُّ رَحِمَهُ اللَّهُ تَعَالَى : « لَوْ مَا أَنْزَلَ اللَّهُ حُجَّةً عَلَى خَلْقِهِ إِلاَّ هَذِهِ السُّورَةَ لَكَفَتْهُمْ ». وَ قَالَ الْبُخَارِيُّ رَحِمَهُ اللَّهُ:

Ash-Shaafi'ee,[16] may Allaah, the Most High, have mercy upon him, said: "If Allaah had sent down to His creation no other proof besides this *Soorah*, it would have been sufficient for them."[17]

Al-Bukhaaree[18] may Allaah have mercy upon him, said:

---

[16] Ash-Shaafi'ee: He is Aboo 'Abdullaah, Muhammad ibn Idrees ibn al-'Abbaas ibn 'Uthmaan ibn Shaafi' al-Haashimee, al-Qurashee. He was born in Ghaza in the year 150 H, and died in Egypt in the year 204 H, and he was one of the 'four *imaams*', may Allaah have mercy upon all of them.

[17] What he means is that this *Soorah* is sufficient for the creation as an encouragement to adhere to the Religion of Allaah by true Faith (*eemaan*), righteous action, calling to Allaah and patiently persevering upon that. He does not mean that this *Soorah* is sufficient for the creation with regard to all matters of the Religion and its prescriptions. He said this because an intelligent and discerning person who hears this *Soorah* or recites it must necessarily hasten to free himself from the state of loss by attainment of these four characteristics: True faith (*eemaan*), righteous action, mutual encouragement upon the truth, and mutual enjoinment of patient perseverance.

[18] Al-Bukhaaree: He is Aboo 'Abdullaah, Muhammad ibn Ismaa'eel ibn Ibraaheem ibn al-Mugheerah al-Bukhaaree. He was born in Bukhaaraa in the month of Shawwal of the year 194 H. He grew up an orphan in the care of his mother. He died, may Allaah have mercy upon him, in the town of Khartank which is about two leagues distance away from Samarqand, on the night preceding 'Eidul-Fitr, in the year 256 H.

» بَابُ العِلْمُ قَبْلَ القَوْلِ وَالعَمَلِ «. وَالدَّلِيْلُ قَوْلُهُ تَعَالَى :

﴿ فَاعْلَمْ أَنَّهُ لاَ إِلَهَ إِلاَّ اللَّهُ وَاسْتَغْفِرْ لِذَنْبِكَ ﴾ فَبَدَأَ بِالعِلْمِ قَبْلَ

القَوْلِ وَالعَمَلِ. اِعْلَمْ رَحِمَكَ اللَّهُ ، أَنَّهُ يَجِبُ عَلَى كُلِّ مُسْلِمٍ وَ

مُسْلِمَةٍ تَعَلُّمُ ثَلاَثِ هَذِهِ المَسَائِلِ وَالعَمَلُ بِهِنَّ ،

'Chapter: Knowledge precedes speech and action' and the proof is the saying of Allaah, the Most High, **"*Know* that none has the right to be worshipped except Allaah, and ask forgiveness of your Lord for your sins."** [Soorah Muḥammad (47):19]. So He began by mentioning knowledge before speech or action.'[19]

Know, may Allaah have mercy upon you, that it is obligatory upon every Muslim, male and female, to learn and act upon the following three matters:

---

[19] Al-Bukhaaree, *raḥimahullaah*, uses this *Aayah* as proof for the obligation of beginning with knowledge before sayings and actions, and this is a textual proof that a person must first have knowledge and then act. There is an intellectual proof to show that knowledge must precede sayings and actions, and it is that sayings and actions will not be correct and acceptable unless they are in conformity with the *Sharee'ah*, and a person can only be sure that his actions accord with the *Sharee'ah* through knowledge. However there are also some things which a person can know through his innate nature, such as the knowledge that Allaah is a single God, since this is a fact ingrained in mans nature. It does not, therefore, require a great deal of effort to teach this. But as for further and more detailed matters, then they require learning and exertion.

الأُولَى : أَنَّ اللَّهَ خَلَقَنَا

THE FIRST: That Allaah created us[20]

---

20 The proofs for this, i.e. that Allaah created us are textual and intellectual. As for the textual proofs, then they are many. From them are the Sayings of Allaah, the Mighty and Majestic,

هُوَ الَّذِى خَلَقَكُم مِّن طِينٍ ثُمَّ قَضَىٰٓ أَجَلاً وَأَجَلٌ مُّسَمًّى عِندَهُۥ ثُمَّ أَنتُمْ تَمْتَرُونَ ۞

"Allaah it is Who created you, O mankind, from clay, (i.e. created Aadam from clay and then produced his offspring from him) then He declared an appointed life-span, and there is - known only to Him - another determined time (until the Resurrection). Yet you still doubt about the Resurrection."

[Soorah al-An'aam (6):2]

وَلَقَدْ خَلَقْنَاكُمْ ثُمَّ صَوَّرْنَاكُمْ

"And We created you and fashioned you."

[Soorah al-A'raaf (7):11]

وَلَقَدْ خَلَقْنَا الْإِنسَانَ مِن صَلْصَالٍ مِّنْ حَمَإٍ مَّسْنُونٍ ۞

"And We created man (Aadam) from dry clay from blackened mud."

[Soorah al-Hijr (15):26]

وَمِنْ ءَايَـٰتِهِۦٓ أَنْ خَلَقَكُم مِّن تُرَابٍ ثُمَّ إِذَآ أَنتُم بَشَرٌ تَنتَشِرُونَ ۞

"And amongst His signs is that he created you from clay, then you, the offspring of your father Aadam, are human beings scattered upon the earth."

[Soorah ar-Room (30):20]

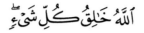

"Allaah created man from dry clay like that of a potter."

[Soorah ar-Rahmaan (55):14]

اَللَّهُ خَٰلِقُ كُلِّ شَىْءٍ

"Allaah is the creator of everything."

[Soorah az-Zumar (39):62]

وَٱللَّهُ خَلَقَكُمْ وَمَا تَعْمَلُونَ ۝

"And Allaah created you and your handiwork."

[Soorah as-Saaffaat (37):96]

وَمَا خَلَقْتُ ٱلْجِنَّ وَٱلْإِنسَ إِلَّا لِيَعْبُدُونِ ۝

"And I did not create *jinn* and mankind except that they should worship Me."

[Soorah adh-Dhaariyaat (51):56]

As for the intellectual proof that Allaah created us, then it is indicated in the Saying of Allaah, the Most High,

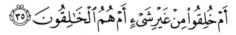

"Were they created by nothing, or did they create themselves?"

[Soorah at-Toor (52):35]

Man did not create himself, since before coming into this life he did not exist; and that which does not exist is nothing; and that which is nothing cannot create anything at all. Nor was it the case that his father or his mother or anyone from creation created him. Nor did he randomly appear without a creator to bring him into existence, since for everything which comes into existence or occurs there must be one who brings it into existence or causes it to occur. The presence of all that exists in this creation and the amazing order found in it and its harmonious structure makes it impossible that it came about randomly. This is because that which would come into existence randomly and by chance is not in principle and origin something well-ordered. This produces the certain conclusion that Allaah alone is

وَرَزَقْنَا

and provided sustenance for us,21

---

the creator, and there is no creator, nor anyone who orders and commands except Allaah. Allaah, the Most High, says,

أَلَا لَهُ ٱلْخَلْقُ وَٱلْأَمْرُ

"Certainly creation and the Command are His."

[Soorah al-A'raaf (7):54]

It was not known that any of the creation denied the Lordship of Allaah, the One free of all imperfections and the Most High, except conceitedly, as was the case with the Pharaoh. Also when Jubayr ibn Mut'im, who was a *mushrik* at the time, heard Allaah's Messenger (ﷺ) reciting Soorah at-Toor (52) when he (ﷺ) reached the Saying of Allaah, the Most High,

أَمْ خُلِقُوا مِنْ غَيْرِ شَىْءٍ أَمْ هُمُ ٱلْخَـٰلِقُونَ ﴿٣٥﴾ أَمْ خَلَقُوا ٱلسَّمَـٰوَٰتِ وَٱلْأَرْضَ بَل لَّا يُوقِنُونَ ﴿٣٦﴾ أَمْ عِندَهُمْ خَزَآئِنُ رَبِّكَ أَمْ هُمُ ٱلْمُصَيْطِرُونَ ﴿٣٧﴾

"Were they created by nothing, or did they create themselves?! Or did they create the heavens and the earth?! Nay they have no certainty, or do they have possession of the treasures of your Lord?! or are they the ones having power and control over the affairs?!"

[Soorah at-Toor (52):35-37]

Jubayr said upon hearing this, *"My heart almost flew, and this was when eemaan first settled in my heart."* [Reported by al-Bukhaaree [Eng. transl. 6/357/no. 377)]

21 The proofs for this in the Book, the *Sunnah* and the intellect are very many. As for the Book, then Allaah, the Most High, says,

$$\text{إِنَّ ٱللَّهَ هُوَ ٱلرَّزَّاقُ ذُو ٱلْقُوَّةِ ٱلْمَتِينُ}$$

"Indeed Allaah is the sole Sustainer of His creation, the All-Powerful, the Mighty."

[Soorah adh-Dhaariyaat (51):58]

$$\text{قُلْ مَن يَرْزُقُكُم مِّنَ ٱلسَّمَوَتِ وَٱلْأَرْضِ قُلِ ٱللَّهُ}$$

"Say, O Muḥammad, to those who associate others in worship along with Allaah: Who gives you provision from the heavens (by sending down rain) and the earth (by bringing out its produce)? Say: Allaah!"

[Soorah Sabaa (34):24]

$$\text{قُلْ مَن يَرْزُقُكُم}$$
$$\text{مِّنَ ٱلسَّمَاءِ وَٱلْأَرْضِ أَمَّن يَمْلِكُ ٱلسَّمْعَ وَٱلْأَبْصَرَ وَمَن يُخْرِجُ}$$
$$\text{ٱلْحَيَّ مِنَ ٱلْمَيِّتِ وَيُخْرِجُ ٱلْمَيِّتَ مِنَ ٱلْحَيِّ وَمَن يُدَبِّرُ ٱلْأَمْرَ}$$
$$\text{فَسَيَقُولُونَ ٱللَّهُ}$$

"Say, O Muḥammad, to those who associate others in worship along with Allaah: Who gives you provision from the heavens and the earth? or who is it that grants you hearing and sight? And who brings out the living from the dead, and brings out the dead from the living? And Who controls the affairs? Then they will say: Allaah."

[Soorah Yoonus (10):31]

The *Aayaat* concerning this are many. As for the *Sunnah*, then from this is his (ﷺ) saying about the fetus, that the angel is sent to it to write down four things about it: its provision, its life-span, its actions, and whether it will be from the blessed or the wretched (in the Hereafter). [Reported by al-Bukhaaree (Eng. transl. 8/387/ no.593) and Muslim (Eng. transl. 4/1391/no.6390)]

As for the intellectual proof that Allaah provides sustenance for us, then it is that we cannot survive except with food and drink, and both of these are created by Allaah, the Mighty and Majestic, as Allaah, the Most High, says,

وَلَمْ يَتْرُكْنَا هَمَلًا ،

and He did not leave us without a purpose[22]

أَفَرَءَيْتُم مَّا تَحْرُثُونَ

ءَأَنتُمْ تَزْرَعُونَهُ أَمْ نَحْنُ الزَّارِعُونَ ۞ لَوْ نَشَآءُ لَجَعَلْنَٰهُ حُطَٰمًا فَظَلْتُمْ تَفَكَّهُونَ ۞ إِنَّا لَمُغْرَمُونَ ۞ بَلْ نَحْنُ مَحْرُومُونَ ۞ أَفَرَءَيْتُمُ الْمَآءَ الَّذِى تَشْرَبُونَ ۞ ءَأَنتُمْ أَنزَلْتُمُوهُ مِنَ الْمُزْنِ أَمْ نَحْنُ الْمُنزِلُونَ ۞ لَوْ نَشَآءُ جَعَلْنَٰهُ أُجَاجًا فَلَوْلَا تَشْكُرُونَ

"Consider that which you cultivate: is it you who causes it to grow or is it that We cause it to spring forth and grow? If We wished We would turn it to dry chaff, so that you would be left in a state of regret, saying: 'Indeed we have been punished, we have indeed been deprived of our harvest.' Consider the water which you drink: is it you who sent it down from the clouds to the earth, or is it We Who sent it down? If We wished We could make it salty, so will you not give thanks to your Lord?"

[Soorah al-Waaqi'ah (56):63-70]

So these *Aayaat* show clearly that our provision, both food and drink, is from Allaah, the Mighty and Majestic.

---

22 This is the reality proven by the textual and intellectual evidences. As for the textual proofs, then from them are the Sayings of Allaah, the Most High,

أَفَحَسِبْتُمْ أَنَّمَا خَلَقْنَٰكُمْ عَبَثًا وَأَنَّكُمْ إِلَيْنَا لَا تُرْجَعُونَ ۞ فَتَعَٰلَى اللَّهُ الْمَلِكُ الْحَقُّ لَا إِلَٰهَ إِلَّا هُوَ

"Did you think that We created you without any purpose, and that you would not be brought back to Us? High and far removed is Allaah, the True King, from what they attribute to Him. None has the right to be worshipped except Him."

[Soorah al-Mu'minoon (23):115-116]

55

بَلْ أَرْسَلَ إِلَيْنَا رَسُوْلاً

rather He sent a Messenger to us.[23]

أَيَحْسَبُ ٱلْإِنسَٰنُ أَن يُتْرَكَ سُدًى ۝ أَلَمْ يَكُ نُطْفَةً مِّن مَّنِيٍّ يُمْنَىٰ ۝ ثُمَّ كَانَ عَلَقَةً فَخَلَقَ فَسَوَّىٰ ۝ فَجَعَلَ مِنْهُ ٱلزَّوْجَيْنِ ٱلذَّكَرَ وَٱلْأُنثَىٰٓ ۝ أَلَيْسَ ذَٰلِكَ بِقَادِرٍ عَلَىٰٓ أَن يُحْۦِىَ ٱلْمَوْتَىٰ ۝

"Does man think he will be left aimlessly, not being given orders and prohibitions and commanded to worship Allaah? Was the denier of Allaah's power to resurrect not merely a drop of semen emitted, then he was a clot of blood, then Allaah shaped and fashioned him and made him a man. Then from his seed created male and female offspring. Is not Allaah, Who does all of this, able to restore them to life after death?"

[Soorah al-Qiyaamah (75):36-40]

As for the intellect, then it shows that the idea that mankind is brought to life merely to eat, drink and pass the time like cattle, and is not then resurrected in the Hereafter or brought to account for their deeds, this is something not befitting the Wisdom of Allaah, the Mighty and Majestic, rather it would be entirely aimless and futile. It is not possible that Allaah should create this creation, then send messengers to them, and then make lawful the spilling of the blood of those who reject and oppose the messengers, and then the final result of everything is nothing. This is impossible due to the Wisdom of Allaah, the Mighty and Majestic.

23 Allaah, the Mighty and Majestic, sent to us, the people of this *Ummah*, the Messenger Muhammad (ﷺ), relating the signs and *Aayaat* of our Lord to us, purifying us, and teaching us the Book and the Wisdom. Just as He had sent messengers to those before us. Allaah, the Blessed and the Most High, says,

وَإِن مِّنْ أُمَّةٍ إِلَّا خَلَا فِيهَا نَذِيرٌ ۝

"There was not a previous nation except that Allaah sent a warner to them."

[Soorah Faatir (35):24]

So Allaah sent the messengers to the creation in order for the proof to be established upon them, and that they should worship Allaah in a manner that He loves and is pleased with, as Allaah, the Blessed and Most High, says,

إِنَّآ أَوْحَيْنَآ إِلَيْكَ كَمَآ أَوْحَيْنَآ إِلَىٰ نُوحٍ وَالنَّبِيِّنَ مِنۢ بَعْدِهِۦ وَأَوْحَيْنَآ إِلَىٰٓ إِبْرَٰهِيمَ وَإِسْمَٰعِيلَ وَإِسْحَٰقَ وَيَعْقُوبَ وَالْأَسْبَاطِ وَعِيسَىٰ وَأَيُّوبَ وَيُونُسَ وَهَٰرُونَ وَسُلَيْمَٰنَ وَءَاتَيْنَا دَاوُۥدَ زَبُورًا ۝ وَرُسُلًا قَدْ قَصَصْنَٰهُمْ عَلَيْكَ مِن قَبْلُ وَرُسُلًا لَّمْ نَقْصُصْهُمْ عَلَيْكَ وَكَلَّمَ اللَّهُ مُوسَىٰ تَكْلِيمًا ۝ رُّسُلًا مُّبَشِّرِينَ وَمُنذِرِينَ لِئَلَّا يَكُونَ لِلنَّاسِ عَلَى اللَّهِ حُجَّةٌۢ بَعْدَ الرُّسُلِ وَكَانَ اللَّهُ عَزِيزًا حَكِيمًا

"We sent Revelation to you, O Muhammad, just as We sent Revelation to Nooh and the Prophets after him; and We sent Revelation to Ibraaheem, Ismaa'eel, Ishaaq, Ya'qoob, the sons of Ya'qoob, 'Eesaa, Yoonus, Haaroon and Sulaymaan; and We gave the Zaboor to Daawood. And We sent Revelation to messengers about whom We have related to you previously, and to messengers about whom We have not related to you; and Allaah spoke directly to Moosaa, messengers as bearers of good tidings and warners, so that the people should have no excuse before Allaah after the sending of the messengers. And Allaah is always the All-Mighty, the All-Wise."

[Soorah an-Nisaa (4):163-165]

It is not possible for us to worship Allaah in the manner He is pleased with except by means of the messengers, since they are the ones who explained to us what Allaah loves and is pleased with, and whatever will draw us closer to Him, the Mighty and Majestic. Therefore it was from Allaah's Wisdom that He sent the messengers to the creation as bearers of good tidings and warners. The evidence is the Saying of Allaah, the Most High,

فَمَنْ أَطَاعَهُ دَخَلَ الْجَنَّةَ

So whoever obeys him will enter Paradise,[24]

إِنَّآ أَرْسَلْنَآ إِلَيْكُمْ رَسُولًا شَٰهِدًا
عَلَيْكُمْ كَمَآ أَرْسَلْنَآ إِلَىٰ فِرْعَوْنَ رَسُولًا ۝ فَعَصَىٰ فِرْعَوْنُ الرَّسُولَ
فَأَخَذْنَٰهُ أَخْذًا وَبِيلًا ۝

"We sent a Messenger to you, O people, as a witness in favour of you or against you on the Day of Resurrection, just as We sent a messenger to the Pharaoh. But the Pharaoh denied and rejected the messenger, so We seized him with a severe punishment."

[Soorah al-Muzzammil (73):15-16]

24 This is a fact proven by the following Sayings of Allaah, the Most High:

وَأَطِيعُوا اللَّهَ وَالرَّسُولَ لَعَلَّكُمْ تُرْحَمُونَ ۝
۞ وَسَارِعُوٓا إِلَىٰ مَغْفِرَةٍ مِّن رَّبِّكُمْ وَجَنَّةٍ عَرْضُهَا
السَّمَٰوَٰتُ وَالْأَرْضُ أُعِدَّتْ لِلْمُتَّقِينَ ۝

"And obey Allaah and obey the Messenger that you may receive Allaah's Mercy, and hasten to forgiveness from your Lord and to Paradise whose width is that of the heavens and the earth, prepared for the pious who are obedient to Allaah."

[Soorah Aal-'Imraan (3):132-133]

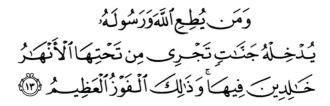

وَمَن يُطِعِ اللَّهَ وَرَسُولَهُ
يُدْخِلْهُ جَنَّٰتٍ تَجْرِي مِن تَحْتِهَا الْأَنْهَٰرُ
خَٰلِدِينَ فِيهَا وَذَٰلِكَ الْفَوْزُ الْعَظِيمُ ۝

"And whoever obeys Allaah and His Messenger, then Allaah will enter him into the gardens of Paradise beneath which rivers flow, in which they will live forever, and that is the great success."

[Soorah an-Nisaa (4):13]

وَمَن

يُطِعِ ٱللَّهَ وَرَسُولَهُ وَيَخْشَ ٱللَّهَ وَيَتَّقْهِ فَأُوْلَٰٓئِكَ هُمُ ٱلْفَآئِزُونَ

"And whoever obeys Allaah and His Messenger, and fears Allaah
and His punishment and is therefore dutiful to Him, then they
are the ones successful on the Day of Resurrection, attaining
Allaah's Pleasure and saviour from the Fire."

[Soorah an-Noor (24):52]

وَمَن يُطِعِ ٱللَّهَ وَٱلرَّسُولَ فَأُوْلَٰٓئِكَ مَعَ ٱلَّذِينَ أَنْعَمَ ٱللَّهُ عَلَيْهِم
مِّنَ ٱلنَّبِيِّـۧنَ وَٱلصِّدِّيقِينَ وَٱلشُّهَدَآءِ وَٱلصَّٰلِحِينَ وَحَسُنَ
أُوْلَٰٓئِكَ رَفِيقًا ﴿٦٩﴾

"So whoever obeys Allaah and His Messenger, by submitting to
their commands and being pleased with their judgement, and
withholding from what they forbid, then he is with those whom
Allaah has blessed with guidance and obedience in this world
and with Paradise in the Hereafter, with the prophets, their sincere followers who were upon their way, the martyrs, and the
righteous; and what an excellent companionship in Paradise are
they."

[Soorah an-Nisaa (4):69]

وَمَن يُطِعِ ٱللَّهَ وَرَسُولَهُ فَقَدْ فَازَ فَوْزًا عَظِيمًا ﴿٧١﴾

"And whoever obeys Allaah and His Messenger has achieved the
greatest success."

[Soorah al-Ahzaab (33):71]

The *Aayaat* in this regard are many.

This fact is also proven by the saying of the Messenger (ﷺ): *"All of my Ummah
will enter Paradise except those who refuse"* So it was said: *"And who would*

وَمَنْ عَصَاهُ دَخَلَ النَّارَ ،

and whoever rejects and disobeys him will enter the Fire,25

---

refuse, O Messenger of Allaah?" He said: *"Whoever obeys me will enter Paradise and whoever disobeys me will enter the Fire."* [Reported by al-Bukhaaree (Eng. transl. 9/284/no.384)]

25 This is also a fact proven by the Sayings of Allaah, the Most High,

$$\text{وَمَن يَعْصِ ٱللَّهَ وَرَسُولَهُ وَيَتَعَدَّ حُدُودَهُ يُدْخِلْهُ نَارًا خَٰلِدًا فِيهَا وَلَهُ عَذَابٌ مُّهِينٌ ﴿١٤﴾}$$

"And whoever disobeys Allaah and His Messenger and transgresses the limits which He has laid down, then Allaah will enter him into the Fire in which he will remain forever and receive a humiliating punishment."

[Soorah an-Nisaa (4):14]

$$\text{وَمَن يَعْصِ ٱللَّهَ وَرَسُولَهُ فَقَدْ ضَلَّ ضَلَٰلًا مُّبِينًا ﴿٣٦﴾}$$

"And whoever disobeys Allaah and His Messenger has indeed strayed into clear error."

[Soorah al-Ahzaab (33):36]

$$\text{وَمَن يَعْصِ ٱللَّهَ وَرَسُولَهُ فَإِنَّ لَهُ خَٰلِدِينَ فِيهَا أَبَدًا ﴿٢٣﴾}$$

"And whoever disobeys and rejects Allaah and His Messenger, then he will burn in the Fire of Hell, remaining in it for eternity."

[Soorah al-Jinn (72):23]

The Messenger of Allaah (ﷺ) said (see previous *hadeeth*): *"And whoever disobeys me will enter the Fire."*

وَالدَّلِيْلُ قَوْلُهُ تَعَالَى:

﴿ إِنَّا أَرْسَلْنَا إِلَيْكُمْ رَسُوْلاً شَاهِدًا عَلَيْكُمْ كَمَا أَرْسَلْنَا إِلَى فِرْعَوْنَ رَسُوْلاً فَعَصَى فِرْعَوْنُ الرَّسُوْلَ فَأَخَذْنَاهُ أَخْذًا وَبِيْلاً ﴾. الثَّانِيَةُ: أَنَّ اللَّهَ لاَ يَرْضَى أَنْ يُشْرَكَ مَعَهُ أَحَدٌ فِي عِبَادَتِهِ لاَ مَلَكٌ مُقَرَّبٌ، وَلاَ نَبِيٌّ مُرْسَلٌ، وَالدَّلِيْلُ قَوْلُهُ تَعَالَى: ﴿ وَأَنَّ الْمَسَاجِدَ لِلَّهِ فَلاَ تَدْعُوا مَعَ اللَّهِ أَحَدًا ﴾.

and the proof is the Saying of the Most High: **"We sent a Messenger to you, O people, as a witness in favour of you or against you on the Day of Resurrection, just as We sent a Messenger to the Pharaoh. But the Pharaoh denied and rejected the Messenger, so We seized him with a severe punishment."** [Soorah al-Muzzammil (73):16]

THE SECOND:[26] Allaah is not pleased that anyone should be made a sharer in worship along with Him, neither any angel brought near, nor any prophet sent as a messenger, and the proof is the Saying of Allaah, the Most High, **"And the places of worship are for Allaah alone, so do not invoke anyone along with Allaah."** [Soorah al-Jinn (72):18]

---

[26] i.e. The second matter which it is obligatory upon us to know is that Allaah, the One free of all imperfections, and the Most High, is not pleased that anyone should be given a share of worship besides Him. Rather He alone is the one deserving and having the right to all worship, and the proof is the saying of Allaah, the Most High, mentioned by the author, (may Allaah have mercy upon him),

$$\text{وَأَنَّ ٱلْمَسَٰجِدَ لِلَّهِ فَلَا تَدْعُوا۟ مَعَ ٱللَّهِ أَحَدًا ﴿١٨﴾}$$

"And the places of worship are for Allaah alone, so do not invoke anyone along with Allaah."

[Soorah al-Jinn (72):18]

Allaah, the Most High, forbade that a person should invoke anyone along with Allaah, and Allaah does not forbid anything except that it is something which He, the Most Perfect and Most High, is not pleased with. Allaah, the Mighty and Majestic, says,

$$\text{إِن تَكْفُرُوا۟ فَإِنَّ ٱللَّهَ}$$
$$\text{غَنِيٌّ عَنكُمْ وَلَا يَرْضَىٰ لِعِبَادِهِ ٱلْكُفْرَ وَإِن تَشْكُرُوا۟ يَرْضَهُ لَكُمْ}$$

"If you disbelieve, then Allaah is not in any need of you, and He is not pleased with disbelief for His slaves; and if you are thankful, believing in Allaah and being obedient to Him, then He is pleased with that for you."

[Soorah az-Zumar (39):7]

$$\text{فَإِن تَرْضَوْا۟ عَنْهُمْ فَإِنَّ ٱللَّهَ لَا يَرْضَىٰ عَنِ ٱلْقَوْمِ ٱلْفَٰسِقِينَ}$$

"But if you are pleased with them, then still Allaah is not pleased with those who rebel against obedience to Allaah and His Messenger."

[Soorah at-Tawbah (9):96]

Allaah is not pleased with unbelief (*kufr*) and direction of worship to any besides Him (*shirk*), rather He sent the messengers and sent down the Revealed Books for war to be waged upon *kufr* and *shirk* and so that they should be annihilated. Allaah, the Most High, says,

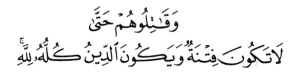

$$\text{وَقَٰتِلُوهُمْ حَتَّىٰ}$$
$$\text{لَا تَكُونَ فِتْنَةٌ وَيَكُونَ ٱلدِّينُ كُلُّهُ لِلَّهِ}$$

"So fight them until their remains no worship of anything be-sides Allaah, and obedience and worship are purely for Allaah."

[Soorah al-Anfaal (8):39]

Since Allaah is not pleased with *kufr* and *shirk* it is obligatory that the Believer is also not pleased with them. This is because the Believers loving and hating must conform to what Allaah loves and hates; so that he is angry with that which angers Allaah, and is pleased with that which pleases Allaah, the Mighty and Majestic. So since Allaah is not pleased with *kufr* and *shirk*, then it is not fitting that the Muslim should be pleased with them. Then *shirk* is something very serious and dangerous, as Allaah, the Mighty and Majestic, says,

إِنَّ ٱللَّهَ لَا يَغْفِرُ أَن يُشْرَكَ بِهِۦ وَيَغْفِرُ مَا دُونَ ذَٰلِكَ لِمَن يَشَآءُ

"Indeed Allaah does not forgive associating anything in worship with Him, but He forgives whatever is lesser than *shirk* to whom-ever He pleases."

[Soorah an-Nisaa' (4):48]

إِنَّهُۥ مَن يُشْرِكْ بِٱللَّهِ فَقَدْ حَرَّمَ ٱللَّهُ عَلَيْهِ
ٱلْجَنَّةَ وَمَأْوَىٰهُ ٱلنَّارُ وَمَا لِلظَّٰلِمِينَ مِنْ أَنصَارٍ ٧٢

"Indeed whoever associates anything in worship with Allaah, then Allaah has forbidden Paradise for him and his abode will be the Fire; and for the wrongdoers who worship others besides Allaah there is none to aid and save them on the Day of Resurrection."

[Soorah al-Maa'idah (5):72]

The Prophet (ﷺ) said: *"Whomever meets Allaah not worshipping anything along with Him will enter Paradise, and whoever meets Him having worshipped others along with Him will enter the Fire"* [Reported by Muslim (Eng. transl. 1/54/ no.168)].

63

الثَّالِثَةُ: أَنَّ مَنْ أَطَاعَ الرَّسُوْلَ وَوَحَّدَ اللَّهَ لاَ يَجُوْزُ

لَهُ مُوَالاَةُ مَنْ حَادَّ اللَّهَ وَ رَسُوْلَهُ وَلَوْ كَانَ أَقْرَبَ قَرِيْبٍ وَالدَّلِيْلُ قَوْلُهُ تَعَالَى:

THE THIRD:[27] That whoever is obedient to the Messenger and singles out Allaah with all worship, upon *tawheed*, then it is not permissible for him to have friendship and alliance with those who oppose Allaah and His Messenger, even if they are those most closely related to him, and the proof is the Saying of Allaah, the Most High:

---

[27] The third matter which is obligatory for us to know is that of 'alliance and disassociation' (*al-Walaa wal-Baraa*) (i.e. alliance with the Believers obedient to Allaah and His Messenger, and enmity and disassociation from the unbelievers and those opposing Allaah and His Messenger). So this alliance and disassociation is a great principle emphasised in many texts. Allaah, the Mighty and Majestic, says:

يَٰٓأَيُّهَا ٱلَّذِينَ
ءَامَنُواْ لَا تَتَّخِذُواْ بِطَانَةً مِّن دُونِكُمْ لَا يَأْلُونَكُمْ خَبَالًا

"O you who believe do not take as friends and protectors those outside your religion, since they will not spare any effort in trying to corrupt you."

[Soorah Aal-'Imraan (3):118]

يَٰٓأَيُّهَا ٱلَّذِينَ
ءَامَنُواْ لَا تَتَّخِذُواْ ٱلَّذِينَ ٱتَّخَذُواْ دِينَكُمْ هُزُوًا وَلَعِبًا مِّنَ ٱلَّذِينَ أُوتُواْ
ٱلْكِتَٰبَ مِن قَبْلِكُمْ وَٱلْكُفَّارَ أَوْلِيَآءَ وَٱتَّقُواْ ٱللَّهَ إِن كُنتُم مُّؤْمِنِينَ ٥٧

"O you who believe do not take as friends and protectors those who take your Religion as mockery and fun, from amongst those who received the Scripture before you, nor from the idolaters; and fear Allaah concerning this if you are truly Believers."

[Soorah al-Maa'idah (5):57]

بِسْمِ اللَّهِ الَّذِينَ ءَامَنُوا لَا تَتَّخِذُوا ءَابَاءَكُمْ

وَإِخْوَٰنَكُمْ أَوْلِيَاءَ إِنِ اسْتَحَبُّوا الْكُفْرَ عَلَى الْإِيمَٰنِ

وَمَن يَتَوَلَّهُم مِّنكُمْ فَأُوْلَٰئِكَ هُمُ الظَّٰلِمُونَ ۩ قُلْ إِن

كَانَ ءَابَاؤُكُمْ وَأَبْنَاؤُكُمْ وَإِخْوَٰنُكُمْ وَأَزْوَٰجُكُمْ وَعَشِيرَتُكُمْ

وَأَمْوَٰلٌ اقْتَرَفْتُمُوهَا وَتِجَٰرَةٌ تَخْشَوْنَ كَسَادَهَا وَمَسَٰكِنُ

تَرْضَوْنَهَا أَحَبَّ إِلَيْكُم مِّنَ اللَّهِ وَرَسُولِهِ وَجِهَادٍ

فِي سَبِيلِهِ فَتَرَبَّصُوا حَتَّىٰ يَأْتِيَ اللَّهُ بِأَمْرِهِ وَاللَّهُ لَا يَهْدِي

الْقَوْمَ الْفَٰسِقِينَ ۩

"O you who believe do not take as friends and protectors your fathers and your brothers if they choose unbelief to belief, and whoever of you takes them as friends and protectors is one of the transgressors. Say, O Mu<u>h</u>ammad, to those who choose to remain in the land of the idolaters and not to emigrate to the land of Islaam: If your fathers; your sons; your brothers; your wives; your families; the wealth which you have earned; the trade which you fear you will lose; and homes which please you are dearer to you than Allaah and His Messenger and fighting *jihaad* in His cause, then wait until Allaah brings about His decree (the Conquest of Makkah) to see the retribution that awaits you, and Allaah does not guide the disobedient."

[Soorah at-Tawbah (9):23-24]

قَدْ كَانَتْ لَكُمْ أُسْوَةٌ حَسَنَةٌ فِي إِبْرَٰهِيمَ وَالَّذِينَ مَعَهُ إِذْ قَالُوا لِقَوْمِهِمْ

إِنَّا بُرَءَٰؤُا مِنكُمْ وَمِمَّا تَعْبُدُونَ مِن دُونِ اللَّهِ كَفَرْنَا بِكُمْ وَبَدَا بَيْنَنَا

وَبَيْنَكُمُ الْعَدَٰوَةُ وَالْبَغْضَاءُ أَبَدًا حَتَّىٰ تُؤْمِنُوا بِاللَّهِ وَحْدَهُ

﴿ لاَ تَجِدُ قَوْمًا يُؤْمِنُوْنَ بِاللَّهِ وَالْيَوْمِ الآخِرِ يُوَادُّوْنَ مَنْ حَادَّ اللَّهَ وَرَسُوْلَهُ وَلَوْ كَانُوْا آبَاءَهُمْ أَوْ أَبْنَاءَهُمْ أَوْ إِخْوَانَهُمْ أَوْ عَشِيْرَتَهُمْ أُوْلَئِكَ كَتَبَ فِي قُلُوْبِهِمُ الإِيْمَانَ وَأَيَّدَهُمْ بِرُوْحٍ مِنْهُ وَيُدْخِلُهُمْ جَنَّاتٍ تَجْرِي مِنْ تَحْتِهَا الأَنْهَارُ خَالِدِيْنَ فِيْهَا رَضِيَ اللَّهُ عَنْهُمْ وَرَضُوْا عَنْهُ أُوْلَئِكَ حِزْبُ اللَّهِ أَلاَ إِنَّ حِزْبَ اللَّهِ هُمُ الْمُفْلِحُوْنَ ﴾.

"You will not find a people who believe in Allaah and the Last Day loving those who oppose Allaah and His Messenger, even if they are their fathers, or their sons, or their brothers, or their kinsfolk. Rather Allaah has decreed true Faith for their hearts, and strengthened them with proof, light and guidance from Him; and He will enter them into the gardens of Paradise beneath whose trees rivers will flow, and they will dwell therein forever. Allaah is pleased with them and they with Him. They are the party of Allaah. Indeed the party of Allaah are the successful." [Soorah al-Mujaadilah (58):22]

"There is a fine example for you to follow in Ibraaheem and those with him when they said to their unbelieving people: 'We are free of you and whatever idols you worship besides Allaah, and we deny and reject what you are upon; and because of your dis-belief in Allaah and your worship of others besides Him, enmity and hatred has arisen between us for ever, unless you believe truly in Allaah, and single Him out, and worship Him alone.'"

[Soorah al-Mumtahinah (60):4]

This is because having friendship and alliance with, and seeking to please one who opposes Allaah is a proof that the belief in Allaah and His Messenger (ﷺ) in

اِعْلَمْ أَرْشَدَكَ اللَّهُ لِطَاعَتِهِ أَنَّ الْحَنِيفِيَّةَ مِلَّةَ إِبْرَاهِيمَ

Know,[28] may Allaah direct[29] you to obedience[30] to Him, that the true and straight Religion,[31] the way[32] of Ibraaheem[33]

---

his heart is indeed weak. This is because it is against reason that a person can have love for anything that is an enemy of the one he truly loves. Alliance with the unbelievers means to help and assist them in the unbelief and misguidance which they are upon; and having love for them is shown by doing those things which will earn their love and friendship by any means. Without a doubt this shows that true belief (*eemaan*) is either totally absent, or is at least deficient. Rather the Believer must be in a state of enmity with those who oppose Allaah and His Messenger, even if the person is the closest of relations to him. He must have hatred for him and separate from him, but this does not prevent him from sincerely advising him and calling him to the truth.

28   Speech concerning Knowledge (*'Ilm*) has preceded, so there is no need to repeat it here.

29   *Ar-Rushd* i.e. may Allaah direct you to uprightness upon the way of truth.

30   *Taa'ah* (obedience): Conformity with what is required by doing what is commanded to be done, and avoiding what is forbidden.

31   *Al-Haneefiyyah*: That is the religion which is free from *shirk*, and founded upon purity and sincerity of intention for Allaah, the Mighty and Majestic.

32   *Al-Millah* i.e. the way which he, Ibraaheem followed in religion.

33   Ibraaheem is the chosen and beloved friend (*Khaleel*) of the Most Merciful. Allaah, the Mighty and Majestic, says,

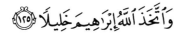

"And Allaah made Ibraaheem a chosen and beloved friend."

[Soorah an-Nisaa' (4):125]

أَنْ تَعْبُدَ اللَّهَ وَحْدَهُ مُخْلِصًا لَهُ الدِّيْنَ ،

is that you worship Allaah alone[34] making the Religion purely and sincerely for Him.[35]

He is the father of the prophets, and his way is mentioned repeatedly so that it should be adhered to.

34 Worship ('*ibaadah*) in its general sense is: 'Submitting oneself to Allaah with love and awe, by doing that which He has ordered and avoiding that which He has forbidden, in the manner laid down and prescribed by Him.' As for the specific meaning of worship, then Shaykh-ul-Islaam Ibn Taymiyyah, *rahimahullaah,* said: "'*ibaadah* (worship) is a comprehensive term covering whatever Allaah loves and is pleased with, both sayings and actions, the apparent and the hidden; such as fearing, having awe, Prayer, *zakaat,* fasting and other practices prescribed by Islaam."

35 *Al-Ikhlaas*: means to purify. What is meant here is that the person by his worship intends and desires the Face of Allaah, the Mighty and Majestic, and to reach the place where He bestows honour and favours (i.e. Paradise). So the person does not worship anything along with Him, neither any angel brought near, nor any prophet sent as a messenger. Allaah, the Most High, says,

ثُمَّ أَوْحَيْنَآ إِلَيْكَ أَنِ ٱتَّبِعْ مِلَّةَ إِبْرَٰهِيمَ حَنِيفًا وَمَا كَانَ مِنَ ٱلْمُشْرِكِينَ ﴿١٢٣﴾

"Then We revealed to you, O Muhammad, that you should follow the Religion of Ibraaheem who was a Muslim upon the true Religion and was not one of those who worshipped idols and associated partners with Allaah."

[Soorah an-Nahl (16):123]

بِذَلِكَ أَمَرَ اللَّهُ جَمِيْعَ النَّاسِ وَخَلَقَهُمْ لَهَا كَمَا قَالَ اللَّهُ تَعَالَى:

This is what Allaah commanded all of the people with,[36] and it was for this that He created them. Allaah, the Most High, says:

وَمَن يَرْغَبُ عَن مِّلَّةِ إِبْرَٰهِـۧمَ إِلَّا مَن سَفِهَ نَفْسَهُۥ وَلَقَدِ ٱصْطَفَيْنَٰهُ فِى ٱلدُّنْيَا وَإِنَّهُۥ فِى ٱلْءَاخِرَةِ لَمِنَ ٱلصَّٰلِحِينَ ﴿١٣٠﴾ إِذْ قَالَ لَهُۥ رَبُّهُۥٓ أَسْلِمْ قَالَ أَسْلَمْتُ لِرَبِّ ٱلْعَٰلَمِينَ ﴿١٣١﴾ وَوَصَّىٰ بِهَآ إِبْرَٰهِـۧمُ بَنِيهِ وَيَعْقُوبُ يَٰبَنِىَّ إِنَّ ٱللَّهَ ٱصْطَفَىٰ لَكُمُ ٱلدِّينَ فَلَا تَمُوتُنَّ إِلَّا وَأَنتُم مُّسْلِمُونَ ﴿١٣٢﴾

"And who turns away from the Religion of Ibraaheem except a fool, ignorant of what benefits him; and We indeed chose Ibraaheem in this world, and made him amongst the righteous in the Hereafter; When his Lord said to him: Make your worship purely for Me and submit obediently to Me, he said in response: I submit obediently and make my worship purely for the Lord of all creation. Then Ibraaheem enjoined this upon his sons, and so did Ya'qoob, saying: 'O my sons, Allaah has chosen the Religion of Islaam for you, so do not abandon Islaam for as long as you live, so that you die as Muslims.'"

[Soorah al-Baqarah (2):130-132]

---

36 i.e. with the true Religion, which is to worship Allaah, making all of the Religion purely for Him. This is what Allaah commanded all of creation with and it was for this He created them. Allaah, the Most High, says,

$$﴿ وَمَا خَلَقْتُ الجِنَّ وَالإِنْسَ إِلاَّ لِيَعْبُدُوْنَ ﴾$$

$$وَمَعْنَى يَعْبُدُوْنَ يُوَحِّدُوْنَ.$$

"I did not create _jinn_ and mankind except that they should worship Me" [Soorah adh-Dhaariyaat (51):56] and the meaning of _worship_ (*'ibaadah*) here is to single Allaah out with all worship (*tawheed*).[37]

$$وَمَا أَرْسَلْنَا مِن قَبْلِكَ مِن رَّسُولٍ إِلَّا نُوحِي إِلَيْهِ أَنَّهُ لَا إِلَٰهَ$$
$$إِلَّا أَنَا فَاعْبُدُونِ ﴿٢٥﴾$$

"We did not send any Messenger before you, O Muḥammad (ﷺ), except that We revealed to him that none has the right to be worshipped except Allaah, so make all of your worship purely for Him."

[Soorah al-Ambiyaa' (21):25]

Allaah, the Mighty and Majestic, made clear in His Book that mankind and _jinns_ were only created for this. Allaah, the Most high, says,

$$وَمَا خَلَقْتُ الْجِنَّ وَالْإِنسَ إِلَّا لِيَعْبُدُونِ ﴿٥٦﴾$$

"I did not create _jinn_ and mankind except that they should worship Me."

[Soorah adh-Dhaariyaat (51):56]

37 Meaning that _tawheed_ is from the meaning of *'ibaadah* (i.e. true worship, which is to make all of it purely for Allaah). The meaning of *'ibaadah* has already preceded, and also what it applies to, and that it is more general than _tawheed_ itself. You should know that *'ibaadah* is of two types:
(i) The servitude of the creation (*'Ibaadah Kawniyyah*), which is submission to what Allaah has commanded and decreed in the creation, and this is the submission that is common to all of the creation, none of them being able to escape it. Allaah, the Most High, says,

وَأَعْظَمُ مَا أَمَرَ اللَّهُ التَّوْحِيْدُ وَهُوَ إِفْرَادُ اللَّهِ بِالعِبَادَةِ ،

And the greatest of all that Allaah has commanded is *tawheed* which is to single out Allaah with all worship.38

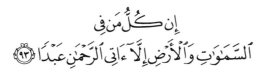

"All the angels in the heavens, and all men and *jinn* upon the earth will come to the Most Merciful on the Day of Judgement as submissive slaves."

[Soorah Maryam (19):93]

This servitude covers the Believers and the unbelievers, the righteous and the wicked.

(ii) Worship and servitude as prescribed by the *Sharee'ah,* and that is to obey and submit to the laws and commands of Allaah, the Most High, and this is particular to those who are obedient to Allaah, and who comply with that which the Messengers came with. Allaah, the Most High, says:

وَعِبَادُ الرَّحْمَنِ الَّذِينَ يَمْشُونَ عَلَى الْأَرْضِ هَوْنًا

"And the believing slaves of the Most Merciful are those who walk upon the earth with calmness and humility."

[Soorah al-Furqaan (25):63]

The first type of servitude is not something for which a servant is commended, since it is not due to any action of his own; however he may be commended for giving thanks in times of ease, and for having patience in times of trial; as opposed to the second type of servitude for which a person is commended.

38 *Tawheed* in the language is a verbal noun from the verb *wahhada* (وَحَّدَ), *yuwahhidu* (يُوَحِّدُ), meaning he unified something and made it one. *Tawheed* cannot be realised except through denial (*nafy*) and affirmation (*ithbaat*). Denial of this ruling for everything other than that which it is made for, and affirmation of it

71

for Him. So we say: A persons *tawheed* is not complete unless he bears witness that none has the right to be worshipped except Allaah, so he denies the right to be worshipped for everything besides Allaah, the Most High, and he affirms that for Allaah alone.

In its technical sense the author has defined it by saying: "*Tawheed* is to single out Allaah with all worship" meaning that you worship Allaah alone, and do not worship anything along with Him: You do not worship any Prophet sent by Him, nor any of the creation. Rather you single Him out with all worship, out of love, veneration, longing and awe. What the Shaykh, *rahimahullaah*, is referring to is the *tawheed* which the Messengers were sent to establish, and it is this that was violated by their peoples.

There is a more general definition of *tawheed* which is that it is: "Singling out Allaah, the Most Perfect, with all that is particular to Him." Thus *tawheed* is of three types:

(1) *Tawheed* **of Allaah's Lordship** (*Tawheed ar-Ruboobiyyah*) which is: 'That Allaah, the one free of all imperfections and the Most High, is singled out with creation, sovereignty and control of the affairs.' Allaah, the Mighty and Majestic, says,

"Allaah is the creator of everything."

[Soorah az-Zumar (39):62]

"Is there any creator besides Allaah, providing you with provision from the heavens (rain) and the earth (its produce)?! Therefore do not worship anything besides Him, but worship Him alone since there is nothing that has the power to harm or benefit you besides Him."

[Soorah Faatir (35):3]

$$\text{تَبَارَكَ ٱلَّذِى بِيَدِهِ ٱلْمُلْكُ وَهُوَ عَلَىٰ كُلِّ شَىْءٍ قَدِيرٌ ﴿١﴾}$$

"Exalted is He in Whose Hand is dominion of everything, and He is fully able to do all things."

[Soorah al-Mulk (67):1]

$$\text{أَلَا لَهُ ٱلْخَلْقُ وَٱلْأَمْرُ ۗ تَبَارَكَ ٱللَّهُ رَبُّ ٱلْعَٰلَمِينَ ﴿٥٤﴾}$$

"Indeed creation and the Command are His. Exalted is Allaah, the Lord of all the creation."

[Soorah al-A'raaf (7):54]

(2) *Tawheed* of Worship (*Tawheed al-Uloohiyyah*) which is: 'To single out Allaah, the one free of all imperfections and the Most High, with all worship, such that a person does not take anyone else besides Allaah and worship him and do acts of devotion for Him as He worships Allaah and does acts of devotion for Him.'

(3) *Tawheed* of Allaah's Names and Attributes (*Tawheed al-Asmaa was-Sifaat*) which is: 'That Allaah, the one free of all imperfections and the Most High, is singled out with whatever names and attributes He has affirmed for Himself in His Book, or upon the tongue of His Messenger (ﷺ); and this involves affirming whatever He has affirmed for Himself, and denying whatever He has denied from Himself, without changing and distorting their meanings, without denying or divesting Allaah of His attributes, without delving into how they are, and without declaring Allaah to be like the creation.'

What the author is referring to here is *tawheed* of worship, and it was with regard to this that the *mushriks* went astray, those whom the Prophet (ﷺ) fought; and whose blood, wealth, lands and homes he made lawful to be taken; and whose womenfolk and children he took as captives. Most of the striving of the messengers with their peoples was with regard to this category of *tawheed*. He, the Most High, says,

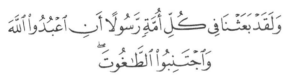

وَأَعْظَمُ مَا نَهَى عَنْهُ الشِّرْكُ وَهُوَ دَعْوَةُ غَيْرِهِ مَعَهُ وَالدَّلِيْلُ قَوْلُهُ تَعَالَى:

The most serious thing that He forbade is *shirk*, which is to invoke others besides Him, along with Him. The proof is His Saying, the Most High:

"We sent a Messenger to every nation, ordering that they should worship Allaah alone."

[Soorah an-Nahl (16):36]

So worship is not correct except for Allaah, the Mighty and Majestic. Whoever violates this *tawheed* is a *mushrik*, an unbeliever, even if he affirms *tawheed* of Lordship and *tawheed* of Allaah's Names and Attributes. So if it were to be the case that a man totally agreed to the *tawheed* of Allaah's Lordship, and His Names and Attributes, but he went to a grave and directed worship to its occupant, or offered a sacrifice as an offering (*nadhr*) for him, then he would be a *mushrik*, an unbeliever, an inhabitant of Hell-Fire forever. Allaah, the Most High, says,

إِنَّهُۥ مَن يُشْرِكْ بِٱللَّهِ فَقَدْ حَرَّمَ ٱللَّهُ عَلَيْهِ ٱلْجَنَّةَ وَمَأْوَىٰهُ ٱلنَّارُ وَمَا لِلظَّٰلِمِينَ مِنْ أَنصَارٍ ﴿٧٢﴾

"Indeed whoever associates anything in worship with Allaah, then Allaah has forbidden Paradise for him, and his abode will be the Fire; and for the transgressors who worship others besides Allaah there will be no one to help and save them from Allaah's punishment on the Day of Resurrection."

[Soorah al-Maa'idah (5):72]

Tawheed is the greatest commandment given by Allaah since it is the foundation upon which the whole Religion is built. Therefore the Prophet (ﷺ) began with it in his call to Allaah, and he ordered those whom he sent out as callers to begin with it also.

﴿ وَاعْبُدُوا اللَّهَ وَلَا تُشْرِكُوا بِهِ شَيْئًا ﴾ .

"Worship Allaah alone, making all worship purely for Him, and do not associate anything in worship along with Him."[39] [Soorah an-Nisaa (4):36]

---

39 The most serious of all that Allaah forbade is *shirk*, and this is because the greatest of all rights are the rights of Allaah, the Mighty and Majestic. So if a person violates the right of Allaah, then he has violated the greatest of all rights, which is the *tawheed* of Allaah, the Mighty and Majestic. Allaah, the Most High, says,

إِنَّ ٱلشِّرْكَ لَظُلْمٌ عَظِيمٌ ١٣

"Shirk is the greatest transgression."

[Soorah Luqmaan (31):13]

وَمَن يُشْرِكْ بِٱللَّهِ فَقَدِ ٱفْتَرَىٰ إِثْمًا عَظِيمًا

"Whoever associates partners in worship along with Allaah has invented a tremendous sin."

[Soorah an-Nisaa' (4):48]

وَمَن يُشْرِكْ بِٱللَّهِ فَقَدْ ضَلَّ ضَلَـٰلَۢا بَعِيدًا

"And whoever associates any partner in worship along with Allaah then he has strayed far from the correct way."

[Soorah an-Nisaa' (4):116]

إِنَّهُۥ مَن يُشْرِكْ بِٱللَّهِ فَقَدْ حَرَّمَ ٱللَّهُ عَلَيْهِ ٱلْجَنَّةَ وَمَأْوَىٰهُ ٱلنَّارُ وَمَا لِلظَّـٰلِمِينَ مِنْ أَنصَارٍ ٧٢

"Indeed whoever associates anything in worship with Allaah, then Allaah has forbidden Paradise for him, and his abode will be the Fire; and for the transgressors who worship others besides Allaah there will be no one to help and save them from Allaah's punishment on the Day of Resurrection."

[Soorah al-Maa'idah (5):72]

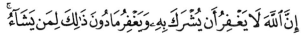

"Allaah does not forgive association of anything in worship with Him, but He forgives what is lesser than *shirk* to whomever He pleases."

[Soorah an-Nisaa' (4):48]

The Prophet (ﷺ) said: *"The greatest sin is that you set up a rival to Allaah when it is He who created you"* [Reported by al-Bukhaaree (Eng. transl. 9/458/no.611) and Muslim (Eng. transl. 1/50/no.156)].

He (ﷺ) also said in the *hadeeth* reported by Muslim from Jaabir, *radiyallaahu 'anhu*: *"Whoever meets Allaah not associating anything in worship with Him will enter Paradise, and whoever meets Him associating anything in worship along with him will enter the Fire"* [*Saheeh* Muslim (Eng. transl. 1/54/no.168)].

The Prophet (ﷺ) further said: *"Whoever dies while still calling upon a rival to Allaah will enter the Fire."* [Reported by al-Bukhaaree (Eng. transl. 6/21/no.24)]

As evidence for Allaah, the Most High's, command that He alone should be worshipped, and for His prohibition of *shirk*, the author, *rahimahullaah*, quotes the Saying of Allaah, the Mighty and Majestic,

وَٱعْبُدُوا۟ٱللَّهَ وَلَا تُشْرِكُوا۟ بِهِۦ شَيْـًٔا

"Worship Allaah alone, making all worship purely for Him, and do not associate anything in worship along with Him."

[Soorah an-Nisaa' (4):36]

So He, the one free of all imperfections and the Most High, commanded that He alone be worshipped and He forbade *shirk*. So this order affirming worship for Him alone means that one who does not worship Allaah is a haughty and obstinate unbeliever (*kaafir*); and that one who worships Allaah and worships others besides Him as well is an unbeliever (*kaafir*) and a polytheist (*mushrik*); and that one who worships Allaah alone is a pure Muslim. *Shirk* is of two types: Greater *shirk* (*shirkun akbar*) and lesser *shirk* (*shirkun asghar*). So the first type: Major *shirk*, which is unrestricted *shirk* termed as such in the *Sharee'ah*, which causes a

76

فَإِذَا قِيْلَ لَكَ مَا الأُصُوْلُ الثَّلاثَةُ

So if it is said to you: What are the three principles[40]

---

person to leave the Religion. The second type: Lesser *shirk* is every action or saying defined by the *Sharee'ah* as being *shirk*, but which does not take a person out of the Religion.

A person must beware of *shirk*, both major and lesser, since Allaah, the Most High, says,

إِنَّ ٱللَّهَ لَا يَغْفِرُ أَن يُشْرَكَ بِهِۦ وَيَغْفِرُ مَا دُونَ ذَٰلِكَ لِمَن يَشَآءُ

"Allaah does not forgive association of anything in worship with Him, but He forgives what is lesser than *shirk* to whomever He pleases."

[Soorah an-Nisaa' (4):48]

Some of the scholars have said that this threat covers all *shirk*, even lesser *shirk*.

40 Principles or fundamentals (*usool*) are that upon which other things are built. From this is the foundation of a wall (*aslul-jidaar*), and the trunk of a tree (*aslush-shajarah*) from which the branches spring. Allaah, the Most High, says,

أَلَمْ تَرَ كَيْفَ ضَرَبَ ٱللَّهُ مَثَلًا كَلِمَةً طَيِّبَةً
كَشَجَرَةٍ طَيِّبَةٍ أَصْلُهَا ثَابِتٌ وَفَرْعُهَا فِى ٱلسَّمَآءِ ﴿٢٤﴾

"Do you not consider the example of a good word (i.e. the testification that none has the right to be worshipped except Allaah) which is like a goodly tree, its trunk (*asl*) is firmly rooted (i.e. the testification is firmly rooted in the heart of the Believer), and its branches reach towards the sky (i.e. the Believers actions are raised up through that to the heavens)."

[Soorah Ibraaheem (14):24]

الَّتِي يَجِبُ عَلَى الإِنْسَانِ مَعْرِفَتُهَا   فَقُلْ مَعْرِفَةُ العَبْدِ رَبَّهُ

which a person must know?,[41] then say the servants knowledge of His Lord[42]

---

41 The author, *rahimahullaah*, introduces this matter in the form of a question, and this is so as to attract ones attention to its importance, since it is of extreme importance and what he discusses are very great and fundamental principles. He declared these three principles to be those which it is obligatory for a person to have knowledge of since they are the principles which the person will be asked about when he is buried in his grave. After burial his companions will leave him, and two angels will come to him and make him sit up and will ask him: 'Who is your Lord?' 'What is your Religion?' and 'Who is your Prophet?' As for the Believer, then he will reply: 'My Lord is Allaah, my Religion is Islaam, and my Prophet is Muhammad.' But as for the doubter or the hypocrite, then he will say 'Haah, Haah, I don't know. I heard the people saying something, so I said it also.' [See the *hadeeth* of Anas, *radiyallaahu 'anhu*, reported by al-Bukhaaree (Eng. transl.2/235/no.422)]

42 Knowledge and awareness of Allaah comes about through various means: From them is reflection and consideration of what He, the Mighty and Majestic, has created, since that leads to awareness of Him and His absolute Sovereignty and perfect Power and Wisdom, and also His Mercy. Allaah, the Most High, says,

أَوَلَمْ يَنظُرُوا۟ فِى مَلَكُوتِ ٱلسَّمَـٰوَٰتِ وَٱلْأَرْضِ وَمَا خَلَقَ ٱللَّهُ مِن شَىْءٍ

"Will those who deny our signs not look and consider Allaah's Sovereignty over the heavens and the earth, and whatever He has created therein."

[Soorah al-A'raaf (7):185]

قُلْ إِنَّمَآ أَعِظُكُم بِوَٰحِـدَةٍ أَن تَقُومُوا۟ لِلَّهِ مَثْنَىٰ وَفُرَٰدَىٰ ثُمَّ تَتَفَكَّرُوا۟ مَا بِصَاحِبِكُم مِّن جِنَّةٍ

"I exhort you (O unbelievers who claim that the Prophet is a madman), to one thing: That you stand up sincerely, and not merely following your desires, in pairs, and ask each other: Have you ever known him to suffer from madness; then that you reflect and consider individually the truth of his affair."

[Soorah Sabaa' (34):46]

إِنَّ فِى خَلْقِ ٱلسَّمَٰوَٰتِ وَٱلْأَرْضِ وَٱخْتِلَٰفِ ٱلَّيْلِ وَٱلنَّهَارِ لَأَيَٰتٍ لِّأُوْلِى ٱلْأَلْبَٰبِ ﴿١٩٠﴾

"Indeed in the heavens and the earth, and the alternation of the night and the day there are clear signs for people of understanding."

[Soorah Aal-'Imraan (3):190]

إِنَّ فِى ٱخْتِلَٰفِ ٱلَّيْلِ وَٱلنَّهَارِ وَمَا خَلَقَ ٱللَّهُ فِى ٱلسَّمَٰوَٰتِ وَٱلْأَرْضِ لَأَيَٰتٍ لِّقَوْمٍ يَتَّقُونَ ﴿٦﴾

"Indeed in the alternation of the day and the night, and in what Allaah has created in the heavens and the earth there are clear signs for those who fear the punishment of Allaah."

[Soorah Yoonus (10):6]

إِنَّ فِى خَلْقِ ٱلسَّمَٰوَٰتِ وَٱلْأَرْضِ وَٱخْتِلَٰفِ ٱلَّيْلِ وَٱلنَّهَارِ وَٱلْفُلْكِ ٱلَّتِى تَجْرِى فِى ٱلْبَحْرِ بِمَا يَنفَعُ ٱلنَّاسَ وَمَا أَنزَلَ ٱللَّهُ مِنَ ٱلسَّمَاءِ مِن مَّاءٍ فَأَحْيَا بِهِ ٱلْأَرْضَ بَعْدَ مَوْتِهَا وَبَثَّ فِيهَا مِن كُلِّ دَابَّةٍ وَتَصْرِيفِ ٱلرِّيَٰحِ وَٱلسَّحَابِ ٱلْمُسَخَّرِ بَيْنَ ٱلسَّمَاءِ وَٱلْأَرْضِ لَأَيَٰتٍ لِّقَوْمٍ يَعْقِلُونَ ﴿١٦٤﴾

"Indeed in the creation of the heavens and the earth, and in the alternation of night and day, and the ships which sail upon the ocean with that which is of use to mankind, and in the rain which Allaah sends down from the sky, and with which He brings life to the earth after its death, and the creatures which He disperses throughout the earth, and the changing state and direction of the winds, and the clouds that proceed as they are commanded between the heavens and the earth, there are indeed clear signs of the sole Lordship of Allaah, for people of sound intellect."

[Soorah al-Baqarah (2):164]

From the means by which a servant may know his Lord is to consider the signs in His *Sharee'ah*, which is the Revelation which His messengers, came with and the immense benefits contained therein which are such that the life of a person in this world and the Hereafter cannot be preserved except through it. So if a person considers this and reflects upon it, and sees how it comprises knowledge and wisdom, and sees how it is perfectly ordered and in full harmony with the needs of the people, then this will lead him to know and to be aware of his Lord, the Mighty and Majestic, as Allaah, the Mighty and Majestic, says,

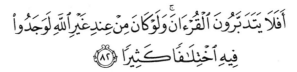

"Will they not carefully consider the Qur'aan: had it been from other than Allaah they would have found a great deal of contradiction in it."

[Soorah an-Nisaa' (4):82]

Also from these means is the knowledge and awareness of Allaah, the one free of all imperfections and the Most High, which He, the Mighty and Majestic, places in the heart of the Believer to the point that it is as if he were seeing his Lord. The Prophet (ﷺ) said, when Jibreel asked him about *ihsaan* (lit. striving to the utmost to do good), he said: *"It is that you worship Allaah as if you were seeing Him, and even though you do not see Him, then He certainly sees you"* [Reported by Muslim (Eng. transl. vol.1, p.1, no.1)].

وَدِينِهِ وَنَبِيَّهُ مُحَمَّدًا ﷺ.

and His Religion (*Deen*),43 and his Prophet Muhammad (ﷺ).44

---

43 i.e. knowledge of the second principle which is the Religion which he is duty bound to act in accordance with; and which comprises wisdom, mercy and takes care of that which is necessary and beneficial for the creation, and which wards off all corruption and evil. Then anyone who truly considers the Religion of Islaam, carefully considering the Book and the *Sunnah* will know for sure that it is the Religion of truth, and that the wellbeing of the servants cannot be attained except through it. It is not fitting that we should judge Islaam according to what the people are upon today since the Muslims have neglected many things and committed tremendous evils, such that it is as if the person living in some Islamic lands is not living in an Islamic environment at all.

However the Religion of Islaam, and all praise and thanks are for Allaah, the Most High, comprehends all benefit that was contained within the previous religions, and excels them in its suitability for every time, every place, and every nation. The meaning of its being suitable for every time, place and nation is that adherence to it in no way conflicts with the wellbeing and benefit of the nation at any time or in any place. Rather in it lies the well being and benefit of that nation. It does not mean that Islaam is subservient to every time, place and nation. So the Religion of Islaam commands every good and righteous action, and forbids every evil action: it commands every noble characteristic and prohibits every despicable characteristic.

44 This is the third principle which is that a person should have knowledge of his Prophet Muhammad (ﷺ). This is achieved by studying the life history of the Prophet (ﷺ), and his worship, his character and manners, how he called to Allaah, the Mighty and Majestic, and how he fought *jihaad* for His cause, and the rest of the aspects of his (ﷺ) life. Therefore every person who wishes to increase his knowledge about his Prophet, and to increase his *eemaan* (true faith) in him should read what he is able to about his life in times of war and times of peace, in his times of difficulty and times of ease, and in all his conditions. Then we ask Allaah, the Mighty and Majestic, that he makes us from those who follow and obey His Messenger (ﷺ), in those things which are hidden and those which are manifest, and that He causes us to die upon that, indeed He is the one rightfully asked for that and the one having full power to grant it.

فَإِذَا قِيْلَ لَكَ مَنْ رَبُّكَ فَقُلْ رَبِّيَ اللَّهُ الَّذِي رَبَّانِي وَرَبَّى جَمِيْعَ العَالَمِيْنَ بِنَعَمِهِ

[THE FIRST PRINCIPLE]

So if it is said to you: 'Who is your Lord?'[45] Then say: 'My Lord is Allaah, who has nurtured[46] me and all of creation with His favours and blessings,

---

[45] i.e. Who is your Lord who created you, and gave you life, and prepared you, and provides you with all your needs.

[46] *'Tarbiyah'* which means to take care of that which is necessary for the development of the one being raised. The authors words indicate that the word *ar-Rabb* (the Lord) is derived from the word *tarbiyah* (to nurture), since he said: "Who has nurtured me and all of creation with His favours and blessings." So Allaah nurtures all of the creation with His favours and blessings, and has prepared them for that for which they were created, and He supported them with all of their needs. Allaah, the exalted and the Most High, said, concerning the conversation between Moosaa and the Pharaoh,

قَالَ فَمَن رَّبُّكُمَا يَـٰمُوسَىٰ ۞ قَالَ رَبُّنَا الَّذِىٓ أَعْطَىٰ
كُلَّ شَىْءٍ خَلْقَهُۥ ثُمَّ هَدَىٰ ۞

"So Pharaoh said: 'O Moosaa who is the Lord of you two?' He answered: 'Our Lord is the One who provided a suitable mate for all creatures which He created, and then guided them to everything they need with regard to procreation, food, drink and habitation."

[Soorah Taa Haa (20):49-50]

So Allaah, the Mighty and Majestic, nurtured and provided for all of creation with His blessings. The blessings of Allaah, the Mighty and Majestic, are so many that they cannot be counted. Allaah, the Exalted and the Most High, says,

وَإِن تَعُدُّوا۟ نِعْمَتَ ٱللَّهِ
لَا تُحْصُوهَآ إِنَّ ٱلْإِنسَـٰنَ لَظَلُومٌ كَفَّارٌ ۞

وَهُوَ مَعْبُودِي لَيْسَ لِي مَعْبُودٌ سِوَاهُ ،

He is the one whom I worship, and there is no other whom I worship besides Him.'47

"And if you were to try to count the blessings of Allaah you would not be able to."

[Soorah Ibraaheem (14):34]

So it is Allaah who created you, prepared you, supported you and provided for your needs, so He alone is deserving of your worship.

47 He is the one whom I worship and humble myself to and submit to, in love and reverence. I do whatever He commands, and abandon whatever He forbids. There is nobody else whom I worship besides Allaah, the Mighty and Majestic. Allaah, the Exalted and the Most High, says,

وَمَآ أَرْسَلْنَا مِن قَبْلِكَ مِن رَّسُولٍ إِلَّا نُوحِىٓ إِلَيْهِ أَنَّهُۥ لَآ إِلَٰهَ إِلَّآ أَنَا۠ فَٱعْبُدُونِ ٢٥

"We did not send any Messenger before you, O Muḥammad, except that We revealed to him that none has the right to be worshipped except Allaah, so make all your worship purely for Him."

[Soorah al-Ambiyaa (21):25]

وَمَآ أُمِرُوٓا۟ إِلَّا لِيَعْبُدُوا۟ ٱللَّهَ مُخْلِصِينَ لَهُ ٱلدِّينَ حُنَفَآءَ وَيُقِيمُوا۟ ٱلصَّلَوٰةَ وَيُؤْتُوا۟ ٱلزَّكَوٰةَ وَذَٰلِكَ دِينُ ٱلْقَيِّمَةِ ٥

"And they were not commanded except that they should worship Allaah alone, making their worship and obedience purely for Him, upon the true Religion and free from *shirk*; and that they should establish the Prayer, and pay the *zakaat*, and that is the straight and true Religion."

[Soorah al-Bayyinah (98):5]

وَالدَّلِيْلُ قَوْلُهُ تَعَالَى: ﴿ الْحَمْدُ لِلَّهِ رَبِّ الْعَالَمِيْنَ ﴾

وَكُلُّ مَا سِوَى اللَّهِ عَالَمٌ وَأَنَا وَاحِدٌ مِنْ ذَلِكَ الْعَالَم

فَإِذَا قِيْلَ لَكَ بِمَ عَرَفْتَ رَبَّكَ؟ فَقُلْ: بِآيَاتِهِ وَمَخْلُوْقَاتِهِ

The proof is the Saying of Allaah, the Most High: **"All praise is for Allaah, the Lord of all creation"**[48] [Soorah al-Faati_h_ah (1):1]. Everything besides Allaah is a created being and I am one of the creation.[49] So if it is said to you: 'How did you arrive at this knowledge of your Lord?' Then say: 'Through His signs and those things which He has created;[50]

---

[48] The author, *ra_h_imahullaah*, presents as proof for the fact that Allaah, the one free of all imperfections and the Most High, is the one who nurtures and sustains all of creation, the Saying of Allaah, the Most High: ٱلْحَمْدُلِلَّهِ "All praise is for Allaah" meaning that description with the attributes of perfection, majesty and greatness are for Allaah, the Most High, alone. رَبِّٱلْعَـٰلَمِينَ "the Lord of all creation" meaning that He is the one who nurtured and sustained them with His blessings, and that He is their creator and their owner and Sovereign-Lord, and that He is the one Who controls their affairs as He, the Mighty and Majestic, wishes.

[49] The creation (*al-'Aalam*: that by which something is known) is so called because they are a sign for their Creator, their sovereign Lord and the one Who controls their affairs. So everything contains a sign showing that Allaah is one, and I am one of the creation, and my Lord has made it obligatory upon me that I should worship Him alone.

[50] Signs (*Aayaat* plural of *Aayah*) are that which indicate something and make it clear. Then the signs of Allaah, the Most High, are of two types: signs in creation, and signs in His Revealed way (*Sharee'ah*). The signs in creation are those things which He created, and the signs in His Revealed way are what is found in His Revelation, which Allaah sent down to His messengers. So the saying of the author, *ra_h_imahullaah*, 'through His signs and those things which He has created' is

وَمِنْ آياتِهِ اللَّيْلُ وَالنَّهارُ وَالشَّمْسُ وَالقَمَرُ ، وَمِنْ مَخْلُوْقاتِهِ السَّمَوَاتُ السَّبْعُ وَالأَرَضُونَ السَّبْعُ وَمَنْ فِيهِنَّ وَمَا بَيْنَهُمَا

and from his signs are the night and the day, the sun and the moon; and from that which He has created are the seven heavens, and the seven earths, and all those within them, and whatever is between them.'51

---

an example of mentioning something particular after that which is general. If we explain the signs to mean both the signs in creation and those in the Revelation; or if we take the signs to refer to the signs in the Revelation in particular, then his saying is a case of addition of that which is separate and different from the first thing mentioned. So whichever the case then knowledge of Allaah, the Mighty and Majestic, is arrived at through His signs in the creation, the tremendous things contained therein which are wondrous creations and clear proofs of perfect wisdom; and likewise through the signs in His Revealed way, and the justice to be seen in it and how it comprises all that is beneficial and repels all that is corrupt.

'And in everything there is a sign for Him, Proving that He is One.'

51 All of these are from Allaah's signs which prove His complete and perfect Power, and complete and perfect wisdom. So the sun is one of Allaah's signs, in its wonderful and well-ordered course which it has followed since Allaah, the Mighty and Majestic, created it, and which it will follow until Allaah, the Most High, grants that the universe is destroyed. So this is its appointed course, as Allaah, the Most High, says,

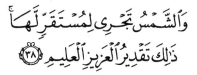

"And the sun proceeds upon its fixed course, (for a term appointed) that is the decree of the All-Mighty, the All-Wise."

[Soorah Yaa Seen (36):38]

Its size and its effects are from the signs of Allaah. As for its size, then it is tremendously great; and as for its effects, then it produces benefit for our bodies, for the

وَالدَّلِيلُ قَوْلُهُ تَعَالَى:

The proof[52] is the Saying of Allaah, the Most High:

---

trees, the rivers, the oceans and other things besides. So if we consider the sun, this great sign, and the great distance that there is between us and it, yet despite this we feel its great heat. Then consider the light it produces which saves the people huge amounts of wealth in the daylight hours when they have no need of other sources of light, so it is indeed a very great sign, and most people perceive only very few of the signs. Likewise the moon is also from the signs of Allaah, the Mighty and Majestic, and He decreed for it measured stations. Each night it has its particular station,

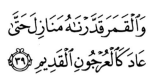

"We have prescribed measured phases for the moon till it re-turns like an old withered palm-stalk."

[Soorah Yaa Seen (36):39]

So it first appears very fine, then its increases stage by stage until it becomes full, then it wanes and returns as it was. It resembles man who begins as something weak, and then increases steadily in strength, and finally again returns to being weak, so exalted is Allaah, the best creator.

[52] i.e. the proof that the day and the night, the sun and the moon are from Allaah's signs is the Saying of Allaah, the Most High,

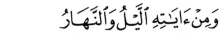

"And from His signs are the night and the day."

[Soorah Fussilat (41):37]

Meaning that the day and the night are from the very clear signs and proofs of Allaah, both in themselves and how they interchange. Also in the benefits which Allaah has placed in them for the servants, and in their changing states. Likewise with regard to the sun and the moon which are signs both in themselves; and in the courses which they proceed upon; and in their order; and the benefit which they

﴿ وَمِنْ آيَاتِهِ اللَّيْلُ وَالنَّهَارُ وَالشَّمْسُ وَالقَمَرُ لَا تَسْجُدُوا لِلشَّمْسِ وَلَا لِلْقَمَرِ وَاسْجُدُوا لِلَّهِ الَّذِي خَلَقَهُنَّ إِنْ كُنْتُمْ إِيَّاهُ تَعْبُدُونَ ﴾ وَقَوْلُهُ تَعَالَى: ﴿ إِنَّ رَبَّكُمُ اللَّهُ الَّذِي خَلَقَ السَّمَاوَاتِ وَالْأَرْضَ فِي سِتَّةِ أَيَّامٍ ثُمَّ اسْتَوَى عَلَى العَرْشِ يُغْشِي اللَّيْلَ النَّهَارَ يَطْلُبُهُ حَثِيثًا وَالشَّمْسَ وَالقَمَرَ وَالنُّجُومَ مُسَخَّرَاتٍ بِأَمْرِهِ أَلَا لَهُ الخَلْقُ وَالأَمْرُ تَبَارَكَ اللَّهُ رَبُّ العَالَمِينَ ﴾.

"And from His signs are the night and the day, and the sun and the moon. Do not prostrate to the sun, nor to the moon, but prostrate to Allaah who created them, if you truly worship Him" [Soorah Fuṣṣilat (41):37] and His, the Most High's Saying: **"Your Lord is Allaah who created the heavens and the earth in six days, then ascended upon the Throne. He causes the night to cover the day which it follows with haste; and the sun, the moon and the stars are subservient and subject to His command. Certainly creation and commandment are His alone. Exalted is Allaah the Lord of all creation."**[53] [Soorah al-A'raaf (7):54]

---

provide for the servants and the harm which that keeps away. Then Allaah, the Most High, forbids the servants from prostrating to the sun or the moon, even though they are very great, yet they are not deserving of and do not have the right to be worshipped, since they are two created things, and the one Who is alone deserving and has the right to worship is Allaah, the Most High, Who created them.

53 Meaning, from the proofs that Allaah created the heavens and the earth is this Saying of Allaah, the Most High which mentions the following signs of Allaah:

    (i) That Allaah created these tremendous entities in six days, and if He

وَالرَّبُّ هُوَ الْمَعْبُودُ

The Lord is the one who is worshipped,[54]

---

wished He could have created them in a single moment, but instead from His wisdom He connected effects to their causes.

(ii) That He ascended upon the Throne, i.e. He ascended upon it in particular in a manner befitting His Majesty and Exaltedness, and this shows the perfection of His Kingship and Sovereignty.

(iii) That He causes the night to envelop and cover the day, so that it is like a garment which descends upon the light of day and covers it up.

(iv) That He has made the sun, the moon and the stars subservient to His command. He commands them as He wills for the benefit of the servants.

(v) That His Sovereignty comprehends everything and His Kingship is perfect, such that creation and commandment are His alone and for no one else.

(vi) That His Lordship comprehends all of creation.

[54] The author, is indicating to the *Aayah*:

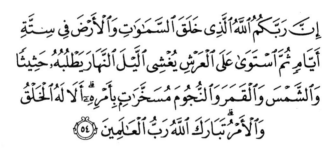

"Your Lord is Allaah who created the heavens and the earth in six days, then ascended upon the Throne. He causes the night to cover the day which it follows with haste; and the sun, the moon and stars are subservient and subject to His command. Certainly creation and commandment are His alone. Exalted is Allaah the Lord of all creation."

[Soorah al-A'raaf (7):54]

وَالدَّلِيْلُ قَوْلُهُ تَعَالَى: ﴿ يَا أَيُّهَا النَّاسُ اعْبُدُوْا

رَبَّكُمُ الَّذِي خَلَقَكُمْ وَالَّذِيْنَ مِنْ قَبْلِكُمْ لَعَلَّكُمْ تَتَّقُوْنَ

and the proof[55] is the Saying of Allaah, the Most High, **"O man-kind,[56] single out your Lord with all worship; He who created you[57] and all those who came before you, so that you may be of those who seek to avoid Allaah's anger and punishment, those whom Allaah is pleased with.[58]**

So the Lord is the one who is worshipped, meaning that He is the One Who alone has the right to be worshipped, or that He is the One who is worshipped rightfully and deservingly, the meaning is not that everything which is worshipped is a Lord, since those gods which are worshipped besides Allaah and which are taken as lords by those who worship them are not Lords. Rather the Lord (*ar-Rabb*) is the creator, the sovereign, the one in control and command of all the affairs.

55 i.e. the proof that the Lord is the one who deserves to be worshipped.

56 The address is to all people from the descendants of Aadam: Allaah, the Mighty and Majestic, commands them to worship Him alone, having no partner, so they are not to attribute rivals in their worship with Allaah. He makes it clear that He alone deserves to be worshipped since He is the sole Creator, having no partner.

57 His Saying: (الَّذِي خَلَقَكُمْ) (i.e. the One Who created you) this is a description explaining the reason for what has preceded, meaning: Worship Him because He is your Lord Who created you. So because He is the Lord and Creator, then it is a necessary duty upon you that you should worship Him. Therefore we say that it is unavoidably binding upon anyone who affirms the Lordship of Allaah that he should worship Him alone, otherwise the person will be contradicting himself.

58 Meaning that you should attain *taqwaa*, and *taqwaa* is to take protection from the punishment of Allaah, the Mighty and Majestic, by doing whatever He commands and keeping away from whatever He forbids.

الَّذِي جَعَلَ لَكُمُ الأَرْضَ فِرَاشًا وَالسَّمَاءَ بِنَاءً وَأَنْزَلَ مِنَ السَّمَاءِ مَاءً فَأَخْرَجَ بِهِ مِنَ الثَّمَرَاتِ رِزْقًا لَكُمْ فَلاَ تَجْعَلُوا لِلَّهِ أَنْدَادًا وَأَنْتُمْ تَعْلَمُونَ ﴿

He who has made the earth a resting place[59] for you and has made the sky a canopy,[60] and sent down rain from the sky,[61] and brought out with it crops and fruits from the earth as provision for you.[62] So do not set up rivals with Allaah in your worship[63] whilst you know that you have no Lord besides Him."[64] [Soorah al-Baqarah (2):21-22]

---

[59] Meaning He has made it a resting place spread out for us, which we may use as such without any difficulty or hardship, just as a person sleeps upon his bed.

[60] i.e. above us, so the sky is a canopy for the people of the earth and it is a safe and protected ceiling, as Allaah, the Most High, says:

وَجَعَلْنَا السَّمَاءَ سَقْفًا مَحْفُوظًا وَهُمْ عَنْ آيَاتِهَا مُعْرِضُونَ ﴿٣٢﴾

"And We made the sky a raised ceiling, safe and guarded, yet the unbelievers turn away from considering the clear signs."
[Soorah al-Ambiyaa' (21):32]

[61] i.e. He sends down from above, from the clouds, pure water for you to drink, and which causes vegetation to grow which you allow your cattle to graze upon, as is mentioned in *Soorah an-Nahl* (16):10.

[62] i.e. As a gift for you, and as stated in another *Aayah*,

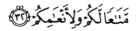

"As provision for you and your cattle"
[Soorah 'Abasa (80):32]

قَالَ ابْنُ كَثِيرٍ رَحِمَهُ اللَّهُ تَعَالَى » الْخَالِقُ لِهَذِهِ الْأَشْيَاء

هُوَ الْمُسْتَحِقُّ لِلْعِبَادَةِ « وَأَنْوَاعُ الْعِبَادَةِ الَّتِي أَمَرَ اللَّهُ بِهَا

مِثْلُ الْإِسْلَامِ ، وَالْإِيمَانِ ، وَالْإِحْسَانِ ، وَمِنْهُ الدُّعَاءُ

Ibn Katheer,[65] *rahimahullaah,* said: "The creator of these things is the One Who deserves to be worshipped." All the types of worship which Allaah commanded[66] - like Islaam (submission and obedience to Allaah), *eemaan* (true Faith comprising belief of the heart, speech of the tongue and action of the limbs), and *ihsaan* (perfection of worship), and from that is invocation/supplication (*du'aa*),

---

63 Meaning, do not set up rivals for the One Who created you, and created those before you, and made the earth a resting place for you and the sky a canopy, and sent down rain from the sky for you, and produced fruits and produce for you, so do not set up for Him rivals which you worship just as you worship Allaah, or which you love just as you love Allaah, since that is not fitting for you, neither according to sound intellect, nor according to Revelation.

64 i.e. when you know that He has no rival, and that creation, provision and control of the affairs is in His Hand alone, so do not set up any partner along with Him in worship.

65 He is 'Imaaduddeen Abul-Fidaa' Ismaa'eel ibn 'Umar al-Qurashee, *al-Haafidh,* the famous author of the *Tafseer* and *Taareekh* (*al-Bidaayah wan-Nihaayah*). He was one of the students of Shaykh-ul-Islaam Ibn Taymiyyah, and died in the year 774H.

66 Having made clear that it is obligatory upon us to worship Allaah, alone, giving no share of worship to anyone besides Allaah, the author, *rahimahullaah* goes on to explain some of the different types of worship. So he said: "And all the types of worship... like Islaam, *eemaan* and *ihsaan.*"

These three: Islaam, *eemaan* and *ihsaan* are the Religion (*Deen*), as occurs in the

وَالْخَوْفُ ، وَالرَّجَاءُ ، وَالتَّوَكُّلُ ، وَالرَّغْبَةُ ،وَالرَّهْبَةُ ، وَالْخُشُوْعُ ،
وَالْخَشْيَةُ وَالإِنَابَةُ ، وَالإِسْتِعَانَةُ ، وَالإِسْتِعَاذَةُ ، وَالإِسْتِغَاثَةُ ، وَالذَّبْحُ ،
وَالنَّذْرُ وَغَيْرُ ذَلِكَ مِنْ أَنْوَاعِ الْعِبَادَةِ الَّتِي أَمَرَ اللَّهُ بِهَا كُلَّهَا لِلَّهِ تَعَالَى

reverential fear (*khawf*), hope and longing (*rajaa*), trust and reliance (*tawakkul*), fervent desire (*raghbah*), dread (*rahbah*), reverence and humility (*khushoo'*), awe (*khashyah*), turning repentantly (*inaabah*), appealing for aid and assistance (*isti'aanah*), seeking refuge (*isti'aadhah*), seeking deliverance and rescue (*istighaathah*), sacrificing (*dhabh*), vows (*nadhr*) and the rest of the types of worship commanded by Allaah, all of them are to be done exclusively for Allaah, the Most High.

---

narration reported by Muslim from the *hadeeth* of 'Umar ibn al-Khattaab, *radiyallaahu 'anhu*, who said: *"Whilst we were sitting with Allaah's Messenger (ﷺ) one day, a man came having very white clothes and very black hair. No trace of having travelled could be seen upon him, and none of us knew him. So he sat down before the Prophet (ﷺ) and joined his knees with his knees, and placed his palms upon his thighs and said: "O Muhammad, tell me about Islaam." So Allaah's Messenger (ﷺ) said: "Islaam is that you testify that none has the right to be worshipped but Allaah, and that Muhammad is the Messenger of Allaah; that you establish the Prayer; pay the zakaat; fast Ramadaan; and make pilgrimage (hajj) to the House if you are able to do so." He said: "You have spoken correctly." He (i.e. 'Umar) said: 'So we were amazed at how he asked, and then told him that he had spoken correctly.' He said: "Then tell me about eemaan," He said: "It is that you have true faith in Allaah, His angels, His Books, His Messengers, the Last Day, and that you have true faith in pre-decree (al-qadr), its good and its evil." He said: "You have spoken correctly." He said: "Then tell me about ihsaan." He said: "It is that you worship Allaah as if you were seeing Him, and even though you do not see Him, yet He certainly sees you." He said: "Then tell me about the Hour." He said: "The one who is questioned about it knows no better than the one who is asking." He said: "Then tell me about the signs." He said: "That the*

وَالدَّلِيْلُ قَوْلُهُ تَعَالَى: ﴿ وَأَنَّ المَسَاجِدَ لِلَّهِ فَلاَ تَدْعُوْا مَعَ اللَّهِ أَحَدًا ﴾

فَمَنْ صَرَفَ مِنْهَا شَيْئًا لِغَيْرِ اللَّهِ فَهُوَ مُشْرِكٌ كَافِرٌ وَالدَّلِيْلُ قَوْلُهُ تَعَالَى:

﴿ وَمَنْ يَدْعُ مَعَ اللَّهِ إِلَهًا آخَرَ لاَ بُرْهَانَ لَهُ بِهِ فَإِنَّمَا حِسَابُهُ عِنْدَ

رَبِّهِ إِنَّهُ لاَ يُفْلِحُ الكَافِرُوْنَ ﴾

The proof for this is the Saying of Him, the Most High:[67] **"And the places of Prayer are for Allaah alone, so do not invoke anyone along with Allaah"** [Soorah al-Jinn (72):18].

Anyone who directs any part of that to anything besides Allaah, then he is a *mushrik* (associationist), an unbeliever (*kaafir*), and the proof is the Saying of Him, the Most High, **"And whoever worships along with Allaah any other object of worship has no proof for that; his reckoning will be with his Lord. Indeed the unbelievers will never prosper"**[68] [Soorah al-Mu'minoon (23):117].

---

slave-girl will give birth to her mistress, and that you will see the bare-footed, naked, and destitute, shepherds competing in building tall buildings." Then he *went off. Then he (i.e. the Prophet (ﷺ)) remained for a long while, then he said: "O 'Umar, do you know who the questioner was?" I said: "Allaah and His Messenger know best." He said: "He was Jibreel, he came to you to teach you your Religion (Deen).""*

So the Prophet (ﷺ) declared all of these things to be the Religion, and that is because they comprehend all of the Religion.

67 Meaning that all types of worship, those mentioned by the author and all other types also, are exclusively for Allaah alone, and there is no partner for Him, so it is not permissible to direct them to anyone other than Allaah, the Most High.

68 The author, may Allaah, the Most High, have mercy upon him, mentions a

93

number of types of worship, and mentions that whoever directs anything from them to other than Allaah is a *mushrik,* an unbeliever, and he proves this with the Sayings of Allaah, the Most High,

وَأَنَّ ٱلۡمَسَٰجِدَ لِلَّهِ فَلَا تَدۡعُواْ مَعَ ٱللَّهِ أَحَدًا ۱۸

"And the places of Prayer (*masaajid*) are for Allaah alone, so do not invoke anyone along with Allaah."

[Soorah al-Jinn (72):18]

وَمَن يَدۡعُ مَعَ ٱللَّهِ إِلَٰهًا
ءَاخَرَ لَا بُرۡهَٰنَ لَهُۥ بِهِۦ فَإِنَّمَا حِسَابُهُۥ عِندَ رَبِّهِۦٓ إِنَّهُۥ لَا يُفۡلِحُ
ٱلۡكَٰفِرُونَ ۱۱۷

"And whoever worships along with Allaah any other object of worship has no proof for that; his reckoning will be with his Lord. Indeed the unbelievers will never prosper."

[Soorah al-Mu'minoon (23):117]

The first *Aayah* is a proof, since Allaah, the Most High, informs that the *masaajid,* which are either the places in which prostration (*sujood*) is made (i.e. the places of Prayer), or the limbs which prostrate, are for Allaah alone. Then He stated as a consequence of that: فَلَا تَدۡعُواْ مَعَ ٱللَّهِ أَحَدًا that is: so do not worship and prostrate to anything else along with Him.

The second *Aayah* is a proof since Allaah, the one free of all imperfections and the Most High, explains that whoever supplicates and invokes something else besides Allaah is an unbeliever (*kaafir*), because He says: **"Indeed the unbelievers will never prosper."** Furthermore His Saying لَا بُرۡهَٰنَ لَهُۥ **"(They have) no proof for that"** indicates that it is not possible for there to be any proof supporting worship of other gods. So this is a description to make the matter clear and manifest, and it is not a qualifying description meant to exclude that which is supported by proof. This is the case since it is not possible for there to be any proof allowing worship of anything along with Allaah.

وَفِي الحَدِيثِ « الدُّعَاءُ مُخُّ العِبَادَةِ » وَالدَّلِيْلُ قَوْلُهُ تَعَالَى : ﴿ وَقَالَ
رَبُّكُمُ ادْعُوْنِي أَسْتَجِبْ لَكُمْ إِنَّ الَّذِيْنَ يَسْتَكْبِرُوْنَ عَنْ عِبَادَتِي
سَيَدْخُلُوْنَ جَهَنَّمَ دَاخِرِيْنَ ﴾.

In the _hadeeth_ there occurs: _"Invocation is the core of worship."_*
And the evidence for this is the Saying of Allaah, the Most High:
**"Your Lord says: O people, invoke Me and supplicate to Me mak-
ing your worship sincerely for Me alone, and I will answer you,
and pardon you and have mercy upon you. Indeed those who disdain to worship Me alone will enter Hell-Fire in disgrace"**[69] [Soorah
Ghaafir (40):60].

---

* Translator's note: The hadeeth is reported with this wording by at-Tirmidhee
and declared weak (_da'eef_) by Shaykh Muḥammad Naaṣiruddeen al-Albaanee in
al-Mishkaat (no. 2331) due to the weakness of one of its narrators, Ibn Lahee'ah.
Imaam Aḥmad and the four _Sunan_ report an authentic _hadeeth_ with the wording:
"Invocation is Worship." (Declared authentic (_saheeh_) by Shaykh al-Albaanee in
Saheehul-Jaami' (no. 3407)).

[69] Here the author, _raḥimahullaah_, begins to quote evidences for the types of
worship which he mentioned in his saying: "And the types of worship which Allaah
commanded, such as Islaam, _eemaan_ and _iḥsaan_, and from that is supplication
(_du'aa_)..." So he began by mentioning the evidences for supplication/invocation
(_du'aa_), and the proofs for Islaam, _eemaan_ and _iḥsaan_ in detail will follow, if
Allaah wills. So the author used as evidence what is related from the Prophet (ﷺ)
as his saying: _"Invocation is the core of worship"_ and he used as evidence the
Saying of Allaah, the Most High,

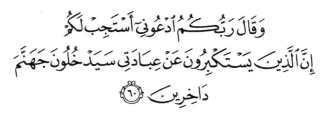

"Your Lord says: O people, invoke Me and supplicate to Me making your worship sincerely for Me alone, and I will answer you, and pardon you and have mercy upon you. Indeed those who disdain to worship Me alone will enter Hell-Fire in disgrace."
[Soorah Ghaafir (40):60]

So the noble *Aayah* proves that invocation/supplication (*du'aa*) is worship, and if that were not the case it would not be said (إِنَّ ٱلَّذِينَ يَسْتَكْبِرُونَ عَنْ عِبَادَتِي) **"those who disdain to worship Me alone...."** So whoever called upon anyone besides Allaah, the Mighty and Majestic, requesting something which none but Allaah has power over, then he is a *mushrik* (one who worships others besides Allaah), an unbeliever (*kaafir*), whether the one he calls upon is living or dead. Whoever requests a living person for something which he is able to do, such as the saying: 'O so and so give me food' or 'O so and so give me a drink,' then there is no harm in that. But whoever asks a dead person or someone who is absent for that, then he is a *mushrik*, since the deceased or the absent cannot possibly do that. So in such a case his supplicating to them shows that he believes that they have some control over the creation, and he is therefore a *mushrik.*

It must be noted that *du'aa* is of two types: (i) Supplication, when a request is made (*du'aa-u mas'alah*) and, (ii) invocation through worship (*du'aa-u 'ibaadah*).

So supplication is to request ones needs, and is worship when the servant requests that from his Lord. This is because it involves showing ones poverty before Allaah, the Most High, and ones need to turn to Him, and ones certain faith that He is the one having full power, the Most Generous, the one who gives bounteously and is Most Merciful. Seeking ones needs from someone else from the creation is permissible if the one to whom the request is made is able to hear and understand it, and has the power to respond to it, like the saying: 'O so and so give me food.'

As for invocation through worship, then it is that the person does an act of worship seeking reward and fearing punishment, and this is not correct unless directed to Allaah alone. To direct this to anyone else besides Allaah is major *shirk* which takes a person out of the Religion, and he falls under the threat in the Saying of Allaah, the Most High,

وَدَلِيْلُ الخَوْفِ قَوْلُهُ تَعَالَى : ﴿ فَلاَ تَخَافُوْهُمْ

فَلاَ تَخَافُوْهُمْ وَخَافُوْنِ إِنْ كُنْتُمْ مُؤْمِنِيْنَ ﴾

The evidence for reverential fear (*khawf*) is the Saying of Allaah, the Most High: **"So do not fear them, but fear Me and beware of disobeying Me, if you are truly Believers"**[70] [Soorah Aal-'Imraan (3):175].

وَقَالَ رَبُّكُمُ ادْعُونِي أَسْتَجِبْ لَكُمْ
إِنَّ الَّذِينَ يَسْتَكْبِرُونَ عَنْ عِبَادَتِي سَيَدْخُلُونَ جَهَنَّمَ
دَاخِرِينَ ﴿٦٠﴾

"Your Lord says: O people, invoke Me and supplicate to Me making your worship sincerely for Me alone, and I will answer you, and pardon you and have mercy upon you. Indeed those who disdain to worship Me alone will enter Hell-Fire in disgrace."
[Soorah Ghaafir (40):60]

70 Fear is to be frightened and is a result of expecting something which will bring about destruction, harm or injury, and Allaah, the one free of all imperfections and the Most High, forbade having fear of the allies of the Satan, and He commanded fear of Himself alone. Fear is of three types:

(i) Natural fear, such as a persons fear of predatory animals, fire, or drowning. This is something for which a person is not to be blamed. Allaah, the Most High, said about Moosaa,

فَأَصْبَحَ فِي الْمَدِينَةِ خَائِفًا يَتَرَقَّبُ

"So he entered in the morning in Pharaoh's city in a state of fear, awaiting events."

[Soorah al-Qasas (28):18]

97

However if this fear is, as mentioned by the author, a cause of his leaving an obligation or doing something forbidden, then it is forbidden. Since whatever causes an obligation to be abandoned, or causes something forbidden to be done is itself forbidden (*haraam*). The evidence here is the Saying of Allaah, the Most High,

$$\text{فَلَا تَخَافُوهُمْ وَخَافُونِ إِن كُنتُم مُّؤْمِنِينَ ﴿١٧٥﴾}$$

"So do not fear them, but fear Me and beware of disobeying Me, if you are truly Believers."

[Soorah Aal-'Imraan (3):175]

Furthermore fear of Allaah, the Most High, is sometimes something praiseworthy, and is sometimes something that is not praiseworthy. It is praiseworthy when it prevents you from being disobedient to Allaah, and causes you to fulfil the obligatory duties and to avoid what is forbidden. So if this goal is reached, then the heart settles and is at peace, and is dominated by joy at the blessings of Allaah and hope for His reward.

It is something that is not praiseworthy when it causes a person to despair of Allaah's Mercy and to give up hope altogether. In such a case the person will give up and may continue in sin due to the fact that he totally gives up hope.

(ii) Reverential fear, that he fears something and takes that as his religion. This is to be for Allaah, the Most High, alone. Directing such reverential fear to anyone other than Allaah, the Most High, is *major shirk*.

(iii) Secret supernatural fear, such as fearing someone buried in a grave, or a person thought to be pious, who is far away and cannot affect him, yet still he has secret fear for him. This is also mentioned by the scholars as being a case of *shirk*.

وَدَلِيلُ الرَّجَاءِ قَوْلُهُ تَعَالَى: ﴿ فَمَنْ كَانَ يَرْجُو لِقَآءَ رَبِّهِ فَلْيَعْمَلْ عَمَلاً صَالِحًا وَلاَيُشْرِكْ بِعِبَادَةِ رَبِّهِ أَحَدًا ﴾

The evidence for hope and longing (ar-rajaa) is the Saying of Allaah the Most High: **"So whoever hopes to see His Lord and be rewarded by Him, then let him make his worship correct and make it purely and sincerely for Him; and let him not make any share of it for anyone other than Him"**[71] [Soorah al-Kahf (18):110].

---

[71] Hope and longing (ar-rajaa') is that a person wishes for something that may be attained and is close, and it may be something that is far off but treated as being something close. This earnest hope which comprises humility and submission may not be directed except to Allaah, the Mighty and Majestic, and directing it to anyone other than Allaah, the Most High, is *shirk*. This *shirk* will either be lesser *shirk* or major *shirk* depending upon the state of the heart of the person in this case. The author uses as evidence the Saying of Allaah, the Most High,

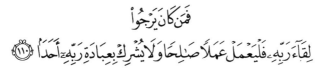

"So whoever hopes to see His Lord and be rewarded by Him, then let him make his worship correct and make it purely and sincerely for Him; and let him not make any share of it for anyone other than Him."

[Soorah al-Kahf (18):110]

'Hope' which is praiseworthy is only that which is found in a person who acts in obedience to Allaah and hopes for reward from Him, or a person who repents from sin and hopes that his repentance is accepted. As for a person who hopes despite the fact that he does not act, then this is delusion and false hopes, and is something blameworthy.

وَدَلِيلُ التَّوَكُّلِ قَوْلُهُ تَعَالَى: ﴿ وَعَلَى اللَّهِ فَتَوَكَّلُوا إِنْ كُنْتُمْ

مُؤْمِنِينَ ﴾ وَقَالَ: ﴿ وَمَنْ يَتَوَكَّلْ عَلَى اللَّهِ فَهُوَ حَسْبُهُ ﴾

The evidence for trust and reliance (*at-tawakkul*) is the Saying of Allaah, the Most High, **"And place your reliance and trust in Allaah if you are true Believers"** [Soorah al-Maa'idah (5):23] and He said: **"And whoever places his reliance and trust in Allaah then He will suffice him"**[72] [Soorah at-Talaaq (65):3].

---

[72] Placing reliance upon something is to depend upon it; and placing reliance upon Allaah, the Most High, is to depend upon Allaah, the Most High, and to accept Him as being the One who suffices you in bringing whatever is beneficial to you and protecting you from whatever is harmful. This is from the completion of true Faith (*eemaan*) and is a sign of it, as He, the Most High, says,

وَعَلَى اللَّهِ فَتَوَكَّلُوٓا۟ إِن كُنتُم مُّؤْمِنِينَ ﴿٢٣﴾

"And place your reliance and trust in Allaah if you are true Believers."

[Soorah al-Maa'idah (5):23]

If the person is sincere in his reliance and trust in Allaah, the Most High, then Allaah, the Most High, will take care of whatever troubles or concerns him, as He, the Most High, says,

وَمَن يَتَوَكَّلْ عَلَى اللَّهِ فَهُوَ حَسْبُهُۥٓ

"And whoever places his reliance and trust in Allaah then He will suffice him."

[Soorah at-Talaaq (65):3]

Meaning that He will suffice him, then He sets the mind of the one who trusts in Him at rest with His Saying,

قَدْ جَعَلَ اللَّهُ لِكُلِّ شَىْءٍ قَدْرًا

"Allaah will certainly bring about whatever He has decreed."

[Soorah at-Talaaq (65):3]

So nothing at all can prevent Him from whatever He wills. Furthermore it should be known that placing reliance and trust is of different types:

(i) Trust and reliance upon Allaah, the Most High, is from the completion of *eemaan*, and one of the signs of its sincerity, it is obligatory since *eemaan* cannot be completed without it, and the proof has preceded.

(ii) Secret trust and dependence, such that he depends upon someone deceased to bring him some benefit or remove some harm, this is major *shirk*. This is because it will not occur except from a person who believes that this deceased person has some hidden control over the creation. There is no difference in this matter whether the deceased is a prophet, a pious person, or an evil enemy of Allaah, the Most High, who is worshipped by the people.

(iii) Placing reliance upon someone else in the affairs, whilst feeling that he himself is of a low standing and the one he depends upon is therefore of higher standing, for example that he depends upon him to bring him sustenance and the like, then this is a type of lesser *shirk* due to the strong connection his heart forms towards him and his dependance upon him. But if he merely relied upon him being certain that he is just a means, and that Allaah, the Most High, is the One Who alone has the power to bring that about in His Hand, then there is no harm in that, since the one on whom he places reliance does have an effect in causing it to occur.

(iv) Relying upon someone else and allowing someone else to act on your behalf with regard to a matter where one is allowed to depute someone. This is something about which there is no harm, as shown by the evidence of the Book, the *Sunnah* and the consensus (*ijmaa'*). Ya'qoob said to his sons:

"O my sons, go back and seek news of Yoosuf and his brother."

[Soorah Yoosuf (12):87]

Also the Prophet (ﷺ) deputed men to take charge of collection and looking after the *zakaat*; he deputed people to establish and carry out the prescribed

وَدَلِيلُ الرَّغْبَةِ وَالرَّهْبَةِ وَالْخُشُوْعِ قَوْلُهُ تَعَالَى: ﴿ إِنَّهُمْ كَانُوْا

يُسَارِعُوْنَ فِي الْخَيْرَاتِ وَيَدْعُوْنَنَا رَغَبًا وَرَهَبًا وَكَانُوْا لَنَا خَاشِعِيْنَ ﴾

وَدَلِيْلُ الْخَشْيَةِ قَوْلُهُ تَعَالَى: ﴿ فَلاَ تَخْشَوْهُمْ وَاخْشَوْنِ ﴾

The evidence for the fervent desire (*ar-raghbah*),[73] dread (*ar-rahbah*)[74] and reverence and humility (*al-khushoo'*)[75] is the Saying of Allaah, the Most High: **"They used to hasten to acts of devotion and obedience to Allaah, and they used to worship Allaah upon love and desire, and upon fear, and were reverent and humble before Allaah"**[76] [Soorah al-Ambiyaa (21):90].

---

punishment; and deputed 'Alee ibn Abee Taalib, *radiyallaahu 'anhu*, to take charge of some of his sacrificial animals during the Farewell Pilgrimage, and to give their skins and covering sheets in charity, and to sacrifice the remainder of the hundred camels after he (ﷺ) had sacrificed sixty three with his own hand. As for the consensus (*ijmaa'*) upon permissibility of this, then it is something known.

[73] *Ar-Raghbah* is the love and desire to reach that which is beloved.

[74] *Ar-Rahbah* is fear which causes one to flee away from the cause of fear. So it is a fear that is accompanied by action.

[75] *Al-Khushoo'* is humility and submissiveness before the Greatness of Allaah, such that the person submits to whatever Allaah has pre-decreed and what He has ordained and commanded.

[76] In this noble *Aayah*, Allaah, the Most High, describes the most loyal and sincere of His servants as worshipping Allaah, the Most High, upon *raghbah* and *rahbah*, whist being humble and submissive to Him. The *du'aa* (invocation) here covers both invoking Allaah through acts of worship, and supplication. So they call upon Allaah out of earnest desire for what is with Him, and hoping for His reward, whilst also fearing His punishment as a result of their sins. So the Believer should hasten to Allaah, the Most High, upon fear and earnest desire; with

وَدَلِيلُ الخَشْيَةِ قَوْلُهُ تَعَالَى : ﴿ فَلاَ تَخْشَوْهُمْ وَاخْشَوْنِ ﴾

The evidence for awe/dread (*al-khashyah*) is the Saying of Allaah, the Most High: **"So do not have awe of them, but have awe of Me"**[77] [Soorah al-Maa'idah (5):3].

---

regard to actions of obedience his hope and earnest desire should predominate, so that he is keen to perform them and hopes that they will be accepted; and with regard to whenever he thinks of committing a sin, then fear should predominate so that he will flee away from doing it and be saved from its consequent punishment.

Some scholars say that the aspect of hope should predominate when a person is ill, and the aspect of fear when he is well. They say this since a person who is ill feels subdued and weakened and it may be that his appointed time is near, so that he may die, and he should do so whilst thinking good of Allaah, the Mighty and Majestic. But when healthy he is energetic and has hope of remaining for a long time, and this may lead him to be exuberant and carefree, so fear should predominate in order to be safe from that. It is also said that the earnest hope and fear should be equal so that his hope does not lead him to feel safe from Allaah, and his fear does not cause him to despair of Allaah's mercy, since both of these are evil and cause a person's destruction.

[77] Awe (*al-khashyah*) is fear founded upon knowledge of the greatness of the One whom he fears, and the complete and perfect Sovereignty and Dominion that is His, since Allaah, the Most High, says,

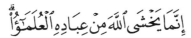

"Only those who have knowledge will truly have awe of Allaah."
[Soorah Faatir (35):28]

Meaning those who know of His greatness and perfect Sovereignty. It is something more particular than fear, and the difference between it and fear will become clear by giving an example: If you fear someone, but you do not know whether he is able to catch you or not, then this is fear (*khawf*). But when you fear someone and know that he is fully able to seize hold of you then that is fear/dread (*khashyah*). With regard to speech about the rulings for each class of fear/dread, then it is the same as for what has already been said with regard to reverential fear (*khawf*).

وَدَلِيلُ الإِنَابَةِ قَوْلُهُ تَعَالَى: ﴿ وَأَنِيبُوۡا إِلَى رَبِّكُمۡ وَأَسۡلِمُوۡا لَهُ ﴾

And the evidence for turning repentantly (al-inaabah) is the Saying of Allaah, the Most High: **"So turn, O you people, repentantly and obediently to your Lord, and submit obediently to Him"**[78] [Soorah az-Zumar (39):54].

---

[78] *Al-Inaabah* is to turn to Allaah, the Most High, in obedience, and avoiding disobedience to Him, and its meaning is close to that of repentance (*tawbah*), except that it is more subtle in meaning, and conveys the sense of dependance upon Allaah and fleeing for refuge to Him, and it cannot be except for Allaah, the Most High. Its evidence is the Saying of Allaah, the Most High,

وَأَنِيبُوٓاْ إِلَىٰ رَبِّكُمۡ وَأَسۡلِمُواْ لَهُۥ

"So turn, O you people, repentantly and obediently to your Lord, and submit obediently to Him"

[Soorah az-Zumar (39):54]

What is meant by the Saying of Allaah, the Most High, وَأَسۡلِمُواْ لَهُۥ **"...submit obediently to Him"** is: Islaam as prescribed and required of us in the *Sharee'ah* and that is to submit to the laws and commandments of Allaah. This is because submission to Allaah, the Most High, is of two types:

(i) Submission of all the creation, which is to submit to whatever He has decreed should exist and occur in the creation about which the creation has no choice. So this is general and covers everyone in the heavens and the earth, the Believers and the unbelievers, the righteous and the wicked. No one can possibly disdain and depart from this. The evidence for it is the Saying of Allaah, the Most High,

وَلَهُۥٓ أَسۡلَمَ مَن فِي ٱلسَّمَٰوَٰتِ
وَٱلۡأَرۡضِ طَوۡعٗا وَكَرۡهٗا وَإِلَيۡهِ يُرۡجَعُونَ ۝

"And to Him everyone in the heavens and the earth submit, willingly or unwillingly, and to Him you will all be returned."

[Soorah Aal-'Imraan (3):83]

وَدَلِيلُ الاِسْتِعَانَةِ قَوْلُهُ تَعَالَى : ﴿ إِيَّاكَ نَعْبُدُ وَإِيَّاكَ نَسْتَعِيْنُ ﴾ وَفِي

الْحَدِيْثِ « إِذَا اسْتَعَنْتَ فَاسْتَعِنْ بِاللَّهِ »

The evidence for appealing for aid and assistance (*al-isti'aanah*) is the Saying of Allaah, the Most High: **"O Allaah You alone we worship, and to You alone we appeal for aid"** [Soorah al-Faatihah (1):5] and in the *hadeeth* there occurs: *"If you seek help, then seek the help of Allaah."*[79] [Reported by at-Tirmidhee and declared *Saheeh* by Shaykh al-Albaanee in *al-Mishkaat* (no.5302)]

(ii) Submission to the laws and prescriptions of Islaam, and this is to submit in obedience. This is particular to those who are obedient to Allaah, the Messengers and those who follow them upon good. The evidences for this in the Qur'aan are many, and from them is the *Aayah* mentioned by the author [Soorah az-Zumar (39):5].

[79] *Al-Isti'aanah* is to appeal for assistance, and it is of various types:
(i) Appealing for aid and assistance from Allaah - this is an appeal for aid and assistance that comprises complete humility of the servant before his Lord, and to submit and entrust the affair to Him, and to be certain that He is fully sufficient for him. This is not to be except for Allaah, the Most High, alone, and the evidence is the Saying of Allaah, the Most High,

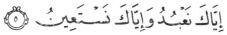

"O Allaah You alone we worship, and to You alone we appeal for aid."

[Soorah al-Faatihah (1):5]

The fact that this is to be for Allaah, the Most High, alone is shown by the fact that He mentions the word upon which the verb acts before the verb itself, and according to the principles of grammar of the Arabic language, in which the Qur'aan came down, bringing forward that which usually comes afterwards indicates restriction and particularisation. So directing this type to other than Allaah, the Most High, is *shirk* which takes a person out of the Religion.

(ii) Seeking the help of a person from the creation, in something which he is capable of helping in. Then this will be in accordance with the action in which help is sought. If it is a good action then it is permissible for the person to seek help upon it, and prescribed for a person to help in that, as Allaah, the Most High, says,

وَتَعَاوَنُواْ عَلَى ٱلْبِرِّ وَٱلتَّقْوَىٰ وَلَا تَعَاوَنُواْ عَلَى ٱلْإِثْمِ وَٱلْعُدْوَٰنِ

"And assist one another upon righteous actions and avoidance of sins."

[Soorah al-Maa'idah (5):2]

If it is a sinful thing, then it is forbidden for the person doing it and for the one who assists, as Allaah, the Most High, says,

وَلَا تَعَاوَنُواْ عَلَى ٱلْإِثْمِ وَٱلْعُدْوَٰنِ

"And do not assist one another in abandoning what Allaah has commanded and upon transgressing the limits laid down in the Religion."

[Soorah al-Maa'idah (5):2]

If it is something permissible, then it is allowed for the person to seek help and to be assisted, and the one who is helping may be rewarded for kind treatment and thus it becomes something prescribed for him as Allaah, the Most High, says,

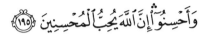

وَأَحْسِنُوٓاْ إِنَّ ٱللَّهَ يُحِبُّ ٱلْمُحْسِنِينَ ١٩٥

"And do good, indeed Allaah loves those who do good."

[Soorah al-Baqarah (2):195]

(iii) Seeking the help of a person from the creation who is alive and present, except that it is something which he is incapable of, then this is futile and useless. For example that he seeks the help of a weak person in order to carry something very heavy.

وَدَلِيلُ الِاسْتِعَاذَةِ قَوْلُهُ تَعَالَى:

﴿ قُلْ أَعُوذُ بِرَبِّ الفَلَقِ ﴾ و ﴿ قُلْ أَعُوذُ بِرَبِّ النَّاسِ ﴾

The evidence for seeking refuge (al-isti'aadhah) is the Saying of Allaah, the Most High: **"Say: I seek refuge with the Lord of the dawn"** [Soorah al-Falaq (113):1] and: **"Say: I seek refuge with the Lord of mankind"**[80] [Soorah an-Naas (114):1].

(iv) Seeking the aid of any deceased person, or the aid of the living in a matter of the hidden and unseen, which they cannot reach. Then this is *shirk* since it will only be done by a person who believes that those whose help he seeks have some hidden control over the creation.

(v) Seeking help by performing deeds that are beloved to Allaah, the Most High. This is something that is prescribed due to the Saying of Allaah, the Most High,

وَٱسْتَعِينُواْ بِٱلصَّبْرِ وَٱلصَّلَوٰةِ

"And seek assistance through patience and Prayer."

[Soorah al-Baqarah (2):45]

The author, *rahimahullaah*, uses as evidence for the first type the Saying of Allaah, the Most High,

إِيَّاكَ نَعْبُدُ وَإِيَّاكَ نَسْتَعِينُ ٥

"O Allaah You alone we worship, and to You alone we appeal for aid."

[Soorah al-Faatihah (1):5]

And the saying of the Prophet (ﷺ) saying: *"If you seek help then seek the help of Allaah."*

80 *Al-Isti'aadhah* is to seek refuge, which is to seek protection against that which one hates and involves seeking refuge and shelter and protection from someone, and is of various types:

(i) Seeking the refuge of Allaah, the Most High, and this involves ones complete need of Him, attachment to Him, and ones certain faith in His being sufficient and His perfect protection from everything, whether in the present or the future, small or large, human or not, and the proof is the Sayings of Allaah, the Most High,

$$قُلْ أَعُوذُ بِرَبِّ ٱلْفَلَقِ ۝ مِن شَرِّ مَا خَلَقَ ۝$$

"Say: I seek refuge with the Lord of the dawn, from the evil of that which He created..."

[Soorah al-Falaq (113):1-2]

$$قُلْ أَعُوذُ بِرَبِّ ٱلنَّاسِ ۝ مَلِكِ ٱلنَّاسِ ۝ إِلَٰهِ ٱلنَّاسِ ۝ مِن شَرِّ ٱلْوَسْوَاسِ ٱلْخَنَّاسِ ۝$$

"Say: I seek refuge with the Lord of mankind; the king of mankind; the one who is worshipped rightfully by mankind; from the evil of Satan who whispers into the hearts of mankind and then withdraws when they remember Allaah..."

[Soorah an-Naas (114):1-4]

(ii) Seeking refuge in one of Allaah's attributes, such as His Speech, His Greatness, His Might, and so on. The evidence for this are his (ﷺ) sayings:

The Prophet (ﷺ) said, *"I seek refuge in the perfect Words of Allaah from the evil of that which He created"* [Reported by Muslim (Eng. transl. 4/1421/no.6541)].

He (ﷺ) said, *"I seek refuge in Your Might that I should not be assailed from below"* [Reported by Aboo Daawood (Eng. transl. 3/1408/no. 5056) and declared _Saheeh_ by Shaykh al-Albaanee in _Saheeh Sunan Abee Dawood_ (no. 4239)].

Also his (ﷺ) saying in the supplication recited when suffering from pain, *"I seek refuge in the Might and Power of Allaah from the evil of what I feel and am wary of."* [Reported by Muslim (Eng. transl. 3/1198/ no. 5462) and Ibn Maajah (no. 3522)].

The Prophet (ﷺ) said, *"I seek refuge in Your Pleasure from Your Wrath"* [Reported by Muslim (Eng. transl. 1/255/no.986)].

His (ﷺ) saying, when Allaah, the Most High, sent down His Saying:

$$ قُلْ هُوَ ٱلْقَادِرُ عَلَىٰٓ أَن يَبْعَثَ عَلَيْكُمْ عَذَابًا مِّن فَوْقِكُمْ $$

"Say He is the One fully able to send punishment upon you from above."

[Soorah al-An'aam (6):65]

He (ﷺ) said: *"I seek refuge in Your Face."* [Collected by al-Bukhaaree (Eng. transl. 9/370/503)].

(iii) Seeking refuge either with the dead, or with living people who are not present and able to grant refuge, then this is *shirk*. In this regard Allaah, the Most High, says,

$$ وَأَنَّهُۥ كَانَ رِجَالٌ مِّنَ ٱلْإِنسِ يَعُوذُونَ بِرِجَالٍ مِّنَ ٱلْجِنِّ فَزَادُوهُمْ رَهَقًا ٦ $$

"And there were men from mankind who used to seek refuge with men of the *jinn*, and so that only increased them in transgression."

[Soorah al-Jinn (72):6]

(iv) Seeking shelter with some person or in some place, or the like, as long as it is something which can serve the purpose of providing shelter. Then this is permissible and the evidence is his (ﷺ) saying, speaking about tribulations, *"Whoever exposes himself to them will be destroyed by them, and whoever finds a place of shelter or refuge from them, then let him take shelter in it"* [Reported by al-Bukhaaree (Eng. transl. vol. 9/p.158/no.203) and Muslim (Eng. transl. 4/1495/no.6893)]. He (ﷺ) also explained this place of shelter or refuge in his (ﷺ) saying, *"So whoever has camels should stick*

وَدَلِيلُ الإِسْتِغَاثَةِ قَوْلُهُ تَعَالَى: ﴿ إِذْ تَسْتَغِيْثُوْنَ رَبَّكُمْ فَاسْتَجَابَ لَكُمْ ﴾

The evidence for seeking deliverance and rescue (*al-istighaathah*) is the Saying of Allaah, the Most High: **"When you sought aid and deliverance of your Lord and He responded to you"**[81] [Soorah al-Anfaal (8):9].

---

to his camels..." [Reported by Muslim (Eng. transl. 4/1495-1496/no.6896)]. There also occurs in *Saheeh Muslim* (Eng. transl. 3/911/no.4190) from Jaabir, *radiyallaahu 'anhu*, that a woman from the tribe of Banoo Makhzoom stole something, so then she was brought to the Prophet (ﷺ) and she sought refuge with Umm Salamah. He also reports in his *Saheeh* (Eng. transl. 4/1494/no.6996) from Umm Salamah, *radiyallaahu 'anhaa*, from the Prophet (ﷺ) that he said: *"A man will seek refuge in the House and an army detachment will be sent against him..."* However if it is the case that someone is seeking refuge from the evil of an oppressor, then it is obligatory to shelter him and grant him refuge as far as is possible. But if he seeks refuge in order to help him to commit something forbidden, or to flee away from an obligation, then it is forbidden to shelter him.

81 *Al-Istighaathah* is to seek rescue and deliverance from severe difficulty and destruction, and is of various types:

(i) Seeking deliverance and rescue from Allaah, the Mighty and Majestic, is one of the most excellent and most perfect deeds, and it was the continual practice of the messengers and their followers. The evidence for it is what the Shaykh, *rahimahullaah*, mentioned,

إِذْ تَسْتَغِيثُونَ رَبَّكُمْ فَاسْتَجَابَ لَكُمْ أَنِّي مُمِدُّكُم بِأَلْفٍ مِّنَ الْمَلَائِكَةِ مُرْدِفِينَ ۝

"When you sought aid and deliverance of your Lord and He responded to you that He was sending you a thousand angels in succession to assist you."

[Soorah al-Anfaal (8):9]

110

This occurred at the battle of *Badr* when the Prophet (ﷺ) saw the *mushriks* numbering a thousand men, whist his companions were a few more than three hundred and ten. So he entered the palm grove calling earnestly upon his Lord, the Mighty and Majestic, raising up his hands and facing the *qiblah*, and saying: *"O Allaah fulfil that which You have promised me. O Allaah if this small group who are the people of Islaam are destroyed you will not be worshipped upon the earth."* Then he continued calling upon his Lord earnestly, with his hands raised such that his cloak fell from his shoulders. So Aboo Bakr, *radiyallaahu 'anhu*, took up his cloak and cast it back upon his shoulders and embraced him from behind and said: *"O Prophet of Allaah, your earnest supplication to your Lord will be sufficient for you since he will fulfil what He has promised you,"* so this *Aayah* was sent down. [Reported by Muslim (Eng. transl. 3/960/no.4360)]

(ii) Seeking rescue and deliverance, either from the dead or from those who are living but are not present and able to give aid and rescue, then this is *shirk*. This is so because it will not be done except by one who believes that those people have some unseen control over the creation, and they have therefore attributed to them a share of the Lordship that is for Allaah, the Most High, alone. Allaah, the Most High, says,

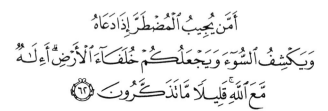

"Or is that which you falsely worship along with Allaah better than He Who responds to the one in distress when he calls Him; who removes the harm; and who makes you to succeed those who came before you?! Is there anything that is worshipped besides Allaah that can do these things for you?! Little do you consider the greatness of Allaah and His favours upon you, and the clear proofs He has given you, so you therefore associate others in worship with Him."
[Soorah an-Naml (27):62]

وَدَلِيْلُ الذَّبْحِ قَوْلُهُ تَعَالَى: ﴿ قُلْ إِنَّ صَلَاتِي وَنُسُكِي وَمَحْيَايَ وَمَمَاتِي لِلَّهِ رَبِّ الْعَالَمِيْنَ لَا شَرِيْكَ لَهُ ﴾ الآيَةُ،

The evidence for sacrificing (*adh-dhabh*) is the Saying of Allaah, the Most High: **"Say, O Muḥammad (ﷺ), indeed my Prayer, my sacrifice, my living and my dying are all purely and solely for Allaah, Lord of all creation. There is no share of any of that for other than him.[82]"** [Soorah al-An'aam (6):162-3].

(iii) Seeking aid and rescue from those who are alive, aware of the situation and capable of assistance and rescue. It is permissible to seek aid and rescue from them: Allaah, the Most High, says in the story of Moosaa:

فَٱسْتَغَٰثَهُ ٱلَّذِى مِن شِيعَتِهِۦ عَلَى ٱلَّذِى مِنْ عَدُوِّهِۦ فَوَكَزَهُۥ مُوسَىٰ فَقَضَىٰ عَلَيْهِ

"So the man who was upon the same Religion as Moosaa sought the aid of Moosaa against his enemy the copt, so Moosaa struck him forcefully and killed him."

[Soorah al-Qaṣaṣ (28):15]

(iv) Seeking rescue and aid from a living person who is not capable of assisting him, without believing that he has some hidden power. For example that a drowning person calls for rescue from a person who is paralysed. This is futility and is a mockery of the one whom he seeks rescue from, and is therefore prohibited for this reason. A further reason for its prohibition is that anyone who saw him seeking rescue from the paralysed man may be deceived into thinking that the paralysed man must have some hidden power enabling him to rescue people.

[82] Sacrifice is to kill by spilling the blood of the animal in a particular manner, and is done for a number of reasons:

(i) That it is done as an act of worship, such that he intends by it veneration of the one for whom he sacrifices, and intends it as an act of submission to him and a means of nearness to him. So this may not be done except for

Also the Prophet (ﷺ) said: *"Allaah has cursed anyone who sacrifices for other than Allaah."* [Reported by Muslim (Eng. transl. 3/1093-1094/no.4876)]

Allaah, the Most High, and has to be done in the manner which Allaah, the Most High, has prescribed. Directing it to other than Allaah is major *shirk* and the evidence (as mentioned by the author) is the Saying of Allaah, the Most High,

$$قُلْ إِنَّ صَلَاتِي وَنُسُكِي وَمَحْيَايَ وَمَمَاتِي لِلَّهِ رَبِّ الْعَالَمِينَ ۝ لَا شَرِيكَ لَهُ$$

"Say, O Muhammad (ﷺ), indeed my Prayer, my sacrifice, my living and my dying are all purely and solely for Allaah, Lord of all creation. There is no share of any of that for other than Him."

[Soorah al-An'aam (6):162-3]

(ii) That it is done out of hospitality for the guest, or for as wedding feast (*waleemah*) or the like, then this is something commanded, either as an obligation or a recommendation, as he (ﷺ) said *"Whoever truly believes in Allaah and the Last Day, then let him treat the guest honourably"* [Reported by al-Bukhaaree (Eng. transl. 8/99/no. 156) and Muslim (Eng. transl. 3/935/no. 4286)]. He (ﷺ) said to 'Abdur-Rahmaan ibn 'Auf, *"Give a wedding, feast (waleemah) even if it is only with a single sheep"* [Reported by al-Bukhaaree (Eng. transl. 7/72/no.96)].

(iii) That it is done to provide food charitably, or to sell the meat and so on, then this falls under that which is permissible and is in principle according to the Saying of Allaah, the Most High,

$$أَوَلَمْ يَرَوْا أَنَّا خَلَقْنَا لَهُم مِّمَّا عَمِلَتْ أَيْدِينَا أَنْعَامًا فَهُمْ لَهَا مَالِكُونَ ۝ وَذَلَّلْنَاهَا لَهُمْ فَمِنْهَا رَكُوبُهُمْ وَمِنْهَا يَأْكُلُونَ ۝$$

وَدَلِيلُ النَّذْرِ قَوْلُهُ تَعَالَى: ﴿ يُوفُونَ بِالنَّذْرِ

وَيَخَافُونَ يَوْمًا كَانَ شَرُّهُ مُسْتَطِيرًا ﴾

The evidence for vows (an-nadhr)[83] is the Saying of Allaah, the Most High: **"They fulfil their vows and they fear a day whose evil is widespread"**[84] [Soorah al-Insaan (76):7].

"Do those _mushriks_ who worship others along with Allaah not see that We have created for them, from what our Hands have created, cattle which they are in charge of, and We have made the cattle subservient to them: so from them are those which they eat the meat of."

[Soorah Yaa Seen (36):71-2]

Furthermore, it may be something desirable or prohibited depending upon what it leads to.

[83] i.e. the evidence that vows are worship is the Saying of Allaah, the Most High,

يُوفُونَ بِالنَّذْرِ وَيَخَافُونَ يَوْمًا كَانَ شَرُّهُ مُسْتَطِيرًا ٧

"They fulfil their vows and they fear a day whose evil is widespread."

[Soorah al-Insaan (76):7]

[84] The _Aayah_ is a proof since Allaah praises them for fulfilling their vows, which shows that Allaah loves that and every action that is beloved to Allaah is worship. This is further supported by the Saying of Allaah, the Most High,

وَيَخَافُونَ يَوْمًا كَانَ شَرُّهُ مُسْتَطِيرًا ٧

"...they fear a day whose evil is widespread."

[Soorah al-Insaan (76):7]

The fulfilling of vows which Allaah, the Most High, has praised are all acts of worship which Allaah, the Mighty and Majestic, has obligated. This is because when a person starts any of the obligatory acts of worship, then he has become

THE SECOND PRINCIPLE[85]

Knowledge of the Religion (*Deen*) of Islaam with the proofs.

---

duty bound to fulfil and complete them. The proof for this is the Saying of Allaah, the Most High,

$$ثُمَّ لْيَقْضُوا تَفَثَهُمْ وَلْيُوفُوا نُذُورَهُمْ وَلْيَطَّوَّفُوا بِالْبَيْتِ الْعَتِيقِ ﴿٢٩﴾$$

"Then let them complete the duties of their *hajj*, and fulfil their vows (e.g. the sacrifice), and let them perform the *tawaaf* of *ifaadah* around the ancient House."

[Soorah al-Hajj (22):29]

Vows by which a person makes a pledge and thus obligates himself to do something or other, or makes some act of obedience to Allaah, that is not obligatory, binding upon himself, then this is disliked, and some of the scholars declared it to be forbidden. This is because the Prophet (ﷺ) forbade making vows and said, *"It does not bring good, it merely causes the miserly person to spend"* [Reported by al-Bukhaaree (Eng. transl. 8/448/no.684) and Muslim (Eng. transl. 3/871/no.4019)]. Yet even so, if a person does go ahead and vow that he will do some act of obedience to Allaah, then it becomes obligatory upon him to perform it as the Prophet (ﷺ) said, *"Whoever vows to act in obedience to Allaah, then let him obey Him"* [Reported by al-Bukhaaree (Eng. transl. 8/449/no.687)].

So in summary vows (*an-nadhr*) applies to the obligatory acts of worship in general, and to making vows in specific, which is that a person obliges himself to do something for the sake of Allaah, the Mighty and Majestic. The scholars divide the vow into various categories and these are laid out in the books of *fiqh* (details of Islamic law and regulations).

85 That is the second of the three principles, which is to attain knowledge of the Religion of Islaam, and to know the Religion of Islaam from its proofs in the Book and the *Sunnah*.

وَهُوَ الاِسْتِسْلاَمُ لِلَّهِ بِالتَّوْحِيْدِ وَالاِنْقِيَادُ لَهُ بِالطَّاعَةِ

وَالْبَرَاءَةُ مِنَ الشِّرْكِ وَأَهْلِهِ.

It is to submit[86] to Allaah with *tawheed*,[87] and to yield obediently[88] to Him, and to free and disassociate oneself from *shirk* and its people.[89]

---

[86] The Religion (*Deen*) of Islaam is "Submission to Allaah with *tawheed*, to yield obediently to Him, and to free and disassociate oneself from *shirk* and its people," so it comprises three matters.

[87] That is that the person must submit to his Lord in the manner prescribed in the *Sharee'ah*, and it is to submit to Allaah, the Mighty and Majestic, with *tawheed*, and by singling Him out with all worship. As for submission to the pre-decree and what Allaah has ordained with regard to laws of creation, then there is no reward attached to that since the person has no choice or ability to escape that. In this regard Allaah, the Most High, says,

وَلَهُۥ أَسْلَمَ مَن فِى ٱلسَّمَٰوَٰتِ وَٱلْأَرْضِ طَوْعًا وَكَرْهًا وَإِلَيْهِ يُرْجَعُونَ ۝

"And to Him everyone in the heavens and the earth submit willingly or unwillingly, and to Him you all will be returned."

[Soorah Aal-'Imraan (3):83]

[88] That is by doing whatever He has commanded, and avoiding everything which He has forbidden, since obedience means to carry out His orders and avoid what He forbids.

[89] Freeing and disassociating oneself from *shirk* means to absolve oneself of it, and totally remove oneself from it and this necessitates separation and disassociation from its people. Allaah, the Most High, said,

قَدْ كَانَتْ لَكُمْ أُسْوَةٌ حَسَنَةٌ فِىٓ إِبْرَٰهِيمَ وَٱلَّذِينَ مَعَهُۥٓ إِذْ قَالُوا۟ لِقَوْمِهِمْ إِنَّا بُرَءَٰٓؤُا۟ مِنكُمْ وَمِمَّا تَعْبُدُونَ مِن دُونِ ٱللَّهِ كَفَرْنَا بِكُمْ وَبَدَا بَيْنَنَا وَبَيْنَكُمُ ٱلْعَدَٰوَةُ وَٱلْبَغْضَآءُ أَبَدًا حَتَّىٰ تُؤْمِنُوا۟ بِٱللَّهِ وَحْدَهُ

وَهُوَ ثَلَاثُ مَرَاتِبَ: الإِسْلَامُ ، وَالإِيْمَانُ ،

وَالإِحْسَانُ ، وَكُلُّ مَرْتَبَةٍ لَهَا أَرْكَانٌ   فَأَرْكَانُ الإِسْلَامِ خَمْسَةٌ

And it is of three levels:[90] Islaam (submission and obedience to Allaah),
eemaan (true faith comprising belief of the heart, speech of the tongue
and action of the limbs), and *ihsaan* (perfection of worship). Each
level has its pillars.[91]

[The first level] The pillars of Islaam are five:[92]

"There is a fine example for you to follow in Ibraaheem and those
with him when they said to their unbelieving people: 'We are
free of you and whatever you worship besides Allaah, and we
deny and reject what you are upon; and because of your disbelief
in Allaah and your worship of others besides Him enmity and
hatred has arisen between us for ever, unless you believe truly in
Allaah, and single Him out and worship Him alone.'"

[Soorah al-Mumtahinah (60):4]

90 The author explained that the Religion of Islaam is of three levels, one above
the other, and they are: Islaam, *eemaan* and *ihsaan*.

91 The proof for that is his (ﷺ) saying in the *hadeeth* related by 'Umar ibn al-
Khattaab, *radiyallaahu 'anhu*, concerning the time when Jibreel came and asked
the Prophet (ﷺ) about Islaam, *eemaan* and *ihsaan*, and he (ﷺ) explained that and
said, *"That was Jibreel, he came to you to teach you your Religion"* [al-Bukhaaree
(Eng. transl. 1/42/no.47) and Muslim (Eng. transl. 1/1-2/1)].

92 The proof for that is the *hadeeth* of Ibn 'Umar, *radiyallaahu 'anhumaa*, who
said that the Prophet (ﷺ) said, *"Islaam is built upon five: the testification that
none has the right to be worshipped except Allaah and that Muhammad is the
Messenger of Allaah; establishment of the Prayer; payment of the zakaat; fasting
Ramadaan; and hajj to Allaah's sacred House"* [Reported by al-Bukhaaree (Eng.
transl. 1/17/no.7) and Muslim (Eng. transl. 1/9/no.18)].

شَهَادَةُ أَنْ لاَ إِلَهَ إِلاَّ اللّهُ وَأَنَّ مُحَمَّدًا رَسُولُ اللّهِ وَإِقَامُ الصَّلاَةِ ، وَإِيْتَاءُ الزَّكَاةِ ، وَصَوْمُ رَمَضَانَ وَحَجُّ بَيْتِ اللّهِ الحَرَامِ. فَدَلِيْلُ الشَّهَادَةِ قَوْلُهُ تَعَالَى: ﴿ شَهِدَ اللّهُ أَنَّهُ لاَ إِلَهَ إِلاَّ هُوَ وَالمَلاَئِكَةُ وَأُوْلُوْا العِلْمِ قَائِمًا بِالقِسْطِ لاَ إِلَهَ إِلاَّ هُوَ العَزِيْزُ الحَكِيْمُ ﴾

The testification that none has the right to be worshipped except Allaah, and that Muhammad is the Messenger of Allaah;93 to establish the Prayer; to pay the *zakaat*; to fast Ramadaan; and to make *hajj* to the sacred House of Allaah.

So the proof for the testification (*shahaadah*) is the Saying of Allaah, the Most High, **"Allaah bears witness that none has the right to be worshipped but Him; and likewise the angels and the people of knowledge bear witness: He Who maintains justice, none has the right to be worshipped but Him, the All-Mighty, the All-Wise."**94 [Soorah Aal-'Imraan (3):18].

---

93 The testification that none has the right to be worshipped except Allaah and that Muhammad is the Messenger of Allaah is a single pillar, and they are a single pillar, even though they are two complementary parts, since all acts of worship depend upon implementation of them together. Thus no worship will be accepted without: (i) sincerity and purity of ones intention for Allaah, the Mighty and Majestic, and this is comprised in the testification that none has the right to be worshipped except Allaah, and (ii) Following and adherence to the way of the Messenger (ﷺ), and this is what is comprised in the testification that none has the right to be worshipped except Allaah.

94 In this Noble *Aayah* Allaah bears witness for Himself that none has the right to be worshipped but Him, and likewise that the angels and the people of knowledge bear witness to that also, and that He, the Most High, maintains justice, and He affirms that with His Saying,

وَمَعْنَاهَا لاَ مَعْبُوْدَ بِحَقٍّ إِلاَّ

اللَّهُ « لاَ إِلَهَ » نَافِيًا جَمِيْعَ مَا يُعْبَدُ مِنْ دُوْنِ اللَّهِ « إِلاَّ اللَّهُ » مُثْبِتًا العِبَادَةَ

لِلَّهِ وَحْدَهُ لاَ شَرِيْكَ لَهُ فِي عِبَادَتِهِ كَمَا أَنَّهُ لاَ شَرِيْكَ لَهُ فِي مُلْكِهِ.

Its meaning is that none has the right to be worshipped except Allaah: *"laa ilaaha"* (Nothing has the right to be worshipped besides Allaah), and *"illallaah"* (except Allaah) affirms worship for Allaah alone, and that there is to be no one given any share of His Dominion and Sovereignty.[95]

شَهِدَ

اللَّهُ أَنَّهُ لاَ إِلَهَ إِلاَّ هُوَ وَالْمَلَائِكَةُ وَأُولُو الْعِلْمِ قَائِمًا بِالْقِسْطِ

لاَ إِلَهَ إِلاَّ هُوَ الْعَزِيزُ الْحَكِيمُ ﴿١٨﴾

"Allaah bears witness that none has the right to be worshipped but Him; and likewise the angels and the people of knowledge bear witness: He Who maintains justice, none has the right to be worshipped but Him, the All-Mighty, the All-Wise."

[Soorah Aal-'Imraan (3):18]

The *Aayah* also contains a great commendation for the people of knowledge since He informs that they bear witness along with His witness and that of the angels. At the forefront of the people of knowledge are His noble messengers. This testification is the greatest testification due to the exaltedness of the One testifying and of that which is being testified, since the witness is Allaah, and His angels, and the people of knowledge; and that which is witnessed to is the *tawheed* of Allaah in worship.

95 His saying, 'Its meaning (the meaning of *laa ilaaha illallaah*) is that none has the right to be worshipped except Allaah' - the testification *laa ilaaha illallaah* is that a person affirms with his tongue and his heart that there is nothing that is worshipped rightfully except Allaah, the Mighty and Majestic, since *ilaah* means that which is worshipped (*ma'bood*). So the sentence *laa ilaaha illallaah* com-

prises a denial and an affirmation. As for the denial it is *laa ilaaha* (None has the right to be worshipped), and as for the affirmation, then it is *illallaah* (except Allaah). So in the sentence there is a word understood in meaning but not stated in words, which is necessary to complete the meaning and it is <u>haqq</u> (rightfully), and when this is understood it clarifies the answer to the following question that may be raised: How can it be said that there is no *ilaah* except Allaah (*laa ilaaha illallaah*) despite the fact that there are false gods worshipped besides Allaah. Furthermore Allaah, the Most High, calls them gods/objects of worship (*aalihah*) and those who worship them call them gods. Allaah, the Exalted and Most High, says,

فَمَآ أَغْنَتْ عَنْهُمْ ءَالِهَتُهُمُ ٱلَّتِي يَدْعُونَ مِن دُونِ ٱللَّهِ مِن شَيْءٍ لَّمَّا جَآءَ أَمْرُ رَبِّكَ

"So their gods which they invoked besides Allaah could not save them from the punishment of their Lord when it came, nor repel any of it from them."

[Soorah Hood (11):101]

So how can other deities be confirmed besides Allaah, the Mighty and Majestic, when all of the messengers said to their people,

ٱعْبُدُواْ ٱللَّهَ مَا لَكُم مِّنْ إِلَٰهٍ غَيْرُهُۥ

"Worship Allaah alone, there is none besides Him deserving and having the right to your worship."

[Soorah al-A'raaf (7):59]

The answer to this question will become clear when we know what is the unstated word or words necessary to complete the meaning of the saying *laa ilaaha illallaah*. So we say: These gods (*aalihah*) which are worshipped besides Allaah are gods, but they are false and futile gods, they are not true gods and do not possess anything of divinity, nor deserve any worship, and the proof for this is the Saying of Allaah, the Most High,

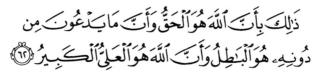

"That is because Allaah is the true God, deserving all worship, having none like Him no sharer and no rival, and those gods which the *mushriks* invoke besides Him are futile and false and not able to create anything, rather they are themselves created things. It is Allaah who is the Most High, above everything, the Most Great."

[Soorah al-Hajj (22):62]

This is also proven by the Saying of Allaah, the Most High,

$$أَفَرَءَيْتُمُ ٱللَّـٰتَ وَٱلْعُزَّىٰ ﴿١٩﴾ وَمَنَوٰةَ الثَّالِثَةَ ٱلْأُخْرَىٰ ﴿٢٠﴾ أَلَكُمُ ٱلذَّكَرُ وَلَهُ ٱلْأُنثَىٰ ﴿٢١﴾ تِلْكَ إِذًا قِسْمَةٌ ضِيزَىٰ ﴿٢٢﴾ إِنْ هِىَ إِلَّا أَسْمَآءٌ سَمَّيْتُمُوهَآ أَنتُمْ وَءَابَآؤُكُم مَّا أَنزَلَ ٱللَّهُ بِهَا مِن سُلْطَـٰنٍ إِن يَتَّبِعُونَ إِلَّا ٱلظَّنَّ وَمَا تَهْوَى ٱلْأَنفُسُ وَلَقَدْ جَآءَهُم مِّن رَّبِّهِمُ ٱلْهُدَىٰ ﴿٢٣﴾$$

"Have you seen, O *mushriks,* (the idols:) al-Laat, al-'Uzzaa, and the other one Manaat, the third of them. You prefer and love the male offspring for yourselves and then falsely attribute daughters, which is something that you hate for yourselves, to Allaah. This is indeed an unjust division. Rather these idols are mere names which you *mushriks* and your forefathers have invented. Allaah has sent down no proof for that."

[Soorah an-Najm (53):19-23]

The Saying of Allaah, the Most High, concerning Yoosuf, *'alayhis-salaam*, provides further proof,

$$مَا تَعْبُدُونَ مِن دُونِهِ إِلَّا أَسْمَآءً سَمَّيْتُمُوهَآ أَنتُمْ وَءَابَآؤُكُم مَّا أَنزَلَ ٱللَّهُ بِهَا مِن سُلْطَـٰنٍ$$

121

وَتَفْسِيرُهَا الَّذِي يُوَضِّحُهَا قَوْلُهُ تَعَالَى: ﴿ وَإِذْ قَالَ إِبْرَاهِيمُ لِأَبِيهِ وَقَوْمِهِ إِنَّنِي بَرَاءٌ مِمَّا تَعْبُدُونَ إِلَّا الَّذِي فَطَرَنِي

The explanation which will make it clear is the Saying of Allaah, the Most High, **"And remember when Ibraaheem[96] said to his father and his people: 'I am totally free[97] from everything that you worship except for the one who created me[98],**

"You do not worship besides Allaah except idols which you call gods, which you and your forefathers give names to, for which Allaah has sent down no authority."

[Soorah Yoosuf (12):40]

So the meaning of *laa ilaaha illallaah* is: None has the right to be worshipped except Allaah, the Mighty and Majestic. As for those things which are worshipped besides Him, then the godship which their worshippers claim for them is not a reality, but rather false and futile.

96 Ibraaheem: the one who was the chosen beloved of Allaah; the *imaam* of those upon the straight and true Religion and free from *shirk*; and the most excellent of the messengers after Muhammad (ﷺ). His father was Aazar.

97 *Baraa*: totally free of that. Also His Saying: (إِنَّنِي بَرَاءٌ مِمَّا تَعْبُدُونَ) **"I am totally free from everything that you worship..."** is synonymous with the saying *laa ilaaha* (none has the right to be worshipped).

98 That is He created me upon the upright nature. Allaah is Saying, (إِلَّا الَّذِي فَطَرَنِي), **"except for the One Who created me"** is synonymous with the saying *illallaah* (except Allaah). So He, the One free of all imperfections and the Most High, is to be given no sharers in His worship just as none has any share in His sovereignty. The proof for this is the Saying of Allaah, the Most High,

أَلَا لَهُ الْخَلْقُ وَالْأَمْرُ تَبَارَكَ اللَّهُ رَبُّ الْعَالَمِينَ ٥٤

"Certainly creation and the command are His. Exalted is Allaah, the Lord of all the creation."

[Soorah al-A'raaf (7):54]

فَطَرَنِي فَإِنَّهُ سَيَهْدِينِ وَجَعَلَهَا كَلِمَةً بَاقِيَةً فِي عَقِبِهِ لَعَلَّهُمْ

يَرْجِعُونَ ﴾ وَقَوْلُهُ: ﴿ قُلْ يَا أَهْلَ الْكِتَابِ تَعَالَوْا إِلَى كَلِمَةٍ

سَوَاءٍ بَيْنَنَا وَبَيْنَكُمْ أَلَّا نَعْبُدَ إِلَّا اللَّهَ وَلَا نُشْرِكَ بِهِ شَيْئًا

He will guide me[99] **upon the true Religion and the way of right-guidance.' And Allaah made this saying,**[100] **that none has the right to be worshipped except Allaah, to persist amongst Ibraaheem's progeny, so that they might remember and return**[101] **to obedience to their Lord, and to worshipping Him alone, and repent from their unbelief and their sins"** [Soorah az-Zukhruf (43):26-28].

And His Saying, **"Say:**[102] **O People of the Book, come to a word**[103] **of justice between us, that we will single Allaah out with all worship and will not worship anything besides Him, and will disasso ciate ourselves from everything that is worshipped besides Him.**

This *Aayah* restricts creation and the command to Allaah, the Lord of all the creation, alone. So all the creation is His, and the creational and legislative command is His.

99 i.e. He will guide and direct me to the truth and grant that I attain it.

100 This saying that is a declaration of being totally free of and disassociated from everything that is worshipped besides Allaah.

101 i.e. return to it from *shirk*.

102 The address being to the Prophet (ﷺ) for him to debate with the People of the Book, the Jews and the Christians.

103 This word is "we will not worship except Allaah, and we will not associate anything in worship along with Him, and will not take one another as Lords besides Allaah." "We will not Worship anything besides Allaah" is the meaning of *laa ilaaha illallaah*, and the meaning of سَوَاءٍ بَيْنَنَا وَبَيْنَكُمْ is that you and us should be the same in that.

وَلاَ يَتَّخِذَ بَعْضُنَا بَعْضًا أَرْبَابًا مِنْ دُوْنِ اللَّهِ فَإِنْ

تَوَلَّوْا فَقُوْلُوا اشْهَدُوا بِأَنَّا مُسْلِمُوْنَ ﴾ وَدَلِيْلُ شَهَادَةِ أَنَّ مُحَمَّدًا

رَسُوْلُ اللَّهِ قَوْلُهُ تَعَالَى: ﴿ لَقَدْ جَاءَكُمْ رَسُوْلٌ مِنْ أَنْفُسِكُمْ

Nor will we take one another as Lords besides Allaah[104] by obeying one another in that which involves disobedience to Allaah. So if they turn away,[105] then say: 'Bear witness that we are Muslims, submitting to Allaah and making our worship purely and sincerely for Him, and not worshipping anything else besides Him'"[106] [Soorah Aal-'Imraan (3):64].

The proof for the testification that Mu<u>h</u>ammad is the Messenger of Allaah, is the Saying of Allaah, the Most High, **"There has indeed come to you Allaah's Messenger, from amongst yourselves[107] and known to you.**

---

104 That is that some of us will not take others as Lords besides Allaah, the Mighty and Majestic, and will not revere one another as we revere Allaah, the Mighty and Majestic, nor worship one another as we worship Allaah, not making judgement and jurisdiction for other than Him.

105 Meaning if they turn away from what you call them to.

106 Then state to them and call them to witness that you are Muslims, submitting to Allaah, and are free from that which they are upon with regard to their obstinate refusal and rejection of this great word *laa ilaaha illallaah* (None has the right to be worshipped except Allaah).

107 Meaning from your race and indeed from amongst you yourselves, just as Allaah, the Most High, says,

عَزِيزٌ عَلَيْهِ مَا عَنِتُّمْ حَرِيصٌ عَلَيْكُمْ بِالْمُؤْمِنِينَ رَؤُوفٌ رَحِيمٌ ۝

It grieves him that you should suffer.[108] **He is eager and anxious**[109] **for the guidance of those of you who are astray, and that they should repent and return to the truth, and he is full of compassion and mercy for the Believers"**[110] [Soorah at-Tawbah (9):128].

هُوَ ٱلَّذِى بَعَثَ فِى ٱلْأُمِّيِّنَ رَسُولًا مِّنْهُمْ يَتْلُوا۟
عَلَيْهِمْ ءَايَٰتِهِۦ وَيُزَكِّيهِمْ وَيُعَلِّمُهُمُ ٱلْكِتَٰبَ وَٱلْحِكْمَةَ وَإِن كَانُوا۟
مِن قَبْلُ لَفِى ضَلَٰلٍ مُّبِينٍ ۝

"It is Allaah Who sent amongst the unlettered Arabs a Messenger from themselves (Muh**ammad (ﷺ)) who recited to them the *Aayaat* which Allaah sent down, and purified them from the pollution of unbelief, and taught them the Book of Allaah and the *Sunnah*; and before Allaah sent him to them as a Messenger they were clearly astray."**

[Soorah al-Jumu'ah (62):2]

108 i.e. whatever grieves you grieves him.

109 i.e. that you should attain that which is beneficial to you, and that harm should be repelled from you.

110 Compassionate and merciful towards the Believers, and that is particular to the Believers since he (ﷺ) was commanded to fight *jihaad* against the unbelievers and the hypocrites. So these attributes of Allaah's Messenger (ﷺ) prove that he was truly the Messenger of Allaah, as is clearly shown from the Saying of Allaah, the Most High,

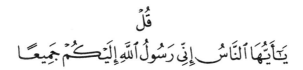

قُل
يَٰٓأَيُّهَا ٱلنَّاسُ إِنِّى رَسُولُ ٱللَّهِ إِلَيْكُمْ جَمِيعًا

وَمَعْنَى شَهَادَةِ أَنَّ مُحَمَّدًا رَسُولُ اللّهِ: طَاعَتُهُ فِيمَا أَمَرَ وَتَصْدِيقُهُ فِيمَا أَخْبَرَ

، وَاجْتِنَابُ مَا نَهَى عَنْهُ وَزَجَرَ ، وَأَلَّا يُعْبَدَ اللّهُ إِلَّا بِمَا شَرَعَ.

The meaning of the testification that Muḥammad is the Messenger of Allaah is: to obey him in whatever he commands; to believe and testify to the truth of everything he informs of; to avoid whatever he forbade and prohibited; and that you worship Allaah only with that which he prescribed.111

"Say, O Muḥammad (ﷺ), to all the people: I am Allaah's Messenger to you all."

[Soorah al-A'raaf (7):158]

The *Aayaat* in this regard proving that Muḥammad is truly the Messenger of Allaah are very many.

111` The meaning of the testification that Muḥammad (ﷺ) is the Messenger of Allaah is to affirm with the tongue and to truly believe with the heart that Muḥammad ibn 'Abdullaah al-Qurashee, al-Haashimee, is the Messenger of Allaah, the Mighty and Majestic, to all of the creation, to the *jinn* and mankind. As Allaah, the Most High, says,

وَمَا خَلَقْتُ الْجِنَّ وَالْإِنسَ إِلَّا لِيَعْبُدُونِ ۝

"I did not create the *jinn* and mankind except that they worship Me."

[Soorah adh-Dhaariyaat (51):56]

There cannot be any worship for Allaah, the Most High, except by way of the Revelation which Muḥammad (ﷺ) came with, as Allaah, the Most High, says,

تَبَارَكَ الَّذِى نَزَّلَ الْفُرْقَانَ عَلَى عَبْدِهِ لِيَكُونَ لِلْعَالَمِينَ نَذِيرًا

"Exalted is He Who sent down the Criterion (i.e. the Qur'aan) between truth and falsehood, in stages, to His slave Muḥammad, so that he should be a warner to men and *jinn* that they will be punished by Allaah if they do not single Him out with all worship and keep away from the worship of everything else besides Him."

[Soorah al-Furqaan (25):1]

126

This testification necessitates that a person believes whatever Allaah's Messenger (ﷺ) informed of; that he obeys him in whatever he orders; and keeps away from whatever he forbade and prohibited; and that he does not worship Allaah except with that which he prescribed. This testification also necessitates that he does not believe that Allaah's Messenger (ﷺ) has any share of, or any right to, Lordship or control over the creation, nor any right to be worshipped at all. Rather he (ﷺ) is a slave and worshipper, not one to be worshipped; and he is a Messenger who is not to be belied. He does not possess, either for himself or for anyone else, the power to bring harm or benefit, except as Allaah wills. Allaah, the Most High, says,

$$قُل لَّآ أَقُولُ لَكُمْ عِندِى خَزَآئِنُ ٱللَّهِ وَلَآ أَعْلَمُ ٱلْغَيْبَ$$
$$وَلَآ أَقُولُ لَكُمْ إِنِّى مَلَكٌ إِنْ أَتَّبِعُ إِلَّا مَا يُوحَىٰٓ إِلَىَّ$$

"Say, O Muḥammad (ﷺ), to those who deny your prophethood: I do not say that I am the Lord who possesses the treasure-houses of the heavens and the earth, so that I should know the secrets of that which is hidden and known only to Allaah; nor do I say to you that I am an angel. Rather in what I say to you and call you to I follow only the Revelation which Allaah sends to me."

[Soorah al-An'aam (6):50]

He is a slave who acts as he is commanded and follows the orders he is given, and Allaah, the Most High, says,

$$قُلْ إِنِّى لَآ أَمْلِكُ لَكُمْ ضَرًّا وَلَا رَشَدًا ۝ قُلْ إِنِّى$$
$$لَن يُجِيرَنِى مِنَ ٱللَّهِ أَحَدٌ وَلَنْ أَجِدَ مِن دُونِهِۦ مُلْتَحَدًا ۝$$

"Say, O Muḥammad (ﷺ): It is not in my power to bring about harm for you, nor guidance, rather that is for Allaah. Say, O Muḥammad, none from Allaah's creation could save or protect me if I was to disobey Him, nor could I find any refuge except with Him."

[Soorah al-Jinn (72):21-22]

$$قُل لَّآ أَمۡلِكُ لِنَفۡسِى نَفۡعًا وَلَا ضَرًّا إِلَّا مَا شَآءَ ٱللَّهُ وَلَوۡ كُنتُ أَعۡلَمُ ٱلۡغَيۡبَ لَٱسۡتَكۡثَرۡتُ مِنَ ٱلۡخَيۡرِ وَمَا مَسَّنِىَ ٱلسُّوٓءُ إِنۡ أَنَا۠ إِلَّا نَذِيرٌ وَبَشِيرٌ لِّقَوۡمٍ يُؤۡمِنُونَ ١٨٨$$

"Say, O Mu<u>h</u>ammad (ﷺ): It is not within my power to bring benefit to myself nor to keep away harm, except as Allaah wills; and if I knew what the future holds I could amass a great deal of wealth, and harm would not befall me. But I am just a Messenger from Allaah sent by Him to warn those who disobey Him of His punishment; and to give glad tidings of His reward for those who truly believe in Him and are obedient to Him."

[Soorah al-A'raaf (7):188]

From this it is known that nothing from the creation deserves or has the right to be worshipped not Allaah's Messenger (ﷺ), nor any of the creation lesser than him; and that worship may only be for Allaah, the Most High, alone,

$$قُلۡ إِنَّ صَلَاتِى وَنُسُكِى وَمَحۡيَاىَ وَمَمَاتِى لِلَّهِ رَبِّ ٱلۡعَٰلَمِينَ ١٦٢ لَا شَرِيكَ لَهُۥ وَبِذَٰلِكَ أُمِرۡتُ وَأَنَا۠ أَوَّلُ ٱلۡمُسۡلِمِينَ$$

"Say, O Mu<u>h</u>ammad (ﷺ): Indeed my Prayer, my sacrifice, my living and my dying, are all purely and solely for Allaah, Lord of all creation. There is no share of any of that for other than Him. That is what my Lord ordered me, and I am the first of this nation to submit to Allaah as a Muslim."

[Soorah al-An'aam (6):162-3]

The right of the Prophet (ﷺ) is that you give him the position and standing which Allaah, the Most High, gave to him, which is that he is the slave of Allaah and His Messenger, may Allaah extol and send blessings of peace upon him.

وَدَلِيلُ الصَّلَاةِ وَالزَّكَاةِ وَتَفْسِيرُ التَّوْحِيدِ قَوْلُهُ تَعَالَى: ﴿ وَمَا أُمِرُوْا إِلاَّ

لِيَعْبُدُوا اللَّهَ مُخْلِصِينَ لَهُ الدِّينَ حُنَفَآءَ وَيُقِيمُوا الصَّلَاةَ وَيُؤْتُوا الزَّكَاة

The evidence for the Prayer (as-salaat) and the zakaat,[112] and the explanation of tawheed is the Saying of Allaah, the Most High, **"And they were not commanded except that they should worship Allaah alone, making their worship and obedience purely for Him, upon the true Religion and free from *shirk*; and that they should establish the Prayer, and pay the zakaat** [113] -

---

[112] That is, the evidence that the Prayer and the zakaat are from the Religion, is the Saying of Allaah, the Most High,

وَمَآ أُمِرُوٓاْ إِلَّا لِيَعْبُدُواْ ٱللَّهَ مُخْلِصِينَ

لَهُ ٱلدِّينَ حُنَفَآءَ وَيُقِيمُواْ ٱلصَّلَوٰةَ وَيُؤْتُواْ ٱلزَّكَوٰةَ

"And they were not commanded except that they should worship Allaah alone, making their worship and obedience purely for Him, upon the true Religion and free from *shirk*; and that they should establish the Prayer, and pay the zakaat."

[Soorah al-Bayyinah (98):5]

This *Aayah* is general and covers all types of worship, so a person must perform all of them purely and sincerely for Allaah, the Mighty and Majestic, being upon the straight and true Religion and following the Revealed way prescribed by Him.

[113] This is an example of something particular being mentioned after the general. So establishment of the Prayer and payment of the zakaat are types of worship, however Allaah, the one free of all imperfections, mentioned them specifically due to their great importance. So the Prayer is a bodily worship, and the zakaat is a worship involving giving wealth, and they are mentioned jointly in the Book of Allaah, the Mighty and Majestic.

وَذَلِكَ دِيْنُ الْقَيِّمَةِ ﴾ وَدَلِيْلُ الصِّيَامِ قَوْلُهُ تَعَالَى:

and that[114] is the straight and true Religion"[115] [Soorah al-Bayyinah (98):5].

And the evidence for Fasting (*siyaam*)[116] is the Saying of Allaah, the Most High,

---

[114] i.e. the worship of Allaah, making the Religion purely for Him, keeping aloof from *shirk*, and establishment of the Prayer and payment of the *zakaat*.

[115] The true and straight Religion, containing no crookedness since it is the Religion laid down by Allaah, the Mighty and Majestic, and Allaah's Religion is straight and upright, just as Allaah, the Most High, says,

وَأَنَّ هَذَا صِرَاطِي مُسْتَقِيمًا فَاتَّبِعُوهُ وَلَا تَتَّبِعُوا السُّبُلَ

فَتَفَرَّقَ بِكُمْ عَن سَبِيلِهِ

"This is My Straight Path, so follow it and do not follow any of the other paths, for they will split you and take you away from that way which He prescribed for you."

[Soorah al-An'aam (6):153]

Just as the noble *Aayah* mentioned by the author contains a mention of worship, and the Prayer and the *zakaat,* then it comprises the reality of *tawheed* and that it is to make worship purely for Allaah, the Mighty and Majestic, without any inclination to *shirk*. So whoever does not make his worship purely for Allaah is not a *muwahhid* (person upon *tawheed*), and whoever makes his worship for other than Allaah is not a person upon *tawheed*.

[116] The proof for its obligation is the saying of Allaah, the Most High,

يَٰأَيُّهَا الَّذِينَ ءَامَنُوا كُتِبَ

عَلَيْكُمُ الصِّيَامُ كَمَا كُتِبَ عَلَى الَّذِينَ مِن قَبْلِكُمْ

﴿ يَا أَيُّهَا الَّذِيْنَ آمَنُوْا كُتِبَ عَلَيْكُمُ الصِّيَامُ كَمَا كُتِبَ عَلَى الَّذِيْنَ مِنْ قَبْلِكُمْ لَعَلَّكُمْ تَتَّقُوْنَ ﴾

"O you who believe Fasting is prescribed as an obligation for you as it was prescribed as an obligation for those who came before you, so that you may attain *taqwaa* (obedience to Allaah and avoidance of whatever He has forbidden)"[117] [Soorah al-Baqarah (2):183].

"O you who believe Fasting is prescribed as an obligation for you as it was prescribed as an obligation for those who came before you."

[Soorah al-Baqarah (2):183]

His Saying كَمَا كُتِبَ عَلَى الَّذِينَ مِن قَبْلِكُمْ "as it was prescribed as an obligation for those who came before you" contains a number of beneficial lessons:

(i) The importance of Fasting since Allaah, the Mighty and Majestic, made Fasting obligatory upon the nations before us. This shows that it is something which Allaah, the Mighty and Majestic, loves, and that it was binding upon every nation.

(ii) Ease for this *ummah* (nation) since it is not alone in having this duty to fast placed upon it, a duty which may be difficult for the souls and the bodies.

(iii) An indication that Allaah, the Most High, perfected the Religion for this *ummah* and completed it with the virtues which were given to earlier nations.

117 In this *Aayah* Allaah, the Mighty and Majestic, makes clear the wisdom behind fasting, in His Saying لَعَلَّكُمْ تَتَّقُونَ, i.e. that you should fear Allaah through fasting, and attain the characteristics of *taqwaa* resulting from it. This benefit was indicated by the Prophet (ﷺ) in his Saying, *"Whoever does not abandon falsehood and evil actions, then Allaah has no need that he should abandon his food and drink"* [Reported by al-Bukhaaree (Eng. transl. 3/70/127)].

وَدَلِيْلُ الحَجِّ قَوْلُهُ تَعَالَى: ﴿ وللَّهِ عَلَى النَّاسِ حِجُّ البَيْتِ مَنْ
اِسْتَطَاعَ إِلَيْهِ سَبِيْلاً وَمَنْ كَفَرَ فَإِنَّ اللَّهَ غَنِيٌّ عَنِ العَالَمِيْنَ ﴾

The evidence for *hajj*[118] is the Saying of Allaah, the Most High, **"And *hajj* to Allaah's sacred House is an obligation upon those able to perform it; and whoever refuses and rejects the obligation of *hajj* to Allaah's House, then Allaah has no need of him or of any of the creation"**[119] [Soorah Aal-'Imraan (3):97].

---

118 The proof for its obligation is the Saying of Allaah, the Most High,

وَلِلَّهِ عَلَى ٱلنَّاسِ حِجُّ ٱلۡبَيۡتِ

مَنِ ٱسۡتَطَاعَ إِلَيۡهِ سَبِيلًا وَمَن كَفَرَ فَإِنَّ ٱللَّهَ غَنِيٌّ عَنِ ٱلۡعَٰلَمِينَ

"And *hajj* to Allaah's sacred House is an obligation to those able to perform it; and whoever refuses and rejects the obligation of *hajj* to Allaah's House, then Allaah has no need of him or of any of the creation."

[Soorah Aal-'Imraan (3):97]

This *Aayah* was sent down in the ninth year after the *hijrah*, when the *hajj* became an obligation. However Allaah, the Mighty and Majestic, says, مَنِ ٱسۡتَطَاعَ إِلَيۡهِ سَبِيلًا **"those able to perform it."** So it shows that *hajj* is not an obligation upon one unable to perform it.

119 In the Saying of Allaah, the Most High, وَمَن كَفَرَ فَإِنَّ ٱللَّهَ غَنِيٌّ عَنِ ٱلۡعَٰلَمِينَ **"then Allaah has no need of him or of any of the creation"** there is a proof that whoever abandons performance of *hajj*, from those able to perform it, is guilty of *kufr* (infidelity). However it is *kufr* (infidelity) which does not take a person out of the Religion according to the saying of the majority of the scholars, due to the saying of 'Abdullaah ibn Shaqeeq, *"The Companions of Allaah's Messenger (ﷺ) had not used to regard the abandonment of any action to be infidelity, except for (abandonment of) the Prayer"* [Reported by at-Tirmidhee, and declared *Saheeh* by Shaykh al-Albaanee in *Saheeh Sunan at-Tirmidhee* (no.2114)].

132

الْمَرْتَبَةُ الثَّانِيَةُ: الْإِيْمَانُ وَهُوَ بِضْعٌ وَسَبْعُوْنَ شُعْبَةً

فَأَعْلَاهَا قَوْلُ لَا إِلَهَ إِلَّا اللَّهُ وَأَدْنَاهَا إِمَاطَةُ الْأَذَى عَنِ الطَّرِيْقِ ،

وَالْحَيَاءُ شُعْبَةٌ مِنَ الْإِيْمَانِ

The second level:[120] *Eemaan*[121] - and it has seventy and odd[122] branches,[123] the highest of them is the saying that 'none has the right to be worshipped except Allaah' (*laa ilaaha illallaah*), the lowest of them is removal of that which is harmful[124] from the path, and a sense of shame (*al-hayaa*)[125] is a branch of *eemaan*.

---

[120] i.e. the second level of the Religion.

[121] *Eemaan* in the Arabic language means: attestation/belief (*at-tasdeeq*) and in the *Sharee'ah* it means: "Certain Faith in the heart, speech of the tongue and action of the parts of the body; and it has seventy and odd branches."

[122] 'and odd' (*bid'un*) means: an un-stated number between three and nine.

[123] i.e. parts.

[124] i.e. removal of rocks and thorns, scrap and rubbish, and that which gives off an offensive smell, and all that causes harm to those who pass by.

[125] Sense of shame (*al-hayaa*) is something which is experienced when one is embarrassed and prevents a person from doing that which is contrary to good manners. Then the way in which the words of the author, that *eemaan* consists of seventy and odd branches is harmonised with the fact that *eemaan* has six pillars is to say: *Eemaan* which is ones creed and belief (*'aqeedah*), has six fundamentals. These are what are mentioned in the *hadeeth* of Jibreel, *'alayhis-salaam*, when he asked the Prophet (ﷺ) about *Eemaan*, and he replied: *"Eemaan is that you truly believe in Allaah, His angels, His Books, His Messengers, the Last Day, and that you truly believe in pre-decree (al-qadr), the good and the evil of it"* [Reported by al-Bukhaaree (Eng. transl. 1/42/no.47) and Muslim (Eng. transl. 1/ 1-2/no. 1)].

وَأَرْكَانُهُ سِتَّةٌ أَنْ تُؤْمِنَ بِاللَّهِ

Its pillars are six: to truly believe in Allaah;126

As for the *eemaan* which covers actions and their various types and different kinds, then it has seventy and odd branches. Therefore Allaah, the Most High, called the Prayer (*Salaat*) *eemaan* in His Saying,

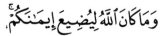

"And Allaah will not cause your *eemaan* (i.e. your Prayers) to be lost and to go unrewarded."

[Soorah al-Baqarah (2):143]

The scholars of *tafseer* (explanation of the Qur'aan) say that it means: your Prayers towards Jerusalem, since before the Companions were commanded to turn towards the *ka'bah* they used to pray towards Jerusalem.

126 *Eemaan* in Allaah comprises four matters:

(1) Belief in the existence of Allaah, the Most High. The existence of Allaah, the Most High, is proven by:
     (i) the natural disposition,
     (ii) the intellect,
     (iii) the Revelation, and,
     (iv) what is experienced and perceived.

(i) As for the proof of the natural disposition for His existence: then every created being is created upon the natural disposition of belief in its Creator, without any previous thought or education. No one turns away from this natural disposition except when his heart is taken over by that which will turn him away from it, as he (ﷺ) said, *"Every child is born upon the natural disposition (al-fitrah), then his parents change him into a Jew, or a Christian, or a Magian"* [Reported by al-Bukhaaree (Eng. transl. 2/262/no.467)].

(ii) As for the proof of the intellect (*al-'aql*) for the existence of Allaah, the Most High, it is due to the fact that all these created things, the earlier ones and the later ones, must have a Creator who brought them into being, since it is not possible for any being to create itself, nor that it should just appear by chance without a cause.

It is not possible for anything to bring itself into existence since something cannot create itself; this is because before its existence it did not exist, so how could it be a creator?!

Nor is it possible that it just appeared by chance without a cause, this is because everything coming into existence must have someone that brought it into existence. Furthermore this astounding arrangement and harmonious order, and the coherence between the causes and their effects and between all that exists makes it impossible that it all came into existence randomly and without a cause. When there is something which comes about randomly having no order at the root of its existence, then how can it exist and remain in a state of order and arrangement, and how can it develop in such a state?!

Since it is not possible that the creation brought itself into existence, nor that it came into being randomly and without a cause, then it has to be the case that it has One who brought it into being, and He is Allaah, the Lord of all creation.

Allaah, the Most High, mentions this intellectual proof and this decisive and conclusive argument, He, the Most High, says,

أَمْ خُلِقُوا مِنْ غَيْرِ شَيْءٍ أَمْ هُمُ ٱلْخَٰلِقُونَ ﴿٣٥﴾

"Were they created by nothing or did they create themselves ?!"

[Soorah aṭ-Ṭoor (52):35]

Which means that they did not come into being without a creator, and they did not create themselves, so it is established for certain that their Creator is Allaah, the Exalted and the Most High. This is why when Jubayr ibn Mut'im, *radiyallaahu 'anhu,* heard Allaah's Messenger (ﷺ) recite *Soorah aṭ-Ṭoor* until the *Aayaat:*

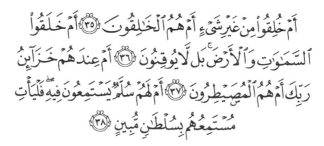

"Were they created by nothing, or did they create themselves?! Or did they create the heavens and the earth?! Nay they have no certainty; or do they have possession of the treasures of your Lord?! or are they the ones having power and control over the affairs?!"

[Soorah at-Toor (52):35-38]

Jubayr was a *mushrik* at the time, he said afterwards, *"My heart almost flew, and this was when eemaan first settled in my heart"* [Reported by al-Bukhaaree (Eng. transl. 6/357/no.377)].

Let us also give an example which will make this clear: If a person told you about a decorated palace, surrounded by gardens, through which rivers flowed, and that it was filled with carpets and couches, and decorated with all sorts of adornments and treasures. Then he said to you that this palace and all within it brought itself into existence, or that it just suddenly appeared like that without any cause or creator. Straight away you would deny that and declare that he was lying, and you would take his words to be foolishness. So can it then be permissible to say that this vast creation, containing the earth and its sky, its stars and all within it, and its amazing and astounding order, brought itself into being, or that it just appeared without anyone creating it?!

(iii) As for the proof of Revelation for the existence of Allaah, the Most High, then all of the Revealed Books state that. Also the rulings and laws sent down in Revelation which ensure the wellbeing of the creation are a proof that they are from a Wise Lord who knows everything that benefits His creation. Also the information about the creation contained in the Revelation, which is testified to by reality proves that it comes from a Lord who is fully capable of creating and bringing about whatever He informed of.

(iv) As for the proof contained in what is experienced and perceived for the existence of Allaah, then that is from two angles:
[a] We hear and see those who supplicate being answered, and those in distress who call upon Him being relieved to such an extent that it is a certain proof of His existence. Allaah, the Most High, says,

$$وَنُوحًا إِذْ نَادَىٰ مِن قَبْلُ فَاسْتَجَبْنَا لَهُ فَنَجَّيْنَاهُ وَأَهْلَهُ مِنَ الْكَرْبِ الْعَظِيمِ ٧٦$$

"And remember Noo<u>h</u>, when he called upon Allaah to destroy his unbelieving folk who obstinately denied and rejected Allaah, so Allaah answered his supplication and saved him and the Believers from his family."

[Soorah al-Ambiyaa (21):76]

Allaah, the Most High, says,

$$إِذْ تَسْتَغِيثُونَ رَبَّكُمْ فَاسْتَجَابَ لَكُمْ$$

"When you sought aid and deliverance of your Lord and He responded to you."

[Soorah al-Anfaal (8):9]

It is reported from Anas ibn Maalik, *radiyallaahu 'anhu*, that a bedouin Arab entered the mosque on the day of *Jumu'ah* whilst the Prophet (ﷺ) was delivering the *khutbah,* and said: *"O Messenger of Allaah, property is being destroyed, the dependants have become hungry, so supplicate to Allaah for us."* So he raised up his hands and supplicated. So clouds like mountains appeared, and he did not come down from his mimbar before I saw rain flowing down his beard. Then on the succeeding Jumu'ah that same bedouin or someone else stood and said: "O Messenger of Allaah, the houses are collapsing and wealth is being flooded, so supplicate to Allaah for us." So he raised his hands and said: "O Allaah, around us and not upon us" and he did not point to any direction except that it cleared"* [Collected by al-Bukhaaree (Eng. transl. 2/26/no.55)].

It has been something always witnessed till this day, that those who call upon Allaah, the Most High, sincerely and fulfil the conditions for the supplication to be answered are indeed responded to.

[b] The clear signs known as 'miracles' brought by the Prophets and seen by the people or heard of by them are a decisive proof for the One Who sent them, i.e.

137

Allaah, the Most High. This is because they were things outside the realm of human ability, and were done by Allaah, the Most High, to aid and help His messengers.

An example is the sign given to Moosaa, 'alayhis-salaam, when Allaah, the Most High, commanded him to strike the sea with his staff. So he struck it and twelve separate dry pathways were opened up through it, the water being like mountains between them Allaah, the Most High, says:

$$\text{فَأَوْحَيْنَآ إِلَىٰ مُوسَىٰ أَنِ ٱضْرِب بِّعَصَاكَ ٱلْبَحْرَ فَٱنفَلَقَ فَكَانَ كُلُّ فِرْقٍ كَٱلطَّوْدِ ٱلْعَظِيمِ ٦٣}$$

"Then we inspired Moosaa, 'Strike the ocean with your staff' and it split into separate parts, and each part was like a huge mountain."

[Soorah ash-Shu'araa (26):63]

A second example was the sign given to 'Eesaa, 'alayhis-salaam, that he used to give life to the dead and bring them out of their graves, by the permission of Allaah. Allaah, the Most High, said about him:

$$\text{وَأُحْىِ ٱلْمَوْتَىٰ بِإِذْنِ ٱللَّهِ}$$

"And I revive the dead by Allaah's permission."

[Soorah Aal-'Imraan (3):49]

$$\text{وَإِذْ تُخْرِجُ ٱلْمَوْتَىٰ بِإِذْنِي}$$

"And when you brought forth the dead by My permission."

[Soorah Aal-Maa'idah (5):110]

A third example: that which was given to Muhammad (ﷺ) when Quraysh asked for a sign, so he pointed to the moon and it split into two and that was seen by the people. Concerning this Allaah, the Most High, says,

$$\text{ٱقْتَرَبَتِ ٱلسَّاعَةُ وَٱنشَقَّ ٱلْقَمَرُ ١ وَإِن يَرَوْاْ ءَايَةً يُعْرِضُواْ وَيَقُولُواْ سِحْرٌ مُّسْتَمِرٌّ ٢}$$

"The Hour has drawn near, and the moon has been split; and if the *mushriks* see a sign proving the truth of the Prophethood of Muhammad (ﷺ) they turn away from it and say: 'This is magic which will pass away.'"

[Soorah al-Qamar (54):1-2]

So these are signs which were seen and perceived which Allaah, the Most High, caused to occur as supporting proof and assistance for His Messengers, and they are decisive proofs of His existence.

(2) *Eemaan* in His Lordship (*ar-Ruboobiyah*). That is that He alone is the Lord, having no sharer in that, nor any helper. So the Lord (*ar-Rabb*) is the One Who creates, is the Sovereign-King, and the Command is His. So there is no creator except Allaah, nor any Sovereign Lord except Him, and there is no command except for Him. Allaah, the Most High, says,

أَلَا لَهُ ٱلْخَلْقُ وَٱلْأَمْرُ

"Certainly creation and the command are His."

[Soorah al-A'raaf (7):54]

"That is Allaah your Lord Who alone has the right to worship. He it is Who has complete Sovereignty, and those whom you worship besides Him do not even possess and control the amount of the thin membrane covering a date-stone."

[Soorah Faatir (35):13]

It is not known that anyone from the creation denied the Lordship of Allaah, the One free of all imperfections, except one who did so out of arrogance and not out of belief in what he said. This was the case with Pharaoh, when he said to his people,

"I am your highest Lord."

[Soorah an-Naazi'aat (79):24]

$$يَـٰٓأَيُّهَا ٱلْمَلَأُ مَا عَلِمْتُ لَكُم مِّنْ إِلَـٰهٍ غَيْرِى$$

"O nobles, I know no other god for you besides me."

[Soorah al-Qasas (28):38]

He did not say this out of belief. Allaah, the Most High, says,

$$وَجَحَدُواْ بِهَا وَٱسْتَيْقَنَتْهَا أَنفُسُهُمْ ظُلْمًا وَعُلُوًّا$$

"They rejected Allaah's clear signs, proving what Moosaa called to, yet in their hearts they knew that they were true and from Allaah; and they did so due to their transgression and arrogance."

[Soorah an-Naml (27):14]

Moosaa said to Pharaoh, as we are told by Allaah,

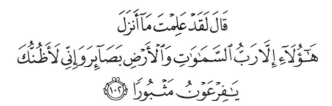

"Moosaa said to Pharaoh: You know for certain that these signs were not sent down except by the Lord of the heavens and the earth, and that they are clear proofs of the truth of what I call you to and that I am Allaah's Messenger. But I think that you O Pharaoh, are one accursed and deprived of good."

[Soorah al-Israa' (17):102]

Therefore the *mushriks* used to affirm the Lordship of Allaah, the Most High, even though they worshipped others along with Him. Allaah, the Most High, says,

قُل لِّمَنِ ٱلۡأَرۡضُ وَمَن فِيهَآ إِن
كُنتُمۡ تَعۡلَمُونَ ۝ سَيَقُولُونَ لِلَّهِ قُلۡ أَفَلَا تَذَكَّرُونَ
۝ قُلۡ مَن رَّبُّ ٱلسَّمَٰوَٰتِ ٱلسَّبۡعِ وَرَبُّ ٱلۡعَرۡشِ ٱلۡعَظِيمِ
۝ سَيَقُولُونَ لِلَّهِ قُلۡ أَفَلَا تَتَّقُونَ ۝ قُلۡ مَن بِيَدِهِۦ
مَلَكُوتُ كُلِّ شَيۡءٍ وَهُوَ يُجِيرُ وَلَا يُجَارُ عَلَيۡهِ إِن
كُنتُمۡ تَعۡلَمُونَ ۝ سَيَقُولُونَ لِلَّهِ قُلۡ فَأَنَّىٰ تُسۡحَرُونَ ۝

"Say, O Mu<u>h</u>ammad (ﷺ), to those *mushriks*: To whom belongs
the Sovereignty of the earth and all the creation upon it, if it is
that you know? They will say: It is Allaah's. Then say: 'Will you
not then realise that He it is Who alone deserves all worship?!
Say to them, O Mu<u>h</u>ammad (ﷺ): Who is the Lord of the seven
heavens and the tremendous Throne which extends over them
all? They will say that it is all for Allaah. Say: Will you not then
fear His punishment for your worship of others besides Him?
Say: In Whose Hand is the Dominion and Control of everything,
and Who protects and none can protect against His punishment,
if it is that you know? They will say: It is for Allaah. Say: Then
how is it that you are turned away from acceptance of the truth
to falsehood, and to the worship of others along with Allaah."

[Soorah al-Mu'minoon (23):84-89]

وَلَئِن سَأَلۡتَهُم مَّنۡ خَلَقَ ٱلسَّمَٰوَٰتِ وَٱلۡأَرۡضَ لَيَقُولُنَّ
خَلَقَهُنَّ ٱلۡعَزِيزُ ٱلۡعَلِيمُ ۝

"And if you, O Mu<u>h</u>ammad (ﷺ), were to ask those *mushriks* from
your people: Who created the heavens and the earth? They will
say: It is Allaah, the Mighty and All-Knowing who created them."

[Soorah az-Zukhruf (43):9]

$$\text{وَلَئِن سَأَلْتَهُم مَّنْ خَلَقَهُمْ لَيَقُولُنَّ ٱللَّهُ فَأَنَّىٰ يُؤْفَكُونَ ﴿٨٧﴾}$$

"And if you, O Muhammad (ﷺ), were to ask those from your people who worship others along with Allaah: Who created them? They will say: 'Allaah created us.' Then have they turned away from the worship of the One Who created them?!"

[Soorah az-Zukhruf (43):87]

The command of the Lord, the One free of all imperfections, covers the creational command and the legislative command. So just as He arranges and controls the creation, and He decrees for it whatever He wishes according to His wisdom, then likewise He is the sovereign Judge therein who lays down and prescribes the acts of worship, and the judgements for social affairs and dealings also according to His wisdom. So whoever takes someone else along with Allaah, the Most High, to prescribe and legislate with regard to acts of worship, or as a sovereign or judge in transactions and social affairs, then he has committed *shirk* in that and has not realized *eemaan*.

(3) *Eemaan* **in Allaah's sole right to worship (al-Uloohiyyah):** That is that He alone is the one who has the right to be worshipped, and no share of any worship is to be directed to anyone else besides Him, *al-Ilaah* means that which is worshipped with love and veneration. Allaah, the Most High, says,

$$\text{وَإِلَٰهُكُمْ إِلَٰهٌ وَاحِدٌ لَّا إِلَٰهَ إِلَّا هُوَ ٱلرَّحْمَٰنُ ٱلرَّحِيمُ ﴿١٦٣﴾}$$

"And the God alone who has the right to be worshipped is a single God (Allaah), so do not worship anything besides Him, nor associate anything in worship with Him, the Most Merciful, the Bestower of Mercy."

[Soorah al-Baqarah (2):163]

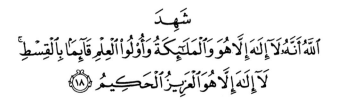

"Allaah bears witness that none has the right to be worshipped but Him; and likewise the angels and the people of knowledge bear witness: He who maintains justice, none has the right to be worshipped but Him, the All-Mighty, the All-Wise."

[Soorah Aal-'Imraan (3):18]

Everything which is taken as a god to be worshipped besides Him is a false and futile object of worship. Allaah, the Most High, says,

$$ ذَٰلِكَ بِأَنَّ ٱللَّهَ هُوَ ٱلْحَقُّ وَأَنَّ مَا يَدْعُونَ مِن دُونِهِ هُوَ ٱلْبَٰطِلُ وَأَنَّ ٱللَّهَ هُوَ ٱلْعَلِيُّ ٱلْكَبِيرُ ۝ $$

"That is because Allaah is the true God, deserving all worship, There is none like Him, no sharer and no rival - and those gods which the *mushriks* invoke besides Him are futile and false and not able to create anything, rather they are themselves created things. And Allaah it is who is the Most High, above everything the Most Great."

[Soorah al-Hajj (22):62]

Furthermore, the fact that they are called gods (*aalihah*) in no way gives them the right to be worshipped. Concerning *al-Laat, al-'Uzzah* and *Manaat*, Allaah, the Most High, says,

$$ إِنْ هِيَ إِلَّا أَسْمَآءٌ سَمَّيْتُمُوهَآ أَنتُمْ وَءَابَآؤُكُم مَّآ أَنزَلَ ٱللَّهُ بِهَا مِن سُلْطَٰنٍ $$

"Rather these idols are mere names which you *mushriks* and your forefathers have invented. Allaah has sent down no proof of that."

[Soorah an-Najm (53):23]

He says that Hood said to his people,

$$ أَتُجَٰدِلُونَنِى فِىٓ أَسْمَآءٍ سَمَّيْتُمُوهَآ أَنتُمْ وَءَابَآؤُكُم مَّا نَزَّلَ ٱللَّهُ بِهَا مِن سُلْطَٰنٍ $$

"Do you dispute with me about mere idols which you and your fathers have given names to, things which can neither bring harm nor benefit, and Allaah has given no proof or excuse for them to be worshipped."

[Soorah al-A'raaf (7):71]

He says that Yoosuf said to his two companions in the prison,

$$
\text{ءَأَرْبَابٌ مُّتَفَرِّقُونَ خَيْرٌ أَمِ اللَّهُ الْوَاحِدُ الْقَهَّارُ ﴿٣٩﴾ مَا تَعْبُدُونَ مِن دُونِهِ إِلَّا أَسْمَاءً سَمَّيْتُمُوهَا أَنتُمْ وَءَابَآؤُكُم مَّا أَنزَلَ اللَّهُ بِهَا مِن سُلْطَنٍ}
$$

"Is it better that you worship many different lords, or that you worship only Allaah, the one who subdues and has full power over everything?! You do not worship besides Allaah except idols which you call gods, which you and your forefathers gave names to, for which Allaah has sent down no authority."

[Soorah Yoosuf (12):39-40]

Therefore the messengers used to say to their people,

$$
\text{اعْبُدُوا اللَّهَ مَا لَكُم مِّنْ إِلَهٍ غَيْرُهُ}
$$

"Worship Allaah alone, there is none besides Him deserving and having the right to your worship."

[Soorah al-A'raaf (7):59]

But the *mushriks* refused this and worshipped other gods along with Allaah, the One free of all imperfections and the Most High, seeking aid from them and calling upon them to deliver and rescue them.

Allaah, the Most High, has exposed the futility of the *mushriks* worshipping these gods with two clear intellectual proofs:

(i) These gods which they worship do not possess any attributes of Divinity. Rather they are created beings which cannot create; nor can they bring any benefit to those who worship them; nor can they keep any harm away from them; nor do they have any power over their life or death; nor do they own and control anything in the heavens, nor have any share in that. Allaah, the Most High, says,

$$وَٱتَّخَذُوا۟ مِن دُونِهِۦٓ ءَالِهَةً لَّا يَخْلُقُونَ شَيْـًٔا وَهُمْ يُخْلَقُونَ وَلَا يَمْلِكُونَ لِأَنفُسِهِمْ ضَرًّا وَلَا نَفْعًا وَلَا يَمْلِكُونَ مَوْتًا وَلَا حَيَوٰةً وَلَا نُشُورًا ٣$$

"And they have taken idols as gods which they worship, things which do not create anything and are themselves created; and which do not possess the power to bring about benefit for themselves, nor to keep away harm. Nor do they have the power to cause death, nor to give life, nor to resurrect the dead."

[Soorah al-Furqaan (25):3]

$$قُلِ ٱدْعُوا۟ ٱلَّذِينَ زَعَمْتُم مِّن دُونِ ٱللَّهِ لَا يَمْلِكُونَ مِثْقَالَ ذَرَّةٍ فِى ٱلسَّمَٰوَٰتِ وَلَا فِى ٱلْأَرْضِ وَمَا لَهُمْ فِيهِمَا مِن شِرْكٍ وَمَا لَهُۥ مِنْهُم مِّن ظَهِيرٍ ٢٢ وَلَا تَنفَعُ ٱلشَّفَٰعَةُ عِندَهُۥٓ إِلَّا لِمَنْ أَذِنَ لَهُۥ$$

"Say, O Muḥammad (ﷺ), to the *mushriks*: Call upon those whom you claim as associates with Allaah and request them to bring blessings to you and remove harm, and when they are unable to do that then know that you have been confounded. They do not possess an atoms weight of good or evil, harm or benefit in the heavens or the earth, nor do they have any share in that. Nor is there any helper for Him from those whom they call upon besides Him. Nor can the intercession of anyone benefit except that he intercedes for one whom Allaah permits it for."

[Soorah Saba (34):22-3]

$$\text{أَيُشْرِكُونَ مَا لَا يَخْلُقُ شَيْئًا وَهُمْ يُخْلَقُونَ ﴿١٩١﴾}$$

$$\text{وَلَا يَسْتَطِيعُونَ لَهُمْ نَصْرًا وَلَا أَنفُسَهُمْ يَنصُرُونَ ﴿١٩٢﴾}$$

"Do they associate in worship along with Allaah those who create nothing and are themselves created by Allaah?! They are unable to help them and cannot help themselves."

[Soorah al-A'raaf (7):191-2]

So this being the state of these gods, then to worship them is the greatest folly and is totally futile.

(ii) Those *mushriks* used to affirm that Allaah, the Most High, alone is the Lord and the Creator; that in His Hand is the control of everything; and that He protects and none can protect from Him. So this necessitates that they should single Him out with all worship just as they have singled Him out by affirming all Lordship for Him. Allaah, the Most High, says,

$$\text{يَا أَيُّهَا النَّاسُ اعْبُدُوا رَبَّكُمُ الَّذِي خَلَقَكُمْ}$$

$$\text{وَالَّذِينَ مِن قَبْلِكُمْ لَعَلَّكُمْ تَتَّقُونَ ﴿٢١﴾ الَّذِي جَعَلَ لَكُمُ}$$

$$\text{الْأَرْضَ فِرَاشًا وَالسَّمَاءَ بِنَاءً وَأَنزَلَ مِنَ السَّمَاءِ مَاءً فَأَخْرَجَ}$$

$$\text{بِهِ مِنَ الثَّمَرَاتِ رِزْقًا لَّكُمْ فَلَا تَجْعَلُوا لِلَّهِ أَندَادًا وَأَنتُمْ}$$

$$\text{تَعْلَمُونَ ﴿٢٢﴾}$$

"O mankind, single out your Lord with all worship, He who created you and all those who came before you, so that you may be of those who seek to avoid Allaah's punishment and Anger, those whom Allaah is pleased with. He who has made the Earth a resting place for you, and has made the sky a canopy; and who sends down rain from the sky and brings out with it from the Earth crops and fruit as a provision for you. So do not set up rivals with Allaah in your worship whilst you know that you have no Lord besides Him."

[Soorah al-Baqarah (2):21-2]

146

وَلَئِن سَأَلْتَهُم مَّنْ خَلَقَهُمْ لَيَقُولُنَّ ٱللَّهُ فَأَنَّىٰ يُؤْفَكُونَ ۝

"And if you, O Muḥammad (ﷺ), were to ask those from your people who worship others along with Allaah: Who created them? They will say: 'Allaah created us.' Then how have they turned away from the worship of the One who created them?!"

[Soorah az-Zukhruf (43):87]

قُلْ مَن يَرْزُقُكُم

مِّنَ ٱلسَّمَاءِ وَٱلْأَرْضِ أَمَّن يَمْلِكُ ٱلسَّمْعَ وَٱلْأَبْصَارَ وَمَن يُخْرِجُ ٱلْحَيَّ مِنَ ٱلْمَيِّتِ وَيُخْرِجُ ٱلْمَيِّتَ مِنَ ٱلْحَيِّ وَمَن يُدَبِّرُ ٱلْأَمْرَ فَسَيَقُولُونَ ٱللَّهُ فَقُلْ أَفَلَا تَتَّقُونَ ۝ فَذَٰلِكُمُ ٱللَّهُ رَبُّكُمُ ٱلْحَقُّ فَمَاذَا بَعْدَ ٱلْحَقِّ إِلَّا ٱلضَّلَٰلُ فَأَنَّىٰ تُصْرَفُونَ ۝

"Say, O Muḥammad (ﷺ), to those who associate others in worship along with Allaah: Who gives you provision from the heavens (by sending down rain) and the earth (by bringing out its produce)? Or who is it that grants you hearing and sight? Who brings out the living from the dead, and brings out the dead from the living? Who controls the affairs? Then they will say: 'Allaah.' Then say: Will you not then fear Allaah's punishment for your worshipping along with Him others who do not provide sustenance for you and who can neither harm nor benefit you. Rather the One Who provides for you from the heavens and the earth, grants you hearing and sight, brings out the living from the dead, and the dead from the living, and controls the affairs is Allaah - your true Lord, about which there can be no doubt. So besides the truth what is there except misguidance, So how is it that you have turned away from the truth?!"

[Soorah Yoonus (10):31-2]

147

(4) Belief in Allaah's names and attributes. That is to affirm whatever names and attributes Allaah affirmed for Himself in His Book, or in the *Sunnah* of his Messenger (ﷺ), in a manner befitting Him, without changing or twisting their wording or meaning (*tahreef*), without denial of them (*ta'teel*), without asserting how they are (*takyeef*) and without declaring them to be like the attributes of the creation (*tamtheel*). Allaah, the Most High, says,

$$ وَلِلَّهِ ٱلْأَسْمَآءُ ٱلْحُسْنَىٰ فَٱدْعُوهُ بِهَا ۖ وَذَرُوا۟ ٱلَّذِينَ يُلْحِدُونَ فِىٓ أَسْمَٰٓئِهِۦ ۚ سَيُجْزَوْنَ مَا كَانُوا۟ يَعْمَلُونَ ١٨٠ $$

"And Allaah has the most excellent and perfect names, so call on Him by them, and abandon the company of those who deviate and commit *shirk* with regard to them - they will be punished for what they used to do."

[Soorah al-A'raaf (7):180]

$$ وَلَهُ ٱلْمَثَلُ ٱلْأَعْلَىٰ فِى ٱلسَّمَٰوَٰتِ وَٱلْأَرْضِ ۚ وَهُوَ ٱلْعَزِيزُ ٱلْحَكِيمُ ٢٧ $$

"His is the highest and most perfect description (none has the right to be worshipped but Him, and nothing is like Him) in the heavens and the earth, and He is the All-Mighty, the All-Wise."

[Soorah ar-Room (30):27]

$$ لَيْسَ كَمِثْلِهِۦ شَىْءٌ ۖ وَهُوَ ٱلسَّمِيعُ ٱلْبَصِيرُ ١١ $$

"There is nothing like Him, and He is the All-Hearing, the All-Seeing."

[Soorah ash-Shooraa (42):11]

With regard to this issue two groups of people have gone astray:

(i) The *Mu'attillah* - those who deny Allaah's names and attributes, or some of them, claiming that to affirm them necessitates making a resemblance between Allaah, the Most High, and his creation. This is a false and futile claim and its futility is shown in a number of ways, from them:

[a] It would necessitate conclusions that are futile, such as that there is contradiction in the Speech of Allaah, the One free of all imperfections.

148

This is because Allaah, the Most High, affirmed the names and attributes for Himself, and also denied that anything is like Him. So if affirming them necessitated resemblance between Allaah and His creation, then this would mean that there is a contradiction in Allaah's speech and that some of it negates the rest.

[b] If two things have a name or a description that is common to them both, it does not necessitate that they are alike. So you see that two people share the fact that they are humans, and possess hearing, and sight, and speech - but that does not mean that they are alike in their human qualities, and in their hearing, their sight and their speech. Furthermore, you see that animals have hands and feet and eyes, but the fact that this is something common to them does not mean that their hands, feet and eyes are alike. So when it is clear to you that there is a great difference between created beings in the names or attributes common to them, then the difference between the Creator and the creation will be far clearer and greater.

(ii) The *Mushabbihah* - those who affirm the names and attributes and also declare Allaah, the Most High, to be like His creation. They claim that this is what is required by and in accordance with the texts since Allaah, the Most High, addressed the people with that which is understandable to them. This claim of theirs is false and futile and its futility is shown in a number of ways, from them:

[a] That resemblance between Allaah, the Most High, and His creation is something futile and false, disproven by the intellect and the Revelation. It is, further, not possible that the texts of the Book and the *Sunnah* require and necessitate something that is false and futile.

[b] That Allaah, the Most High, addressed the people with that which is in essence understandable to them: however as for its essential reality and how that which is spoken of is, then this is knowledge which Allaah, the Most High, has kept to Himself. This is the case with regard to Allaah's self and His attributes. So Allaah has affirmed for Himself that He hears, and hearing is something understandable to us, and is the ability to perceive sounds. But as for how the reality of Allaah, the Most High's, Hearing is, then this is not known to us. This is because hearing differs even amongst created beings, so the difference in that regard between the Creator and the creation will be far greater. Also Allaah, the Most High, has informed us that He ascended (*istawaa*) upon His Throne (*'Arsh*). So ascension is some-

thing that is in essence understandable to us. However as for the reality of Allaah's having ascended and how that is, then this is something that is not known to us. So ascending or mounting a chair is not the same as mounting a difficult and wild camel. So if it is something wherein the creation differ, then the difference between the Creator and the creation will be far greater.

Eemaan in Allaah, the Most High, as we have described it, will produce great fruits for the Believers, from them:

(i) That he implements and realises the *tawheed* of Allaah, the Most High, such that he is not attached and devoted to other than Him. So he does not place hope in others, fear others, and does not worship any besides Him.

(ii) Completion of ones love for Allaah, the Most High, and to revere Him as is demanded by His perfect names and exalted attributes.

(iii) To accomplish worship of Him by doing whatever He has commanded, and avoiding whatever He has forbidden.

127 The angels (*al-malaa'ikah*) are created beings unseen to us and hidden from us. They are worshippers of Allaah, the Most High, and have none of the qualities of Lordship or Divinity, nor any right to be worshipped. Allaah, the Most High, created them from light, and bestowed upon them complete submission to His commands and the power to carry them out. Allaah, the Most High, says,

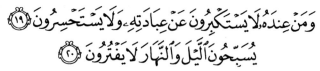

"And the angels who are near Him are not too proud to worship Him, nor do they become weary of worshipping Him. They praise and glorify Him day and night and never slacken in that."

[Soorah al-Ambiyaa (21):19-20]

They are many in number, so many that only Allaah, the Most High, can enumerate them. It is also established in the two *Saheehs* from the *hadeeth* of Anas, *radiyallaahu 'unhu*, concerning the night-journey and ascension (*mi'raaj*) of the Prophet (ﷺ), that the 'Much Frequented House' (*al-Baytul-Ma'moor*) was shown to the Prophet (ﷺ), and that seventy thousand angels pray in it every day, and then when they leave they never return to it, but another group arrives every day [Collected by al-Bukhaaree (Eng transl. 4/287, 290/ no. 429) and Muslim (Eng. transl. 1/100, 103/ no. 309)].

Eemaan in the angels comprises four matters:

(1) To believe in their existence.

(2) To believe specifically in those whose name we know, such as Jibreel. As for those whose names are unknown to us, then we have general and comprehensive belief in all of them.

(3) To believe in whatever has been described to us of their attributes. With regard to Jibreel, the Prophet (ﷺ) informed that he saw him in the appearance that he had been created upon, having six hundred wings and filling up the horizon [Reported by al-Bukhaaree (Eng. transl. 4/301/nos. 455,457)]. It sometimes occurs that an angel changes into the form of a man by the command of Allaah. This occurred with Jibreel when Allaah, the Most High, sent him to Maryam: he took the form of a perfect man. Also when he came to the Prophet (ﷺ) who was sitting with his Companions, he came in the form of a man having very white clothes and very black hair; no signs of having travelled were seen upon him and none of the Companions knew him. So he sat with the Prophet (ﷺ) and placed his knees together with his knees, and placed his palms upon his thighs. Then he asked the Prophet (ﷺ) about Islaam, *eemaan*, *ihsaan*, the Last Hour, and its signs. So the Prophet (ﷺ) answered him, and he departed. Then he (ﷺ) said: *"This was Jibreel. He came to you to teach you your Religion"* [Reported by Muslim (Eng. transl. 1/ 1/no.1)]. Likewise the angels whom Allaah sent to Ibraaheem and Loot were also in the form of men.

(4) To believe in the duties that we know of which they carry out by the command of Allaah, the Most High, such as their glorifying Allaah and declaring Him free and far removed from all imperfections, and their worshipping Him day and night without wearying or slackening. There are some of them who have particular duties, for example Jibreel, who was entrusted to convey the Revelation from Allaah, the Most High, to the prophets and messengers. Meekaa'eel, who is entrusted with the duty of looking after rainfall and the growth of plants. Israafeel, who is entrusted with blowing the Horn (as-Soor) at the Last Hour, and when the creation are to be resurrected. The angel of death whose duty it is to take the souls at the point of death. Maalik, who is entrusted to guard the Hellfire. The angels entrusted with the embryos in the womb, that when the unborn child has attained four months in its mothers womb, then Allaah sends an angel to it to write down its provision, its life-span, its actions and whether it will be wretched or fortunate. The angels entrusted with recording the deeds of each person, and there are two angels for each person - one on his right and one on his left. The angels whose duty it is to question the deceased when he is placed in the grave, two angels come to him and ask him about his Lord, his Religion and his Prophet.

Eemaan in the angels produces very great fruits, from them:

(i) Knowledge of the greatness of Allaah, the Most High, His Power, His authority and His dominion. Since the greatness of any created thing shows the greatness of the Creator.

(ii) Thankfulness to Allaah, the Most High, for His care and concern for the welfare of mankind, since He entrusted some angels with protecting them and recording their deeds and other actions beneficial to them.

(iii) Love of the angels for their worship of Allaah, the Most High.

There are some deviant folk who deny that the angels are physical beings, and claim instead that they are merely an expression referring to the power of good inherent in created beings. This saying is a denial of the Book of Allaah, the Most High, the *Sunnah* of His Messenger (ﷺ), and the consensus (*ijmaa'*) of the Muslims. Allaah, the Most High, says,

$$\text{ٱلْحَمْدُ لِلَّهِ فَاطِرِ ٱلسَّمَٰوَٰتِ وَٱلْأَرْضِ جَاعِلِ ٱلْمَلَٰئِكَةِ رُسُلًا أُو۟لِىٓ}$$
$$\text{أَجْنِحَةٍ مَّثْنَىٰ وَثُلَٰثَ وَرُبَٰعَ}$$

"All praise and thanks are for Allaah, the Sole Creator who brought the heavens and the earth into existence; who made the angels messengers, with His commands and prohibitions, having wings - two or three or four."

[Soorah Faaṭir (35):1]

وَلَوْ تَرَىٰ إِذْ يَتَوَفَّى ٱلَّذِينَ كَفَرُواْ ٱلْمَلَـٰٓئِكَةُ يَضْرِبُونَ وُجُوهَهُمْ وَأَدْبَـٰرَهُمْ

"And if you could see, O Muḥammad (ﷺ), the angels when they take out the souls of the unbelievers at death - striking their faces and their behinds."

[Soorah al-Anfaal (8):50]

وَمَنْ أَظْلَمُ مِمَّنِ ٱفْتَرَىٰ عَلَى ٱللَّهِ كَذِبًا أَوْ قَالَ أُوحِيَ إِلَىَّ وَلَمْ يُوحَ إِلَيْهِ شَىْءٌ وَمَن قَالَ سَأُنزِلُ مِثْلَ مَآ أَنزَلَ ٱللَّهُ وَلَوْ تَرَىٰٓ إِذِ ٱلظَّـٰلِمُونَ فِى غَمَرَٰتِ ٱلْمَوْتِ وَٱلْمَلَـٰٓئِكَةُ بَاسِطُوٓاْ أَيْدِيهِمْ أَخْرِجُوٓاْ أَنفُسَكُمُ

"And if you could see when those who worship others along with Allaah are in the agonies of death, and the angels are spreading their hands and striking them, and saying: Deliver up your souls."

[Soorah al-An'aam (6):93]

حَتَّىٰٓ إِذَا فُزِّعَ عَن قُلُوبِهِمْ قَالُواْ مَاذَا قَالَ رَبُّكُمْ قَالُواْ ٱلْحَقَّ وَهُوَ ٱلْعَلِىُّ ٱلْكَبِيرُ

"Until when the fear is banished from the angels' hearts they say to one another: 'What is it that your Lord has said?' They say: 'The Truth, and He is the Most High, the Most Great.'"

[Soorah Saba (34):23]

Allaah said about the people of paradise,

وَٱلْمَلَـٰٓئِكَةُ يَدْخُلُونَ عَلَيْهِم مِّن كُلِّ بَابٍ ۝ سَلَـٰمٌ عَلَيْكُم بِمَا صَبَرْتُمْ فَنِعْمَ عُقْبَى ٱلدَّارِ

His Books;[128]

"And the angels enter upon them from every gate, greeting them: You are in peace and security due to your having patiently obeyed your Lord in the worldly life, so how excellent a final home is Paradise instead of the Fire."

[Soorah ar-Ra'd (13):23-4]

The Prophet (ﷺ) said, *"If Allaah loves a servant He calls to Jibreel, 'Allaah loves so and so, so love him.' So Jibreel calls out to the inhabitants of the heavens, 'Allaah loves so and so, so love him,' so the inhabitants of the heavens love him. Then acceptance of him is placed on the earth."* [Collected by al-Bukhaaree (Eng. transl. 9/430/no. 577)].

The Prophet (ﷺ) also said, *"On the day of Jumu'ah there are angels at every door of the mosque writing down whoever comes first, and then the succeeding people in order. So when the Imaam sits, then the scrolls are rolled up and they come to hear the Reminder."* [Collected by al- Bukhaaree (Eng. transl. 2/25/no. 51)].

These texts clearly prove that the angels are physical beings and not abstract forces, as claimed by the deviants, and what is clearly shown in the texts is something upon which there is consensus (*ijmaa'*) of the Muslims.

128 The Books (*kutub*, plural of *kitaab*) - meaning that which is written. What is meant here is those Books which Allaah, the Most High, sent down to His messengers as a mercy to the creation, and as guidance for them, in order to enable them to attain success and happiness in this world and in the Hereafter. *Eemaan* in the Books comprises four matters:

(1) To believe that they were sent down by Allaah, the Most High.

(2) To believe in those Books whose names we know: from them the Qur'aan which was sent down to Muhammad (ﷺ) the *Tawraat* which was sent down to Moosaa (Moses), the *Injeel* which was sent down to 'Eesaa (Jesus), and the *Zaboor* which was given to Daawood (David), as for those for which we do not know by name then we have collective and general belief in all of them.

(3) To affirm whatever reports are established as being contained in them, such as whatever is reported in the Qur'aan, and those reports which have not been changed or distorted from the previous Books.

(4) To act upon whatever rulings they contain that have not been abrogated, and to be pleased with that, and to fully submit to it - whether we understand the wisdom behind it or not. All of the previous Books are abrogated by the sublime Qur'aan. Allaah, the Most High, says,

$$وَأَنزَلْنَآ إِلَيْكَ ٱلْكِتَبَ بِٱلْحَقِّ مُصَدِّقًا لِّمَا بَيْنَ يَدَيْهِ مِنَ ٱلْكِتَبِ وَمُهَيْمِنًا عَلَيْهِ فَٱحْكُم بَيْنَهُم بِمَآ أَنزَلَ ٱللَّهُ$$

"And we have sent down the Qur'aan to you, O Muhammad (ﷺ), and it is the truth, as confirmation of the Books sent down before it and as a trustworthy witness testifying to the truth contained therein and exposing the falsehood interpolated by men."
[Soorah al-Maa'idah (5):48]

The meaning of this *Aayah* is that the Qur'aan is a judge upon them, so it is not therefore permissible to act upon any ruling contained in the previous Books, except for that which is proven to be correctly from them and is affirmed and approved by the Qur'aan.

Eemaan in the revealed Books produces great fruits, from them:
(i) The knowledge that Allaah, the Most High, takes care of His servants and sent down to each people a Book for their guidance.
(ii) The knowledge of Allaah, the Most High's great wisdom in prescribing for each people those prescribed laws suitable for their condition. As Allaah, the Most High, says,

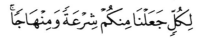

$$لِكُلٍّ جَعَلْنَا مِنكُمْ شِرْعَةً وَمِنْهَاجًا$$

وَرُسُلِهِ

His Messengers;[129]

"And for each people we laid down a prescribed law and a detailed way to be followed."

[Soorah al-Maa'idah (5):48]

(iii) Giving thanks to Allaah for having blessed us with that.

[129] The messengers (*ar-Rusul,* plural of *Rasool*) meaning one who is sent to convey a message and what is meant here is: those of mankind who had Revelation and religious law sent to them and were ordered to convey it to the people. The first of the messengers was Noo<u>h</u> (Noah) and the last of them was Mu<u>h</u>ammad (ﷺ). Allaah, the Most High, says,

إِنَّآ أَوْحَيْنَآ إِلَيْكَ كَمَآ أَوْحَيْنَآ إِلَىٰ نُوحٍ وَٱلنَّبِيِّـۧنَ مِنۢ بَعْدِهِۦ

"We sent Revelation to you O Mu<u>h</u>ammad, just as we sent Revelation to Noo<u>h</u> and the Prophets after him."

[Soorah an-Nisaa' (4):163]

It is reported from Anas ibn Maalik, *radiyallaahu 'anhu,* in the <u>h</u>adeeth about the Intercession, that the Prophet (ﷺ) mentioned that the people will come to Aadam to ask him to intercede on their behalf, but he will excuse himself and say to them, *"Go to Noo<u>h</u>, for he was the first of the messengers whom Allaah sent..."* [Collected by al-Bukhaaree (Eng. transl. 6/3/no.3].

Also Allaah, the Most High, said about Mu<u>h</u>ammad (ﷺ),

مَّا كَانَ مُحَمَّدٌ أَبَآ أَحَدٍ مِّن رِّجَالِكُمْ وَلَٰكِن

رَّسُولَ ٱللَّهِ وَخَاتَمَ ٱلنَّبِيِّـۧنَ

"Mu<u>h</u>ammad is not the father of any of your men, but he is the Messenger of Allaah and the last of the prophets."

[Soorah al-A<u>h</u>zaab (33):40]

Nor was there any nation left without a messenger sent by Allaah, the Most High with a special prescribed law for his people, or a prophet sent to revive prescribed laws given previously. Allaah, the Most High, says,

$$وَلَقَدْ بَعَثْنَا فِي كُلِّ أُمَّةٍ رَسُولًا أَنِ اعْبُدُوا اللَّهَ وَاجْتَنِبُوا الطَّاغُوتَ$$

"We sent a messenger to every nation, ordering that they should worship Allaah alone and that they should avoid everything worshipped besides Allaah."

[Soorah an-Nahl (16):36]

$$وَإِن مِّنْ أُمَّةٍ إِلَّا خَلَا فِيهَا نَذِيرٌ ﴿٢٤﴾$$

"There was not a previous nation except that Allaah sent a warner to them."

[Soorah Faatir (35):24]

$$إِنَّا أَنزَلْنَا التَّوْرَىٰةَ فِيهَا هُدًى وَنُورٌ يَحْكُمُ بِهَا النَّبِيُّونَ الَّذِينَ أَسْلَمُوا لِلَّذِينَ هَادُوا$$

"We sent down the *Tawraat* containing guidance and light, and the prophets who submitted themselves to Allaah judged the Jews thereby."

[Soorah al-Maa'idah (5):44]

The messengers were human and created beings, they had no share at all of Lordship nor any right to a share of worship or divinity. Allaah, the Most High, says about His Prophet Muhammad (ﷺ), and he was the best of all Messengers and had the highest standing amongst them with Allaah,

$$قُل لَّا أَمْلِكُ لِنَفْسِي نَفْعًا وَلَا ضَرًّا إِلَّا مَا شَاءَ اللَّهُ وَلَوْ كُنتُ أَعْلَمُ الْغَيْبَ لَاسْتَكْثَرْتُ مِنَ الْخَيْرِ وَمَا مَسَّنِيَ السُّوءُ إِنْ أَنَا إِلَّا نَذِيرٌ وَبَشِيرٌ لِّقَوْمٍ يُؤْمِنُونَ ﴿١٨٨﴾$$

"Say, O Muhammad (ﷺ), it is not within my power to bring benefit to myself nor to keep away harm - except as Allaah wills; and if I knew what the future holds I could amass a great deal of

157

wealth and harm would not befall me. But I am just a messenger from Allaah sent by Him to warn those who disobey Him of His punishment, and to give glad tidings of His reward for those who truly believe in Him and are obedient to Him."

[Soorah al-A'raaf (7):188]

$$قُلْ إِنِّي لَآ أَمْلِكُ لَكُمْ ضَرًّا وَلَا رَشَدًا ۝$$

$$قُلْ إِنِّي لَن يُجِيرَنِي مِنَ اللَّهِ أَحَدٌ وَلَنْ أَجِدَ مِن دُونِهِ مُلْتَحَدًا ۝$$

"Say, O Muhammad (ﷺ), it is not in my power to bring about harm for you, nor guidance, rather it is for Allaah. Say, O Muhammad (ﷺ), none from Allaah's creation could save or protect me if I were to disobey Him, nor could I find any refuge except with Him."

[Soorah al-Jinn (72):21-22]

So they experience whatever the rest of mankind experience with regard to illness, death, the need for food and drink, and so on. Allaah, the Most High, says about Ibraaheem that he described his Lord, the Most High, saying,

$$وَالَّذِي هُوَ يُطْعِمُنِي وَيَسْقِينِ ۝ وَإِذَا مَرِضْتُ فَهُوَ يَشْفِينِ ۝ وَالَّذِي يُمِيتُنِي ثُمَّ يُحْيِينِ ۝$$

"He is the One who provides me with food and drink, and if I become ill then it is He who cures me; and He is the One Who causes me to die when He wills, then when He wills He will resurrect me to life."

[Soorah ash-Shu'araa (26):79-81]

The Prophet (ﷺ) said, *"I am just a human like yourselves, I forget just as you forget. So if I forget, then remind me"* [Reported by Muslim (Eng. transl. 1/284/ no.1168)].

Furthermore Allaah, the Most High, has described them as being slaves of His, and this is at the height of their honour and in the context of praise of them. So He, the Most High, said about Nooh,

$$إِنَّهُۥ كَانَ عَبْدًا شَكُورًا ٣$$

"He was indeed a thankful *slave* of Allaah."

[Soorah al-Israa' (17):3]

He said about Muhammad (ﷺ),

$$تَبَارَكَ ٱلَّذِى نَزَّلَ ٱلْفُرْقَانَ عَلَىٰ عَبْدِهِۦ لِيَكُونَ لِلْعَٰلَمِينَ نَذِيرًا$$

"Exalted is He who sent down the Criterion (i.e. the Qur'aan) between truth and falsehood, in stages, to His *slave* Muhammad, so that he should be a warner to men and *jinn* that they will be punished by Allaah if they do not single Him out with all worship and keep away from the worship of everything else besides Him."

[Soorah al-Furqaan (25):1]

He also said about Ibraaheem, Ishaaq and Ya'qoob,

$$وَٱذْكُرْ عِبَٰدَنَآ إِبْرَٰهِيمَ وَإِسْحَٰقَ وَيَعْقُوبَ$$
$$أُوْلِى ٱلْأَيْدِى وَٱلْأَبْصَٰرِ ٤٥ إِنَّآ أَخْلَصْنَٰهُم بِخَالِصَةٍ ذِكْرَى$$
$$ٱلدَّارِ ٤٦ وَإِنَّهُمْ عِندَنَا لَمِنَ ٱلْمُصْطَفَيْنَ ٱلْأَخْيَارِ ٤٧$$

"And remember O Muhammad (ﷺ), Our *slaves* Ibraaheem, Ishaaq and Ya'qoob: men strong in their worship of Allaah and their obedience of Him, and men having understanding of the true Religion; and we chose and purified them with the quality of acting solely for the Hereafter, and calling the people to remembrance of the Hereafter and to obedience to Allaah. All of them were amongst those who were excellent and were chosen by Allaah for obedience to Him and as Messengers to the creation."

[Soorah Saad (38):45-47]

Allaah, the Most High also says, concerning 'Eesaa ibn Maryam,

"'Eesaa is not but a *slave* of Ours whom we blessed with guidance and *eemaan*, and we made Him a sign to the children of Israa'eel."

[Soorah az-Zukhruf (43):59]

Eemaan in the messengers comprises four matters:

(1) To believe that they were truly messengers sent by Allaah, the Most High. So whoever disbelieves in the messengership of one of them has disbelieved in all of them. Allaah, the Most High says,

كَذَّبَتْ قَوْمُ نُوحٍ ٱلْمُرْسَلِينَ ﴿١٠٥﴾

"The people of Nooh denied the messengers."

[Soorah ash-Shu'araa (26):105]

So Allaah declared them to be deniers of all of the messengers, even though they had no other messenger sent to them besides Nooh. Because of this the Christians who deny Muhammad (ﷺ) and do not follow him are also denying the Messiah ('Eesaa) ibn Maryam and are not following him either - especially since he gave them the news of the coming of Muhammad (ﷺ); and there is no meaning to his giving them the news of his coming except that he was to be a messenger for them so that Allaah should save them through him from misguidance and guide them to the Straight Path.

(2) To believe in each of them in particular whose name we know, such as Muhammad, Ibraaheem, Moosaa, 'Eesaa and Nooh, *'alayhimus-salaam*; and these five are the ones firmest in their resolve (*oolul-'adhm*) from amongst the messengers. They are mentioned together by Allaah, the Most High, in two places in the Qur'aan,

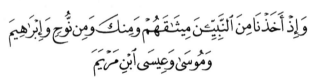

"And when We took the covenant from the prophets, and from you, O Muhammad (ﷺ), and from Nooh, Ibraaheem, Moosaa and 'Eesaa ibn Maryam."

[Soorah al-Ahzaab (33):7]

شَرَعَ لَكُم مِّنَ ٱلدِّينِ مَا وَصَّىٰ بِهِۦ نُوحًا وَٱلَّذِىٓ أَوْحَيْنَآ إِلَيْكَ وَمَا وَصَّيْنَا بِهِۦٓ إِبْرَٰهِيمَ وَمُوسَىٰ وَعِيسَىٰٓ أَنْ أَقِيمُوا۟ ٱلدِّينَ وَلَا تَتَفَرَّقُوا۟ فِيهِ

"Your Lord prescribed for Nooh, and that which We revealed to you - O Muhammad (ﷺ), and that which He prescribed for Ibraaheem, Moosaa, 'Eesaa - that you should establish the Religion, acting upon what is prescribed, and not split into sects with regard to it."

[Soorah ash-Shooraa (42):13]

As for those whose names we do not know, then we have general and comprehensive belief in all of them. Allaah, the Most High, says,

وَلَقَدْ أَرْسَلْنَا رُسُلًا مِّن قَبْلِكَ مِنْهُم مَّن قَصَصْنَا عَلَيْكَ وَمِنْهُم مَّن لَّمْ نَقْصُصْ عَلَيْكَ

"And We sent down messengers before you, O Muhammad (ﷺ): We have narrated to you the stories of some of them, and We did not narrate to you the stories of others."

[Soorah Ghaafir (40):78]

(3) To affirm whatever is narrated authentically from their reports.

(4) To act in accordance with the Revealed Law of the Messenger who was sent to us, and he is the last of them, Muhammad (ﷺ) who was sent to all people. Allaah, the Most High, says,

$$\text{فَلَا وَرَبِّكَ لَا يُؤْمِنُونَ}$$

$$\text{حَتَّىٰ يُحَكِّمُوكَ فِيمَا شَجَرَ بَيْنَهُمْ ثُمَّ لَا يَجِدُوا}$$

$$\text{فِىٓ أَنفُسِهِمْ حَرَجًا مِّمَّا قَضَيْتَ وَيُسَلِّمُوا تَسْلِيمًا ﴿٦٥﴾}$$

"But no, by your Lord, they do not have Faith until they make you, O Muḥammad (ﷺ), judge in all matters of dispute between them, and they find no resistance in themselves against your decisions, and accept them with full submission."

[Soorah an-Nisaa' (4):65]

Eemaan in the messengers produces very great fruits, from them:

(i) Knowledge of the mercy of Allaah, the Most High, and the great care He has for His servants, since He sent messengers to them to guide them to the way of Allaah, the Most High, and to make clear to them how they should worship Allaah, since the human mind alone cannot arrive at knowledge of that.

(ii) Giving thanks to Allaah, the Most High, for this great blessing.

(iii) Love and respect for the messengers, and to give them their due level of praise, since they are messengers sent by Allaah, the Most High, and because they established worship of Him, conveyed His messages and sincerely advised His servants.

But the obstinate rejectors denied their messengers, claiming that messengers from Allaah, the Most High, cannot be from mankind. This false claim is mentioned and refuted by Allaah, the Most High, in His Saying,

$$\text{وَمَا مَنَعَ ٱلنَّاسَ أَن يُؤْمِنُوٓا إِذْ جَآءَهُمُ}$$

$$\text{ٱلْهُدَىٰٓ إِلَّآ أَن قَالُوٓا أَبَعَثَ ٱللَّهُ بَشَرًا رَّسُولًا ﴿٩٤﴾ قُل لَّوْ كَانَ}$$

$$\text{فِى ٱلْأَرْضِ مَلَـٰٓئِكَةٌ يَمْشُونَ مُطْمَئِنِّينَ لَنَزَّلْنَا عَلَيْهِم}$$

$$\text{مِّنَ ٱلسَّمَآءِ مَلَكًا رَّسُولًا ﴿٩٥﴾}$$

162

"And what prevented the *mushriks* from your people, O Muḥammad (ﷺ), from believing truly in Allaah, and in what you brought to them from Him, when the clear proof of the truthfulness of what you called them to came to them - except their ignorant saying, 'Has Allaah sent a man as a messenger?!' Say to them, O Muḥammad (ﷺ), 'If there were angels walking about and residing upon the earth then We would have sent down from the heavens an angel as a messenger.'"

[Soorah al-Israa (17):94-5]

Allaah, the Most High, refutes this claim of theirs, since it has to be the case that the messengers are humans - since each messenger was sent to the people of the earth who are themselves humans. If the inhabitants of the earth were angels, then Allaah would have sent down an angel from the heavens as a messenger to them, so that he would be like them. Likewise Allaah, the Most High, quotes that those who denied the messengers said,

$$\text{إِنْ أَنتُمْ إِلَّا بَشَرٌ مِّثْلُنَا تُرِيدُونَ أَن تَصُدُّونَا}$$

$$\text{عَمَّا كَانَ يَعْبُدُ ءَابَآؤُنَا فَأْتُونَا بِسُلْطَنٍ مُّبِينٍ ﴿١٠﴾}$$

$$\text{قَالَتْ لَهُمْ رُسُلُهُمْ إِن نَّحْنُ إِلَّا بَشَرٌ مِّثْلُكُمْ وَلَكِنَّ ٱللَّهَ}$$

$$\text{يَمُنُّ عَلَى مَن يَشَآءُ مِنْ عِبَادِهِ وَمَا كَانَ لَنَآ أَن نَّأْتِيَكُم}$$

$$\text{بِسُلْطَنٍ إِلَّا بِإِذْنِ ٱللَّهِ}$$

"You are just human beings, like us in your appearance, and you are not angels. All you desire with your saying is to turn us away from the worship of that which our forefathers worshipped, so bring us clear proof of the truth of what you say. The Messengers sent to them said: It is true that we are human beings like you; but Allaah favours whomsoever He wills from His creation with prophethood and wisdom. Nor is it for us to bring any proof in accordance with your demands except by Allaah's command."

[Soorah Ibraaheem (14):10-11]

163

وَالْيَوْمِ الآخِرِ

the Last Day;[130]

---

130 The Last Day (*al-Yawmul-Aakhir*) is the Day of Resurrection when the people will be resurrected, and brought for account, and rewarded or punished. It is called the Last Day since there is no day which comes after it, because on it the people of Paradise will take up residence in their final homes and the people of the Fire in their final abode. *Eemaan* in the Last Day comprises three matters:

(1) *Eemaan* **in the Resurrection (*al-Ba'th*),** this is the reviving of the dead when the Horn (*as-Soor*) is blown for the second time. Then the people will stand before the Lord of creation - barefoot, naked and uncovered, and uncircumcised. Allaah, the Most High, says,

كَمَا بَدَأْنَا أَوَّلَ خَلْقٍ نُّعِيدُهُ وَعْدًا عَلَيْنَا إِنَّا كُنَّا فَاعِلِينَ

"Allaah will return the creation to a state of being naked, barefoot and uncircumcised, on the Day of Resurrection - just as Allaah created them in the beginning. That is a true and certain promise from Allaah - Allaah will certainly carry it out."

[Soorah al-Ambiyaa (21):104]

The Resurrection is a firmly established reality proven by the Book, the *Sunnah* and the consensus of the Muslims. Allaah, the Most High, says,

ثُمَّ إِنَّكُم بَعْدَ ذَٰلِكَ
لَمَيِّتُونَ ۝ ثُمَّ إِنَّكُمْ يَوْمَ الْقِيَامَةِ تُبْعَثُونَ ۝

"Then after that, O mankind, you will die. Then on the Day of Resurrection you will be raised up."

[Soorah al-Mu'minoon (23):15-16]

Also the Prophet (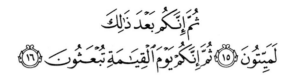) said, *"The people will be raised up on the Day of Resurrection (barefoot), naked and uncircumcised"* [Reported by al-Bukhaaree (Eng. transl. 4/364/no. 568) and Muslim (Eng. transl. 4/1487/no. 6846)].

There is consensus of the Muslims upon it, and it is necessitated by wisdom. It has to be the case that Allaah, the Most High, has laid down an appointed time for the creation to be requited for the duties He bound them with upon the tongues of His messengers. Allaah, the Most High, says,

$$أَفَحَسِبْتُمْ أَنَّمَا خَلَقْنَاكُمْ عَبَثًا وَأَنَّكُمْ إِلَيْنَا لَا تُرْجَعُونَ ۝$$

"Did you think that We created you without any purpose, and that you would not be brought back to us for requital."

[Soorah al-Mu'minoon (23):115]

He said to His Prophet (ﷺ),

$$إِنَّ الَّذِي فَرَضَ عَلَيْكَ الْقُرْءَانَ لَرَادُّكَ إِلَى مَعَادٍ$$

"He Who sent down the Qur'aan to you, O Muhammad (ﷺ), will certainly bring you to the place of return."

[Soorah al-Qasas (28):85]

(2) *Eemaan* **in the accounting and retribution.** The servant will be brought to account for his deeds, and rewarded or punished for them. This is proven by the Book, the *Sunnah* and the consensus of the Muslims. Allaah, the Most High, says,

$$إِنَّ إِلَيْنَا إِيَابَهُمْ ۝ ثُمَّ إِنَّ عَلَيْنَا حِسَابَهُمْ ۝$$

"Indeed to Allaah will be the return of the unbelievers, and it is Allaah Who will bring them to account."

[Soorah al-Ghaashiyah (88)25-6]

$$وَمَنْ جَاءَ بِالسَّيِّئَةِ فَلَا يُجْزَى إِلَّا مِثْلَهَا وَهُمْ لَا يُظْلَمُونَ ۝$$

"Whoever meets his Lord with a good deed, shall receive ten times its like in reward; and whoever meets him with an evil deed shall not receive recompense except with its like; and they shall not be wronged."

[Soorah al-An'aam (6):160]

وَنَضَعُ ٱلْمَوَٰزِينَ

ٱلْقِسْطَ لِيَوْمِ ٱلْقِيَٰمَةِ فَلَا تُظْلَمُ نَفْسٌ شَيْئًا وَإِن كَانَ

مِثْقَالَ حَبَّةٍ مِّنْ خَرْدَلٍ أَتَيْنَا بِهَا وَكَفَىٰ بِنَا حَٰسِبِينَ

"And Allaah will set up the Scales of Justice for the people on the Day of Resurrection, so no soul shall be treated unjustly in the least. Even the extent of the weight of a mustard seed We shall bring it and recompense it. And Allaah is fully sufficient as a Reckoner."

[Soorah al-Ambiyaa' (21):47]

Ibn 'Umar, *radiyallaahu 'anhumaa*, narrates that the Prophet (ﷺ) said, *"Allaah will bring the Believer close and shelter and screen him, and say: 'Did you commit such and such a sin?' 'Did you commit such and such a sin?' So he will say, 'Yes, my Lord' - until he has confessed his sins and will think that he is ruined. (Allaah) will say, 'I screened your sins in the world, and I forgive you for them today.' So he will be given the book of his good deeds. As for the unbelievers and the hypocrites, then they will be exposed in front of the people and it will be said, 'These are the ones who lied against their Lord, indeed the Curse of Allaah is upon the transgressors.'"* [Reported by al-Bukhaaree (Eng. transl. 3/372/no. 621) and Muslim (Eng. transl. 4/1444/no. 6669)].

It is authentically reported from the Prophet (ﷺ) that he said, *"Whoever intends to do a good deed and does it, then Allaah writes it down for him as ten good deeds, or up to seven hundred good deeds, or many more; and whoever intends to do an evil deed, and did it, then Allaah will write it for him as a single evil deed."* [Reported by al-Bukhaaree (Eng. trans. 8/329/ no. 498) and Muslim (Eng. trans. 1/75/no. 233 -237)].

Furthermore there is consensus of the Muslims upon affirmation of the Reckoning and accounting of the deeds. This is also what is necessitated by wisdom since Allaah, the Most High, sent down the Revealed Books, sent the messengers, and obligated the people to accept what the messengers brought and to act upon what was obligatory from it. He also obligated the Muslims to fight those who opposed him, and He made their blood lawful (to be shed), and their offspring and women and wealth (to be taken). So if there was to be no reckoning and no reward or retribution - then all of this would be in vain and futile, and the Lord Who is All-Wise is free from that. This is indicated by Allaah, the Most High, in His Saying,

فَلَنَسْـَٔلَنَّ ٱلَّذِينَ أُرْسِلَ إِلَيْهِمْ وَلَنَسْـَٔلَنَّ ٱلْمُرْسَلِينَ ٦ فَلَنَقُصَّنَّ عَلَيْهِم بِعِلْمٍ وَمَا كُنَّا غَآئِبِينَ ٧

"We shall certainly question those peoples to whom My messengers were sent - did they act obediently as commanded, doing what I ordered them and withholding from what I forbade them? And We shall certainly question the messengers as to whether they conveyed what they were commanded to. And We shall certainly narrate to the messengers and to those whom they were sent to whatever they did in the world - with certain knowledge. We were not absent from them and unaware of their deeds."

[Soorah al-A'raaf (7):6-7]

(3) *Eemaan* in the Paradise and Hell-Fire, and that they are the final and everlasting place of return for the creation. So Paradise (*al-Jannah*) is the place of bliss which Allaah, the Most High, has prepared for the pious and obedient Believers - those who truly believed in whatever Allaah obligated them to believe in, those who were obedient to Allaah and His Messenger, and who sincerely worshipped Allaah alone and followed His Messenger. Paradise contains all types of delights and bounties, "That *which no eye has seen, nor any ear has heard, nor has ever been imagined by a human heart.*" [Reported by al-Bukhaaree (Eng. transl. 4/306/no. 467) and Muslim (Eng. transl. 1/122/no. 363)].

Allaah, the Most High, says,

إِنَّ

ٱلَّذِينَ ءَامَنُوا۟ وَعَمِلُوا۟ ٱلصَّـٰلِحَـٰتِ أُو۟لَـٰٓئِكَ هُمْ خَيْرُ ٱلْبَرِيَّةِ ٧ جَزَآؤُهُمْ عِندَ رَبِّهِمْ جَنَّـٰتُ عَدْنٍ تَجْرِى مِن تَحْتِهَا ٱلْأَنْهَـٰرُ خَـٰلِدِينَ فِيهَآ أَبَدًا رَّضِىَ ٱللَّهُ عَنْهُمْ وَرَضُوا۟ عَنْهُ ذَٰلِكَ لِمَنْ خَشِىَ رَبَّهُۥ ٨

167

"Those who truly believe in Allaah and His Messenger and worship Allaah alone, making their worship purely and sincerely for Him - establishing the Prayer, giving the *zakaat*, and obeying Allaah concerning what He has ordered and forbidden, then they are the best of creation. Their reward is with their Lord on the Day of Resurrection: everlasting gardens with rivers flowing beneath the trees within them. They will live and remain therein forever and will not die. Allaah is pleased with them for their obedience to Him in the worldly life, and they are pleased with Him and the reward He will give them on that Day. That is for those who fear Allaah, openly and secretly, in the world - and therefore do what He commands them and avoid committing sins."

[Soorah al-Bayyinah (98):7-8]

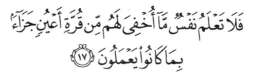

"So no soul knows what delights of the eye Allaah has kept hidden as reward for them for what they used to do."

[Soorah as-Sajdah (32):17]

As for the Hell-Fire, then it is the place of punishment which Allaah, the Most High, has prepared for the unbelievers, for the transgressors who disbelieved in Him and disobeyed His messengers. It contains such punishments and tortures as cannot be imagined. Allaah, the Most High, says,

وَٱتَّقُواْ ٱلنَّارَ ٱلَّتِيٓ أُعِدَّتْ لِلْكَٰفِرِينَ

"And beware of the Fire which Allaah has made ready for those who disbelieve in Him."

[Soorah Aal-'Imraan (3):131]

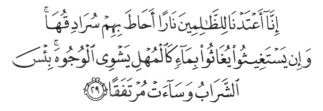

"We have prepared for the unbelievers a Fire whose walls surround them; and if they call out for relief from their raging thirst
they will be given a liquid that is black, foul-smelling, viscid and
unbearably hot, it will scorch away their faces. What an evil drink,
and what an evil resting place."

[Soorah al-Kahf (18):29]

"Allaah has cursed the unbelievers and prepared a blazing Fire
for them in the Hereafter. They will remain in the Fire forever
and will not have anyone to save or rescue them. On the Day
when they are dragged upon their faces in the Fire they will say:
oh would that we had obeyed Allaah and obeyed His Messenger."

[Soorah al-Ahzaab (33):64-66]

Connected to *eemaan* in the Last Day is *eemaan* in everything that will occur after
death, such as:

(a) The trial in the grave. This is that the deceased will be questioned in the grave
by the angels. He will be asked about his Lord, his Religion and his Prophet. As
for the Believers then Allaah will make them firm upon the true saying, and they
will reply: 'My Lord is Allaah, my Religion is Islaam, and my Prophet is
Muhammad (ﷺ).' As for the transgressors then Allaah will misguide them. The
unbeliever will say: 'Aah, Aah, I do not know,' and the hypocrite and the doubter
will say: 'I do not know, I heard the people saying something so I said it too.'

(b) Punishment and bliss in the grave (*'adhaabul-qabr wa na'eemuhu*). The transgressors, the hypocrites and the unbelievers will be tortured in it. Allaah, the Most
High, says,

$$\text{وَلَوْ تَرَىٰٓ إِذِ ٱلظَّٰلِمُونَ فِى غَمَرَٰتِ ٱلْمَوْتِ}$$

$$\text{وَٱلْمَلَٰٓئِكَةُ بَاسِطُوٓا۟ أَيْدِيهِمْ أَخْرِجُوٓا۟ أَنفُسَكُمُ ٱلْيَوْمَ}$$

$$\text{تُجْزَوْنَ عَذَابَ ٱلْهُونِ بِمَا كُنتُمْ تَقُولُونَ عَلَى ٱللَّهِ غَيْرَ ٱلْحَقِّ}$$

$$\text{وَكُنتُمْ عَنْ ءَايَٰتِهِۦ تَسْتَكْبِرُونَ ﴿٩٣﴾}$$

"And if you could but see, O Muhammad (ﷺ), those disbelievers in the throes of death - with the angel striking them with their hands, saying: 'Bring out your soul. This day you will be humiliated and punished for your unbelief - because of your speaking falsely about Allaah and your haughty refusal to obey Allaah's commands and the orders of His Messenger."

[Soorah al-An'aam (6):93]

Allaah, the Most High, said concerning the Pharaoh and his followers,

$$\text{ٱلنَّارُ}$$

$$\text{يُعْرَضُونَ عَلَيْهَا غُدُوًّا وَعَشِيًّا وَيَوْمَ تَقُومُ ٱلسَّاعَةُ أَدْخِلُوٓا۟}$$

$$\text{ءَالَ فِرْعَوْنَ أَشَدَّ ٱلْعَذَابِ ﴿٤٦﴾}$$

"They are exposed to the Fire, morning and evening, and on the Day when the Hour is established it will be said to the angels: Enter Pharaoh and his people into the severest torment."

[Soorah Ghaafir (40):46]

Also it is reported in _Saheeh Muslim_ from the _hadeeth_ of Zayd ibn Thaabit, from the Prophet (ﷺ) that he said: _"If it were not that you would stop burying the dead I would have supplicated so that you should hear the torment of the grave that I am hearing."_ Then he turned his face towards us and said: _"Seek Allaah's refuge from the torment of the grave."_ They said: _"We seek Allaah's refuge from the torment of the grave."_ He said: _"Seek Allaah's refuge from the trials and turmoil - those which are apparent and those which are hidden."_ They said: _"We seek Allaah's refuge from trials and turmoil - those which are apparent and those which_ *are hidden." He said: "Seek Allaah's refuge from the trial of the Dajjaal." They said: "We seek Allaah's refuge from the trial of the Dajjaal"* [Eng. transl. 4/1489/ no. 6859].

As for the bliss experienced by the sincere Believers in the grave, then Allaah, the Most High, says,

إِنَّ ٱلَّذِينَ قَالُوا۟ رَبُّنَا ٱللَّهُ ثُمَّ ٱسْتَقَٰمُوا۟ تَتَنَزَّلُ عَلَيْهِمُ ٱلْمَلَٰئِكَةُ أَلَّا تَخَافُوا۟ وَلَا تَحْزَنُوا۟ وَأَبْشِرُوا۟ بِٱلْجَنَّةِ ٱلَّتِى كُنتُمْ تُوعَدُونَ ﴿٣٠﴾

"Those who declare that their Lord is Allaah, and attribute no partner to Him and free themselves from the false gods and rivals attributed to Him, and they remain upright upon *tawheed*, not polluting it with *shirk*, and they are obedient to Him in whatever He orders and prohibits - then the angels descend upon them at the point of death, saying: 'Do not fear or grieve, and receive good tidings of the Paradise which you were promised in the world'."

[Soorah Fussilat (41):30]

فَلَوْلَآ

إِذَا بَلَغَتِ ٱلْحُلْقُومَ ﴿٨٣﴾ وَأَنتُمْ حِينَئِذٍ تَنظُرُونَ ﴿٨٤﴾ وَنَحْنُ أَقْرَبُ إِلَيْهِ مِنكُمْ وَلَٰكِن لَّا تُبْصِرُونَ ﴿٨٥﴾ فَلَوْلَآ إِن كُنتُمْ غَيْرَ مَدِينِينَ ﴿٨٦﴾ تَرْجِعُونَهَآ إِن كُنتُمْ صَٰدِقِينَ ﴿٨٧﴾ فَأَمَّآ إِن كَانَ مِنَ ٱلْمُقَرَّبِينَ ﴿٨٨﴾ فَرَوْحٌ وَرَيْحَانٌ وَجَنَّتُ نَعِيمٍ ﴿٨٩﴾

"Why then, when the person's soul is leaving him and reaches his throat; and those of you who are present are witnessing; and Our Angels are nearer to him than you - ready to take his soul - but you do not see them. If you are exempt from the Reckoning why then do you not bring back the souls, if you are truthful?! So

if the deceased was one of those brought near by Allaah, then for him there is ease and fine and pleasant provision, and gardens of delight."

[Soorah al-Waaqi'ah (56):83-89]

From al-Baraa ibn 'Aazib, *radiyallaahu 'anhu*, that the Prophet (ﷺ) said, with regard to the Believer when he answers the angels in the grave,: *"A Caller will call from heaven: 'That My servant has spoken truly, so spread out for him a bed from Paradise, and clothe him from Paradise, and open for him a door to Paradise.' He said: So its gentle breeze and its fragrance will come to him, and his grave will be widened for him as far as the eye can see"* [Reported by Ahmad and Aboo Daawood (Eng. transl. 3/1330/no. 4735) within a long *hadeeth*].

Eemaan in the Last Day produces very great fruits, from them:

(i) The desire to do acts of obedience, keenness upon that and to have hope for reward for them on that day.

(ii) Fear of committing sins and fear of being pleased with sins - for fear of receiving punishment on that Day.

(iii) Consolation for the Believer of whatever worldly things he has missed - and solace in the bliss and reward of the Hereafter that he hopes for.

But the unbelievers deny the Resurrection after death claiming that it is not possible. This claim of theirs is futile, and its futility is proven by the Revelation, by what has been witnessed and experienced, and by the intellect.

As for the Revelation, then Allaah, the Most High, says,

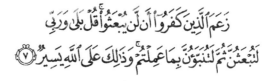

"The unbelievers claim that Allaah will not resurrect them after death. Say to them O Muhammad, by my Lord you will certainly be resurrected from your graves - and then you will be informed of the deeds which you did in the world. That is easy for Allaah."

[Soorah at-Taghaabun (64):7]

This is also something about which all the Revealed Books were agreed upon.

As for what has been witnessed, then Allaah has shown his servants the dead being brought to life in this world. Five examples of this are mentioned in *Soorah al-Baqarah*:

The first example: The people of Moosaa when they said to him:

$$لَن نُّؤْمِنَ لَكَ حَتَّىٰ نَرَى ٱللَّهَ جَهْرَةً$$

"We will never believe you until we see Allaah openly."

[Soorah al-Baqarah (2):55]

So Allaah, the Most High, caused them to die, then He brought them back to life. Concerning this Allaah, the Most High, says, addressing the children of Israaeel:

$$وَإِذْ قُلْتُمْ يَٰمُوسَىٰ لَن نُّؤْمِنَ لَكَ حَتَّىٰ نَرَى ٱللَّهَ جَهْرَةً$$
$$فَأَخَذَتْكُمُ ٱلصَّٰعِقَةُ وَأَنتُمْ تَنظُرُونَ ۝ ثُمَّ بَعَثْنَٰكُم مِّنۢ$$
$$بَعْدِ مَوْتِكُمْ لَعَلَّكُمْ تَشْكُرُونَ ۝$$

"And remember when you said: O Moosaa, we will never believe you until we see Allaah openly, so death seized you whilst you were looking on. Then We raised you back to life after you deaths so that you might give thanks."

[Soorah al-Baqarah (2):55-56]

The second example: In the story of the murdered man concerning whom the Banee Israaeel disputed. So Allaah, the Most High, commanded them to sacrifice a cow and to strike him with a part of it, so that he would be revived and inform them of who had killed him. Concerning this Allaah, the Most High, says,

$$وَإِذْ$$
$$قَتَلْتُمْ نَفْسًا فَٱدَّٰرَٰٔتُمْ فِيهَا وَٱللَّهُ مُخْرِجٌ مَّا كُنتُمْ تَكْتُمُونَ ۝$$
$$فَقُلْنَا ٱضْرِبُوهُ بِبَعْضِهَا كَذَٰلِكَ يُحْىِ ٱللَّهُ ٱلْمَوْتَىٰ وَيُرِيكُمْ$$
$$ءَايَٰتِهِۦ لَعَلَّكُمْ تَعْقِلُونَ ۝$$

"And remember - O Banee Israaeel - when you killed a man and disputed as to the murderer - and Allaah brought forth that which you hid. So We said: Strike the deceased with a part of the slaughtered cow. So they struck him with it and Allaah gave life to him. Thus Allaah brings the dead to life and shows you His clear signs that you may know the truth of the Prophethood of Muḥammad (ﷺ), and what he came with, and so believe in him and follow him."

[Soorah al-Baqarah (2):72-73]

The third example: occurs in the story of those who left their homes fleeing from death - and they were thousands in number, so Allaah, the Most High, caused them to die, and then brought them to life again. Concerning this Allaah, the Most High, says,

أَلَمْ تَرَ
إِلَى ٱلَّذِينَ خَرَجُوا۟ مِن دِيَـٰرِهِمْ وَهُمْ أُلُوفٌ حَذَرَ ٱلْمَوْتِ
فَقَالَ لَهُمُ ٱللَّهُ مُوتُوا۟ ثُمَّ أَحْيَـٰهُمْ إِنَّ ٱللَّهَ لَذُو فَضْلٍ عَلَى
ٱلنَّاسِ وَلَـٰكِنَّ أَكْثَرَ ٱلنَّاسِ لَا يَشْكُرُونَ ﴿٢٤٣﴾

"Did you not consider, O Muḥammad, those who fled from their homes in thousands, fearing death from the plague? So Allaah said to them: 'Die.' Then He restored them to life after their deaths. Indeed Allaah bestows great favour upon the people by making clear to them the way of guidance and warning them from the path of error and by bestowing great blessings upon them. Yet most of the people do not give thanks."

[Soorah al-Baqarah (2):243]

The fourth example: occurs in the story of the one who passed by a town that was ruined and dead and he could not imagine that Allaah, the Most High, would give life to it. So Allaah, the Most High, caused him to die for a hundred years, and then brought him to life. Concerning this Allaah, the Most High, says,

أَوْ كَالَّذِى مَرَّ

عَلَىٰ قَرْيَةٍ وَهِيَ خَاوِيَةٌ عَلَىٰ عُرُوشِهَا قَالَ أَنَّىٰ يُحْىِ هَٰذِهِ ٱللَّهُ بَعْدَ مَوْتِهَا ۖ فَأَمَاتَهُ ٱللَّهُ مِائَةَ عَامٍ ثُمَّ بَعَثَهُ ۖ قَالَ كَمْ لَبِثْتَ ۖ قَالَ لَبِثْتُ يَوْمًا أَوْ بَعْضَ يَوْمٍ ۖ قَالَ بَل لَّبِثْتَ مِائَةَ عَامٍ فَٱنظُرْ إِلَىٰ طَعَامِكَ وَشَرَابِكَ لَمْ يَتَسَنَّهْ ۖ وَٱنظُرْ إِلَىٰ حِمَارِكَ وَلِنَجْعَلَكَ ءَايَةً لِّلنَّاسِ ۖ وَٱنظُرْ إِلَى ٱلْعِظَامِ كَيْفَ نُنشِزُهَا ثُمَّ نَكْسُوهَا لَحْمًا ۚ فَلَمَّا تَبَيَّنَ لَهُ قَالَ أَعْلَمُ أَنَّ ٱللَّهَ عَلَىٰ كُلِّ شَىْءٍ قَدِيرٌ ۩٢٥٩

"Or did you not consider, O Muhammad, the one who passed by
a town and it was desolate and in ruins. He said: 'How will Allaah
give life to this after its death?' So Allaah caused him to die for a
hundred years, then raised him to life again. He said to him: 'How
long have you remained dead?' He said: 'I have remained for a
day, or rather part of a day.' He said: 'Rather you have remained
dead for a hundred years. So look at your food and drink - they
have not become spoiled through the years; and look at your donkey, how Allaah gives life to it while you are looking on. Thus We
have made you a sign for the people, proving the Resurrection.
Look at the bones, how We bring them together and then clothe
them with flesh. So when this was clearly shown to him he said:
'I have certain knowledge that Allaah is fully able to do all
things'."

[Soorah al-Baqarah (2):259]

The fifth example: In the story of Ibraaheem, the chosen beloved of Allaah, when
he asked Allaah, the Most High, to show him how He gives life to the dead. So
Allaah, the Most High, commanded him to sacrifice four birds and to place parts
of them upon the mountains around him. Then he was to call them; and the parts
joined together and they flew quickly to Ibraaheem. Concerning this Allaah, the
Most High, says,

$$وَإِذۡ قَالَ إِبۡرَٰهِـۧمُ رَبِّ أَرِنِى كَيۡفَ تُحۡىِ ٱلۡمَوۡتَىٰ قَالَ أَوَلَمۡ$$

$$تُؤۡمِنۡ قَالَ بَلَىٰ وَلَٰكِن لِّيَطۡمَئِنَّ قَلۡبِى قَالَ فَخُذۡ أَرۡبَعَةً مِّنَ$$

$$ٱلطَّيۡرِ فَصُرۡهُنَّ إِلَيۡكَ ثُمَّ ٱجۡعَلۡ عَلَىٰ كُلِّ جَبَلٍ مِّنۡهُنَّ جُزۡءًا$$

$$ثُمَّ ٱدۡعُهُنَّ يَأۡتِينَكَ سَعۡيًا وَٱعۡلَمۡ أَنَّ ٱللَّهَ عَزِيزٌ حَكِيمٌ ۝$$

"Do you not consider when Ibraaheem said: 'O my Lord, show me how you give life to the dead.' He said: 'Do you not believe, O Ibraaheem that I have the power to do that?' He said: 'Yes, I certainly believe, but I wish to increase in e*emaan* and certainty.' He said: 'Then take four birds, slaughter them and cut them into pieces. Then place a portion of each on every hill and call them. They will come in haste to you. And know that Allaah is All-Mighty, All-Wise."

[Soorah al-Baqarah (2):260]

These were actual visible events proving that it is possible for the dead to be raised to life. An indication of the signs given by Allaah, the Most High, to 'Eesaa ibn Maryam has already preceded: from them being the giving of life to the dead, and raising them from their graves by the permission of Allaah, the Most High.

The proofs of the intellect, are from two angles:

(i) That Allaah, the Most High, originated the heavens and the earth and everything contained in them. So the one who originated and created them and has the power and ability to do that will not be unable to recreate them. Allaah, the Most High, says,

$$وَهُوَ ٱلَّذِى يَبۡدَؤُاْ ٱلۡخَلۡقَ ثُمَّ يُعِيدُهُۥ وَهُوَ أَهۡوَنُ عَلَيۡهِ$$

"It is He (Allaah) who originates the creation, then brings it back again after it has perished, and that is even easier for Him."

[Soorah ar-Room (30):27]

$$كَمَا بَدَأۡنَآ أَوَّلَ خَلۡقٍ نُّعِيدُهُۥ وَعۡدًا عَلَيۡنَآ إِنَّا كُنَّا فَٰعِلِينَ$$

"We shall bring the creation (on the Day of Resurrection) back to the state in which We first created them: naked, barefoot and uncircumcised. That is a promise We have given and We shall certainly carry it out."

[Soorah al-Ambiyaa (21):104]

He also said, commanding a rebuttal to the saying of those who deny the resurrection of the decayed bones,

$$قُلْ يُحْيِيهَا الَّذِىٓ أَنشَأَهَآ أَوَّلَ مَرَّةٍ ۖ وَهُوَ بِكُلِّ خَلْقٍ عَلِيمٌ$$

"Say to the one who denies the resurrection of the decayed bones: They will be revived to life by the One who created them in the first place when they had been nothing. Indeed He has full knowledge of all His creation."

[Soorah Yaa Seen (36):79]

(ii) The earth becomes dead and barren and devoid of greenery, and then the rain falls and it comes to life, sprouting green plants of all kinds. So the One able to give it life after its being dead is the One who is able to bring the dead to life. Allaah, the Most High, says,

$$وَمِنْ ءَايَـٰتِهِۦٓ أَنَّكَ تَرَى ٱلْأَرْضَ خَـٰشِعَةً فَإِذَآ أَنزَلْنَا عَلَيْهَا ٱلْمَآءَ ٱهْتَزَّتْ وَرَبَتْ ۚ إِنَّ ٱلَّذِىٓ أَحْيَاهَا لَمُحْىِ ٱلْمَوْتَىٰٓ ۚ إِنَّهُۥ عَلَىٰ كُلِّ شَىْءٍ قَدِيرٌ ٣٩$$

"And from the signs proving Allaah's ability to bring the dead to life is that you see the earth dry and dusty, devoid of plants and crops. Then when Allaah sends down rain upon it the earth swells and puts forth vegetation. Indeed He who brought it to life will certainly bring the dead back to life. Indeed He is fully able to do all things."

[Soorah Fussilat (41):39]

وَنَزَّلْنَا مِنَ ٱلسَّمَاءِ مَاءً مُّبَرَكًا فَأَنبَتْنَا بِهِ جَنَّتٍ وَحَبَّ ٱلْحَصِيدِ ۝ وَٱلنَّخْلَ بَاسِقَتٍ لَّهَا طَلْعٌ نَّضِيدٌ ۝ رِّزْقًا لِّلْعِبَادِ وَأَحْيَيْنَا بِهِ بَلْدَةً مَّيْتًا كَذَلِكَ ٱلْخُرُوجُ ۝

"And We send down from the clouds water containing blessings; and with it We cause many gardens to grow, and crops of wheat and barley, and tall date-palms having spathes piled one on top of the other, as sustenance for the servants; and We give life with that water to barren land. Likewise will be the Resurrection."

[Soorah Qaaf (50):9-11]

Some of the people of deviation went astray and denied the punishment of the grave, and its bliss, claiming that it is not possible since it is contrary to the reality we experience. They say: If you were to uncover the dead in the grave you would find him just as he was, the grave would not have changed by becoming wider or tighter. So this claim of theirs is rendered futile by the texts, experience and intellect.

The texts proving establishment of punishment and bliss of the grave have preceded under section (b) from those matters pertaining to *eemaan* in the Last Day. Also in *Saheeh al-Bukhaaree* from the *hadeeth* of Ibn 'Abbaas, *radiyallaahu 'anhumaa*, who said: "The *Prophet* (ﷺ) *was passing by a walled garden in al-Madeenah when he heard the sound of two people being tortured in their graves.*" and he mentioned the *hadeeth* and it contains: "*that one of them had not used to save himself from being soiled by urine, and in a narration: from his urine; and as for the other then he used to go about with evil gossip (to cause enmity between people)*" [Eng. transl. vol. 1, p. 141, no. 215].

As for what is experienced, then a person who is asleep may see in his dream that he is in a spacious and splendid place where he is in bliss, or that he is in a restricted and frightening place where he feels pain, and sometimes that which he sees may cause him to awaken. Yet despite this he remains upon his bed, in his room, in the same state that he was in before. Then sleep is the brother of death, and therefore Allaah, the Most High, calls it *wafaat* ('passing away'), Allaah, the Most High, says,

اللَّهُ يَتَوَفَّى ٱلْأَنفُسَ حِينَ مَوْتِهَا وَٱلَّتِي
لَمْ تَمُتْ فِي مَنَامِهَا فَيُمْسِكُ ٱلَّتِي قَضَىٰ عَلَيْهَا ٱلْمَوْتَ
وَيُرْسِلُ ٱلْأُخْرَىٰ إِلَىٰ أَجَلٍ مُّسَمًّى

"Allaah takes the souls when the appointed span for their life is completed, and also those that do not die He takes during their sleep so then He keeps those for which He has ordained death, and sends the others forth for an appointed term."

[Soorah az-Zumar (39):42]

As for the intellect, then a person while sleeping sees true dreams which are consistent with reality. He may even see the Prophet (ﷺ) in his true appearance, and whoever sees him upon his true appearance has truly seen him. Yet despite this the person who is asleep remains in his room upon his bed, far from what he sees. So if this is possible in the worldly life, then how can it not be possible in the life of the Hereafter?!

As for their seeking to support their claim with the saying that if you were to uncover a dead man in his grave you would find him just as he was, and you would find that the grave had not widened or become constricted; then the reply to this is from a number of angles, from them:

(i) It is not allowed to try to contradict the *Sharee'ah* texts with the like of these futile doubts - which are such that if the one who raises them were to carefully consider the *Sharee'ah* texts he would see the futility of these doubts. So it is as has been said: "How many people seek to find fault with a saying that is correct, and their downfall is faulty understanding."

(ii) That the state experienced after death (*al-Barzakh*) is from the affairs of the hidden and the unseen and cannot be reached by the senses. If it could be reached by the senses then the benefit in having *eemaan* in the hidden and the unseen would pass away, and the true Believers and the deniers would be the same in their affirmation of it.

(iii) The punishment and bliss, expansion of the grave and its constriction will be experienced by the deceased and not by others. This is just like the sleeping person who sees in his dream that he is in a frightful and constricted place, or in an extensive and pleasing place, yet in the view of others he has experienced no change whilst asleep and remains in his room under his covers upon his bed. Also the Prophet (ﷺ) used to receive Revelation whilst he was with his Companions, and he would hear the Revelation yet the Companions would hear nothing. Also sometimes the angel would take the form of a man and would speak to him, yet the Companions would not see or hear the angel.

(iv) That the perception of the creation is limited to what Allaah, the Most High, has enabled them to reach and perceive, and they cannot reach and perceive everything that exists. So the seven heavens and the earth and all within them, and everything glorifies and praises Allaah in a true and real sense, and Allaah, the Most High, allows this to be heard sometimes by whomever He wills from His creation, yet this is something hidden from us. Concerning this Allaah, the Most High, says,

$$تُسَبِّحُ لَهُ ٱلسَّمَـٰوَٰتُ ٱلسَّبْعُ وَٱلْأَرْضُ وَمَن فِيهِنَّ وَإِن مِّن شَىْءٍ إِلَّا يُسَبِّحُ بِحَمْدِهِۦ وَلَـٰكِن لَّا تَفْقَهُونَ تَسْبِيحَهُمْ$$

"The seven heavens and the earth and the Believers, from the angels, men and *jinn* - within them praise and glorify Allaah, declaring Him free from all defects. There is nothing from His creation except that it praises and glorifies Him, yet you do not comprehend their praises."

[Soorah al-Israa (17):44]

Likewise the devils and the *jinn* proceed upon the earth, coming and going, and the *jinn* gathered in the presence of the Prophet (ﷺ) and listened quietly to his recitation and then went off as warner's to their people. Yet despite this they are hidden from us. Concerning this Allaah, the Most High, says,

وَ تُؤْمِنَ بِالقَدَرِ خَيْرِهِ وَشَرِّهِ

and that you truly believe in pre-decree (*al-qadar*) its good and its evil.[131]

يَٰبَنِىٓ ءَادَمَ لَا يَفْتِنَنَّكُمُ
ٱلشَّيْطَٰنُ كَمَآ أَخْرَجَ أَبَوَيْكُم مِّنَ ٱلْجَنَّةِ يَنزِعُ عَنْهُمَا لِبَاسَهُمَا
لِيُرِيَهُمَا سَوْءَٰتِهِمَآ إِنَّهُۥ يَرَىٰكُمْ هُوَ وَقَبِيلُهُۥ مِنْ حَيْثُ لَا تَرَوْنَهُمْ
إِنَّا جَعَلْنَا ٱلشَّيَٰطِينَ أَوْلِيَآءَ لِلَّذِينَ لَا يُؤْمِنُونَ ﴿٢٧﴾

"O children of Aadam, do not let Satan deceive you by putting you to trial just as he caused your parents Aadam and Hawaa to be taken out of Paradise, stripping them of their clothing to reveal their private parts - due to their obedience to him. Indeed Satan sees you, he and his tribe the *jinn* from whence you cannot see them. Indeed We have made the devils helpers of those who are unbelievers."

[Soorah al-A'raaf (7):27]

Since the creation cannot reach and perceive all that exists, then it is not permissible to reject those affairs of the Hidden and Unseen that have been affirmed but which they are unable to perceive.

131 *Al-Qadar* (Pre-Decree) is "Allaah, the Most High's, ordainment of the creation, in accordance with His Knowledge that preceded everything, and in accordance with His Wisdom." Belief in q*adar* comprises four matters:

(i) To believe that Allaah, the Most High, has always and eternally known everything, both the general and the specific details, whether with regard to His actions or the actions of His creation.

(ii) To believe that Allaah wrote all of this in the Preserved Tablet (*al-Lawhul-Mahfoodh*); and concerning these two matters Allaah, the Most High, says,

وَالدَّلِيْلُ عَلَى هَذِهِ الأَرْكَانِ السِّتَّةِ قَوْلُهُ تَعَالَى:

﴿ لَيْسَ البِرَّ أَنْ تُوَلُّوْا وُجُوْهَكُمْ قِبَلَ المَشْرِقِ وَالمَغْرِبِ وَلَكِنَّ البِرَّ مَنْ آمَنَ بِاللَّهِ وَاليَوْمِ الآخِرِ وَالمَلاَئِكَةِ وَالكِتَابِ وَالنَّبِيِّيْنَ ﴾

وَدَلِيْلُ القَدَرِ قَوْلُهُ تَعَالَى: ﴿ إِنَّا كُلَّ شَيْءٍ خَلَقْنَاهُ بِقَدَرٍ ﴾

The proof for these six pillars is the Saying of Allaah, the Most High, **"It is not righteousness that you turn your faces to the east or the west, but rather righteousness is the righteousness of those who truly believe in Allaah, and the Last Day, and the Angels, and the Books, and the Prophets."** [Soorah al-Baqarah (2):177]

The proof for pre-decree is the Saying of Allaah, the Most High, **"We have created all things in accordance with a pre-decreed measure."** [Soorah al-Qamar (54):49]

أَلَمْ تَعْلَمْ أَنَّ اللَّهَ يَعْلَمُ مَا فِى السَّمَاءِ وَالْأَرْضِ إِنَّ ذَلِكَ فِى كِتَابٍ إِنَّ ذَلِكَ عَلَى اللَّهِ يَسِيرٌ ﴿٧٠﴾

"Do you not know that Allaah knows whatever is in the seven heavens and the seven earth's, nothing of that is hidden from Him. The knowledge of all that is contained in the Preserved Tablet, and it is something easy for Allaah."

[Soorah al-Hajj (22):70]

It is reported from 'Abdullaah ibn 'Amr ibn al-'Aas, *radiyallaahu 'anhumaa*, who said that I heard Allaah's Messenger (ﷺ) say, *"Allaah wrote the decreed measures for all of the creation before the creation of the heavens and the earth by fifty thousand years."* [Reported by Muslim (Eng. transl. 4/1396/no. 6416)].

(iii) To believe that everything in existence exists by the Will of Allaah, the Most High, whether it is those matters pertaining to His actions, or those matters pertaining to the actions of the creation. Concerning His own actions Allaah, the Most High, says,

وَرَبُّكَ يَخْلُقُ مَا يَشَآءُ وَيَخْتَارُ

"And your Lord creates whatever He wills and chooses.'

[Soorah al-Qasas (28):68]

وَيَفْعَلُ ٱللَّهُ مَا يَشَآءُ ۝

"And Allaah does whatever He wills."

[Soorah Ibraaheem (14):27]

هُوَ ٱلَّذِى يُصَوِّرُكُمْ فِى ٱلْأَرْحَامِ كَيْفَ يَشَآءُ

"It is Allaah who fashions you in the wombs as He wills."

[Soorah Aal 'Imraan (3):6]

Allaah, the Most High, says, with regard to the actions of the created beings,

وَلَوْ شَآءَ ٱللَّهُ لَسَلَّطَهُمْ عَلَيْكُمْ فَلَقَٰتَلُوكُمْ

"And if Allaah had willed He would have given them power over you and they would have fought you."

[Soorah an-Nisaa (4):90]

وَلَوْ شَآءَ ٱللَّهُ مَا فَعَلُوهُ فَذَرْهُمْ وَمَا يَفْتَرُونَ ۝

"And if Allaah had willed He would have kept them from doing that; so leave them and the falsehood which they invent."

[Soorah al-An'aam (6):137]

(iv) To believe that everything in existence is created by Allaah, the Most High, both the things themselves and their attributes and their activities. Allaah, the Most High, says,

ٱللَّهُ خَٰلِقُ كُلِّ شَىْءٍ وَهُوَ عَلَىٰ كُلِّ شَىْءٍ وَكِيلٌ ۝

"Allaah it is Who is the Creator of everything, and He is the Guardian over all things,"

[Soorah az-Zumar (39):62]

$$وَخَلَقَ كُلَّ شَىْءٍ فَقَدَّرَهُ تَقْدِيرًا ﴿٢﴾$$

"And Allaah created everything and gave everything its due and decreed measure."

[Soorah al-Furqaan (25):2]

He said about the Prophet of Allaah Ibraaheem, *'alayhis-salaam*, that he said to his people:

$$وَٱللَّهُ خَلَقَكُمْ وَمَا تَعْمَلُونَ ﴿٩٦﴾$$

"And Allaah created you and your handiwork."

[Soorah as-Saafaat (37):96]

Belief in pre-decree as we have described it does not negate the fact that the servant has will (*mashee'ah*) and ability (*qudrah*) in those actions where he has a choice. Rather both the *sharee'ah* texts and the reality that is witnessed affirm this for him.

As for the texts, then Allaah, the Most High, says about their will,

$$فَمَن شَآءَ ٱتَّخَذَ إِلَىٰ رَبِّهِ مَآبًا ﴿٣٩﴾$$

"So whoever wills shall act and prepare for the day when they return to their Lord."

[Soorah an-Naba (78):39]

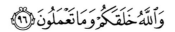

"Enter your wives from any angle you wish ."

[Soorah al-Baqarah (2):223]

$$فَٱتَّقُوا۟ ٱللَّهَ مَا ٱسْتَطَعْتُمْ وَٱسْمَعُوا۟ وَأَطِيعُوا۟$$

"And fear Allaah and fear His punishment, by doing whatever He has obligated, avoiding sins, and doing deeds that will draw one closer to Him, as much as you are able."

[Soorah at-Taghaabun (64):16]

$$\text{لَا يُكَلِّفُ}$$

$$\text{ٱللَّهُ نَفْسًا إِلَّا وُسْعَهَا لَهَا مَا كَسَبَتْ وَعَلَيْهَا مَا ٱكْتَسَبَتْ}$$

"Allaah does not place a burden on any soul greater than that it can bear. It will receive the good that it has earned and is accountable for the evil it has committed."

[Soorah al-Baqarah (2):286]

In the reality that we witness, every person knows that he possesses will and ability, and through them is able to do or leave an action. Furthermore he knows that there is a difference between things that occur with his will, such as his walking along, and things that occur involuntarily, such as his trembling with fear. However the will and ability of the person exist by the Will and Ability/Power of Allaah, the Most High. Allaah, the Most High, says,

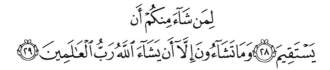

"For whoever from the creation wishes to follow the truth; and you will not wish it unless Allaah, the Lord of all creation, wishes that for you."

[Soorah at-Takweer (81):28-29]

Because all of the creation is part of the Dominion of Allaah, the Most High, and there is nothing within His Dominion that exists without His Knowledge and Will.

Also belief in pre-decree as we have described it does not provide any excuse for a person to abandon obligatory duties, or to commit sins, using the plea that this was pre-decreed for him. Such an argument is futile from a number of angles:

(i) The Saying of Allaah, the Most High,

سَيَقُولُ ٱلَّذِينَ أَشْرَكُواْ
لَوْ شَآءَ ٱللَّهُ مَآ أَشْرَكْنَا وَلَآ ءَابَآؤُنَا وَلَا حَرَّمْنَا مِن شَيْءٍ
كَذَٰلِكَ كَذَّبَ ٱلَّذِينَ مِن قَبْلِهِمْ حَتَّىٰ ذَاقُواْ بَأْسَنَا
قُلْ هَلْ عِندَكُم مِّنْ عِلْمٍ فَتُخْرِجُوهُ لَنَآ إِن تَتَّبِعُونَ إِلَّا
ٱلظَّنَّ وَإِنْ أَنتُمْ إِلَّا تَخْرُصُونَ ۝

"Those who worship others along with Allaah will say: 'If Allaah
had willed us to believe and worship Him alone, then we would
not have worshipped others along with Him, nor would our forefathers; nor would we ourselves have declared things forbidden.
So the fact that He did not prevent us shows that He is pleased
with what we do'. In the same way did the evildoers before them
deny and reject the truth, until our punishment came upon them.
Say to them, O Muhammad (ﷺ): Do you have any proof that you
can produce that Allaah is pleased with that?! Rather you are
just following conjecture and inventing lies against Allaah."

[Soorah al-An'aam (6):148]

If they had been any excuse for them in pre-decree then Allaah would not have
sent down His punishment upon them.

(ii) The Saying of Allaah, the Most High,

رُّسُلًا مُّبَشِّرِينَ وَمُنذِرِينَ لِئَلَّا يَكُونَ
لِلنَّاسِ عَلَى ٱللَّهِ حُجَّةٌۢ بَعْدَ ٱلرُّسُلِ وَكَانَ ٱللَّهُ عَزِيزًا حَكِيمًا

"Messengers who were sent with the good news of Allaah's reward for those who obey Him, do as He commands and believe in
His messengers, and warner's of Allaah's punishment, for those
who disobey Allaah, contravene His commands and disbelieve in
His messengers; so that those who disbelieve in Allaah and wor-

ship others besides Him may have no excuse to avoid punishment after the sending of the messengers, and Allaah is the All-Mighty, All-Wise."

[Soorah an-Nisaa (4):165]

If pre-decree were an excuse for the evildoers, then it would not be removed by the sending of the messengers, since their evil acts after the sending of the messengers would still be according to the pre-decree of Allaah, the Most High.

(iii) Al-Bukhaaree reports from 'Alee ibn Abee Ṭaalib, *radiyallaahu 'anhu*, that the Prophet (ﷺ) said: *"There is not one of you except that his place in the Fire or in Paradise has already been written."* So a man from the people said: *"Shall we not just depend upon it, O Messenger of Allaah?"* He replied: *"No, act for everyone will have that made easy for him"* (Then he recited Aayaat 5-10 of Soorah al-Layl). [Eng. transl. 8/392/no, 602]

In the wording reported by Muslim he said: *"For everyone will have that which he was created for made easy for him"* (Eng. transl. 4/1393/ no. 6398).

So the Prophet (ﷺ) commanded action and forbade inaction and dependence upon pre-decree.

(iv) Allaah, the Most High, gave the servant orders and prohibitions, and did not burden him except with that which he is capable of performing. Allaah, the Most High, says,

فَٱتَّقُوا۟ٱللَّهَ مَٱسْتَطَعْتُمْ

"And fear Allaah and fear His punishment by doing whatever He has obligated, avoiding sins and doing deeds that will draw one closer to Him - as much as you are able."

[Soorah at-Taghaabun (64):16]

لَا يُكَلِّفُ ٱللَّهُ نَفْسًا إِلَّا وُسْعَهَا

"Allaah does not place a burden on any soul greater than it can bear."

[Soorah al-Baqarah (2):286]

So if the servant was compelled to do (evil) actions, then he would have been duty bound with avoiding something which is impossible for him to avoid - and this is futile. Therefore it is the case that if he falls into a sin due to ignorance, forgetfulness or having been compelled then there is no sin upon him, as he is excused.

(v) Allaah's pre-decree is a hidden secret that is not known except after what was decreed comes about; whereas the person's will and desire in his deeds is something that precedes them. So his will to commit the actions is not based upon his having knowledge of what Allaah has decreed. Since this is the case it invalidates his attempt to use pre-decree as an excuse, because there is no proof for a person in something that he doesn't know.

(vi) We see that in a person's worldly affairs he strives to take care of that which is in his best interests, seeking to attain it; and he does not, instead, strive to attain what is not in his best interest and excuse himself in this with pre-decree. So why then does he turn away from what benefits him in the matter of his Religion, and instead does that which will harm him, and then use pre-decree as his excuse?! Are not these two matters the same?!

We will quote an example to make this clear: If a person stood at the head of two roads, one of them led to a land where there was total anarchy, killing and looting, destruction of property, fear and famine; and the second road led to a land of complete order, total stability and security, affluence, and where peoples live and property and wealth were respected, then which road will he take? He will certainly take the second road to the land of order and security. It is not possible that any sane person would take the road to the land of anarchy and fear and then use pre-decree as his excuse. So why with regard to the affairs of the Hereafter does he take the road to the Fire and not the road to Paradise and seek to use pre-decree as his excuse?!

Another example is that of a sick person who is told to take a medicine that he does no like or desire so he drinks it; and he is told to refrain from some food that he likes to avoid its harm, so he refrains from it. He does all of this hoping to be cured and restored to wellbeing. It is not possible that he will abstain from drinking the medicine, and will eat the harmful food, and then seek to use pre-decree as his excuse in this. So why does a person leave that which Allaah and His Messenger have commanded, or do that which Allaah forbade and His Messenger forbade and then seek to use pre-decree as an excuse?!

(vii) That the one who seeks to use Pre-Decree as an excuse for abandoning the obligatory duties or for committing sins, if a person were to transgress against him - either stealing his wealth or violating his rights, and then sought to use Pre-Decree as an excuse for his actions, saying: 'Don't blame me since my transgression was something decreed by Allaah' - then he would not accept this excuse from him. So how is it that he will not accept Pre-Decree as an excuse for someone who transgresses against him, yet he himself seeks to use it as an excuse for himself when he transgresses against that which is the right of Allaah, the Most High?!

In this regard it is mentioned that a thief who deserved the punishment of having his hand amputated was brought before Ameerul-Mumineen 'Umar ibn al-Khattaab, *radiyallaahu 'anhu*, so he ordered that his hand be amputated, so he said: "Wait. O chief of the Believers, I only stole by the pre-decree of Allaah." So 'Umar replied: "And we only amputate by the pre-decree of Allaah."

Belief in pre-decree produces very great fruits, from them:-

(i) Dependence upon Allaah, the Most High, after having carried out the necessary means to an end; so he does not depend upon the means itself, since everything occurs by the pre-decree of Allaah, the Most High.

(ii) That the person is not amazed with himself when that which he wants is attained. Its attainment is a blessing granted by Allaah, the Most High, and came about through the means to good and success which Allaah decreed. So being amazed with his own self will cause him to forget to give thanks for this blessing.

(iii) Peace of mind and being at ease with whatever occurs with him from that which Allaah, the Most High, has decreed for him. So he does not become disturbed by the fact that something he loves does not come to him, nor by something he dislikes coming to him. All of this occurs by the pre-decree of Allaah, to whom belongs the dominion of the heavens and the earth. It was something that was going to happen and could not be avoided. Concerning this Allaah, the Most High, Says,

مَآ أَصَابَ

مِن مُّصِيبَةٍ فِى ٱلْأَرْضِ وَلَا فِىٓ أَنفُسِكُمْ إِلَّا فِى كِتَٰبٍ
مِّن قَبْلِ أَن نَّبْرَأَهَآ إِنَّ ذَٰلِكَ عَلَى ٱللَّهِ يَسِيرٌ ۝ لِّكَيْلَا
تَأْسَوْا۟ عَلَىٰ مَا فَاتَكُمْ وَلَا تَفْرَحُوا۟ بِمَآ ءَاتَىٰكُمْ وَٱللَّهُ
لَا يُحِبُّ كُلَّ مُخْتَالٍ فَخُورٍ ۝ ٱلَّذِينَ يَبْخَلُونَ وَيَأْمُرُونَ

"No calamity befalls you in the earth or in your selves except that it was written in the Preserved Tablet before We created the souls. Indeed creating the souls and recording all the calamities that will befall them is something easy for Allaah. We have informed you of this so that you should not grieve over worldly matters that escape you, nor exult over others due to what He has given to you; and Allaah does not love the proud who exult over others due to the worldly things they have been given."

[Soorah al-Hadeed (57):22-23]

The Prophet (ﷺ) said: *"How amazing is the affair of the Believer, all of his affair is good, and that is not the case for anyone except the Believer: if ease comes to him he gives thanks for it, so that is good for him; and if trouble comes to him he has patience and so that is good for him"* [Reported by Muslim (Eng. transl. 4/1541/no. 7138)].

Two sects have gone astray regarding pre-decree:-

(i): The *Jabariyyah* - those who say that the person is compelled to carry out his actions, and that he has no will or ability with regard to them.

(ii): The *Qadariyyah* - those who say that the person is totally independent and has unrestricted free will and ability regarding his actions, and that Allaah's Will and Power have no effect in this.

The rebuttal of the first group (al-*Jabariyyah*) is found in the texts and the reality of that is witnessed. As for the texts, then Allaah, the Most High, affirmed will and desire and ability for the servant and attributed actions to him. Allaah, the Most High, says,

مِنكُم مَّن يُرِيدُ ٱلدُّنْيَا وَمِنكُم مَّن يُرِيدُ ٱلْأَخِرَةَ

"There are some amongst you who desire this world and some who desire the Hereafter."

[Soorah Aal-'Imraan(3):152]

وَقُلِ ٱلْحَقُّ مِن رَّبِّكُمْ فَمَن شَاءَ فَلْيُؤْمِن وَمَن شَاءَ فَلْيَكْفُرْ إِنَّا أَعْتَدْنَا لِلظَّٰلِمِينَ نَارًا أَحَاطَ بِهِمْ سُرَادِقُهَا

"Say, O Muḥammad: This that I have brought you from your Lord is the truth - it is He who guides and humiliates - so if you wish then believe, and if you wish then disbelieve. If you disbelieve then your Lord has prepared for you a Fire whose walls surround those within it."

[Soorah al-Kahf (18):29]

مَّنْ عَمِلَ صَٰلِحًا فَلِنَفْسِهِ وَمَنْ أَسَاءَ فَعَلَيْهَا وَمَا رَبُّكَ بِظَلَّٰمٍ لِّلْعَبِيدِ ٤٦

"Whoever acts in obedience to Allaah, then it is for the benefit of his own soul and he will be rewarded for it; and whoever acts in disobedience to Allaah, then he has transgressed against his own soul and earned Allaah's Anger; and your Lord will not punish anyone for a sin he did not commit."

[Soorah Fuṣṣilat (41):46]

As for the reality that it witnessed, then every person knows the difference between his actions that he does by choice - such as eating, drinking, buying and selling, and those that happen without his will - such as shivering due to a feverish chill, and falling from a roof. So in the former examples he acted by his own will and choice and was not compelled, and in the latter he neither chose nor desired that which happened to him.

191

As for the rebuttal of the second sect (*al-Qadariyyah*), then it is in the texts and the intellect. As for the texts, then Allaah, the Most High, is the Creator of everything, and everything exists by His Will. Furthermore Allaah, the Most High, has made clear in His Book that the actions of the servants occur in accordance with His Will. He, the Most High, says,

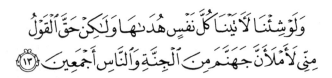

$$وَلَوۡ شَآءَ ٱللَّهُ مَا ٱقۡتَتَلَ ٱلَّذِينَ$$
$$مِنۢ بَعۡدِهِم مِّنۢ بَعۡدِ مَا جَآءَتۡهُمُ ٱلۡبَيِّنَٰتُ وَلَٰكِنِ ٱخۡتَلَفُوا۟$$
$$فَمِنۡهُم مَّنۡ ءَامَنَ وَمِنۡهُم مَّن كَفَرَ وَلَوۡ شَآءَ ٱللَّهُ مَا ٱقۡتَتَلُوا۟$$
$$وَلَٰكِنَّ ٱللَّهَ يَفۡعَلُ مَا يُرِيدُ ۝$$

"And if Allaah had willed those who came after Moosaa and 'Eesaa would not have fought amongst themselves after clear signs had come to them from Allaah. But they differed, some believing in Allaah, and His signs and others disbelieving. So if Allaah had willed He would have prevented them and they would not have fought each other; but Allaah does whatever He wills."

[Soorah al-Baqarah (2):253]

$$وَلَوۡ شِئۡنَا لَءَاتَيۡنَا كُلَّ نَفۡسٍ هُدَىٰهَا وَلَٰكِنۡ حَقَّ ٱلۡقَوۡلُ$$
$$مِنِّى لَأَمۡلَأَنَّ جَهَنَّمَ مِنَ ٱلۡجِنَّةِ وَٱلنَّاسِ أَجۡمَعِينَ ۝$$

"And if We had willed We could have guided every person to true belief in Allaah, but the Word from Me has become binding for them, that I will fill the Fire with the sinners and disbelievers from the *jinn* and mankind."

[Soorah as-Sajdah (32):13]

As for the intellect, then all of the creation is the possession and dominion of Allaah, the Most High, and man is part of this creation and is a slave owned by Allaah, the Most High, and it is not possible for the slave to act within the dominion of the owner except with His Permission and Will.

المَرْتَبَةُ الثَّالِثَةُ الإِحْسَانُ رُكْنٌ وَاحِدٌ

وَهُوَ أَنْ تَعْبُدَ اللَّهَ كَأَنَّكَ تَرَاهُ فَإِنْ لَمْ تَكُنْ تَرَاهُ فَإِنَّهُ يَرَاكَ وَالدَّلِيْلُ

قَوْلُهُ تَعَالَى: ﴿ إِنَّ اللَّهَ مَعَ الَّذِينَ اتَّقَوْا وَالَّذِينَ هُمْ مُحْسِنُوْنَ ﴾

وَقَوْلُهُ: ﴿ وَتَوَكَّلْ عَلَى العَزِيْزِ الرَّحِيْمِ الَّذِي يَرَاكَ حِيْنَ تَقُوْمُ

وَتَقَلُّبَكَ فِي السَّاجِدِيْنَ إِنَّهُ هُوَ السَّمِيْعُ العَلِيْمُ ﴾ وَقَوْلُهُ: ﴿

وَمَاتَكُوْنُ فِي شَأْنٍ وَمَاتَتْلُوْ مِنْهُ مِنْ قُرْآنٍ وَلاَ تَعْمَلُوْنَ مِنْ عَمَلٍ

إِلاَّ كُنَّا عَلَيْكُمْ شُهُوْدًا إِذْ تُفِيْضُوْنَ فِيْهِ ﴾ الآية.

The third level is *al-ihsaan* [lit. to do well or perfectly], it is a single pillar which is: that you worship Allaah as if you were seeing Him, and even though you do not see Him then He certainly sees you. The proof is the Saying of Allaah, the Most High, **"Allaah is with those who fear Him and keep away from what He has forbidden, and those who are people of *ihsaan* - those who do well in carrying out whatever He has obligated, taking care of His rights and being constant in obedience to Him, He aids, guides and assists them"** [Soorah an-Nahl (16):128], and His Saying, **"And place your reliance O Muhammad in the All-Mighty, the Bestower of Mercy. He Who sees you when you stand to pray, and sees your movements along with those who follow you in the Prayer - in your standing, bowing, prostration and sitting. Your Lord is the One who hears whatever you recite and mention in your Prayer, and Who knows whatever you and those following you do in your Prayer - so recite the Qur'aan in it, and correctly perform it, since your Lord sees and hears you"** [Soorah ash-Shooraa (26):217-220], and His Saying, **"You are not involved in any matter, O Muhammad, nor**

do you recite the Book of Allaah, nor do you do any action - O people - whether it is good or evil, except that We are witnessing your deeds when you do them..."132 [Soorah Yoonus (10):61]

---

132 *Al-Ihsaan* is the opposite of behaving badly, and it means that a person strives to do what is good and to repel harmful things. So he strives to benefit the servants of Allaah through his wealth, position, knowledge and his person. So as for the case of doing good with ones wealth, then he spends and gives in charity, and pays the *zakaat*, and the best of the types of doing good through wealth is the *zakaat* since it is one of the pillars of Islaam, and one of its great foundations. A person's Islaam will not be complete without it. It is the charity most loved by Allaah, the Mighty and Majestic, and that is followed by that which it is obligatory upon a person to spend upon his wife, mother, father, children, brothers, children of his brothers, sisters, paternal uncles, paternal aunts, maternal aunts, and so on. Then by charity given to the poor and to the rest of those deserving of charity - such as students of knowledge for example.

As for the case of doing good by means of ones position, then it is that people are found in different levels. Some of them have status with someone in authority and so strive to benefit the people by means of his position. So if a man comes to him and requests that he should intercede for him with the one in authority then he does so, either to repel some harm from him or to attain some good for him. As for doing good by means of his knowledge, then it is that he strives to pass on his knowledge to Allaah's servants, in open and private gatherings and assemblies. Even if people sit socially, to drink coffee, then it pertains to good and fine behaviour that he should teach the people. Even if you are in a public gathering it is from what is good that you teach the people. However wisdom is to be used in this matter. So you should not weary the people making it a habit that every single time you sit in a gathering you admonish and address the people, since the Prophet (ﷺ) used to give them admonition now and then, and not too frequently. This is because the souls become weary and bored. When they become bored they become languid and weak and may even come to dislike what is good merely because of the frequency with which the person stands and addresses them.

As for seeking to benefit the people with ones person, then the Prophet (ﷺ) said: "*... that you help a man to mount and ride his riding beast, or you lift up his luggage on to it for him, is a charity*" [Reported by al-Bukhaaree (Eng. transl. 4/

90-91/ no. 141) and Muslim (Eng. transl. 2/483-484/ no. 2204)]. So you help this man to carry his luggage, or you guide him to the correct road to take and so on, all of this pertains to *ihsaan*. So this is with regard to striving to do good to the servants of Allaah.

As for *ihsaan* in the worship of Allaah, then it is that you worship Allaah as if you were seeing Him, as the Prophet (ﷺ) said. So worship done in this way, that a person worships his Lord as if he were actually seeing Him is worship that is accompanied by yearning and seeking. So a person will find that his soul encourages him upon worship done in this way, since he is yearning for the one he loves. Therefore he worships Him as if he were seeing Him, and he directs his heart to Him and turns to Him and seeks to draw near to Him, He the One free of all imperfections and the Most High.

"Then even though you do not see Him, then He certainly sees you." This part shows worship done whilst fleeing and fearing, and is therefore the second level of *ihsaan*. So if you do not worship Allaah, the Mighty and Majestic, as if you are seeing Him and seeking Him and your soul is encouraging you towards Him, then worship Him keeping in mind that He sees you. So you will then worship Him as one who fears Him and seeks to flee from His retribution and punishment.

This level is held by those having knowledge of these affairs to be lower than the first level. Worship of Allaah, the Perfect and Most High, is, as Ibn al-Qayyim, *rahimahullaah*, said: 'Worship of the Most Merciful is utmost love of Him, along with the worshippers submission and humility, they are its two pillars.' So worship is built upon these two matters: utmost love, and utmost humility and submission. Love causes one to desire and seek, and humility causes one to fear and flee. This is *ihsaan* in the worship of Allaah, the Mighty and Majestic. If a person worships Allaah in this manner, then he will become one who is pure and sincere in his worship of Allaah, the Mighty and Majestic. He will not desire with his worship that he is seen by the people, or heard of, nor will he desire their praise. It will be the same to him whether the people notice him or do not notice him.

He will worship with *ihsaan* in every condition. Indeed part of the completion of purity and sincerity of worship (*al-ikhlaas*) is that a person should seek not to be seen by the people when he worships, and that his worship should be a secret between him and his Lord. That is unless there is some benefit for the Muslims or for Islaam in his performing it openly, for example if he is a person who is fol-

الآيَةُ. وَالدَّلِيْلُ مِنَ السُّنَّةِ

حَدِيْثُ جِبْرَائِيْلَ الْمَشْهُوْرُ عَنْ عُمَرَ رَضِيَ اللَّهُ عَنْهُ قَالَ: بَيْنَمَا نَحْنُ جُلُوْسٌ عِنْدَ رَسُوْلِ اللَّهِ صَلَّى اللَّهُ عَلَيْهِ وَسَلَّمَ ذَاتَ يَوْمٍ إِذْ طَلَعَ عَلَيْنَا رَجُلٌ شَدِيْدُ بَيَاضِ الثِّيَابِ شَدِيْدُ سَوَادِ الشَّعْرِ لاَ يُرَى عَلَيْهِ أَثَرُ السَّفَرِ وَلاَ يَعْرِفُهُ مِنَّا أَحَدٌ ، حَتَّى جَلَسَ إِلَى النَّبِيِّ صَلَّى اللَّهُ عَلَيْهِ وَسَلَّمَ فَأَسْنَدَ رُكْبَتَيْهِ إِلَى رُكْبَتَيْهِ وَوَضَعَ كَفَّيْهِ عَلَى فَخِذَيْهِ وَقَالَ: يَا مُحَمَّدُ أَخْبِرْنِي عَنِ الإِسْلاَمَ ،

The proof from the *sunnah* is the well-known *hadeeth* of Jibraa'eel, reported from 'Umar, *radiyallaahu 'anhu*, that he said, *"Whilst we were sitting in the presence of Allaah's Messenger (ﷺ) one day a man came to us having very white clothes and very black hair. No trace of having travelled was to be seen upon him, nor did any of us know him. So he came and sat down with the Prophet (ﷺ) and put his knees against his knees, and placed his palms upon his thighs and said: "O Muhammad, inform me about Islaam."*

---

lowed and taken as an example and he wishes to manifest his worship to the people so that they should take it as an example to follow; or that he manifests his worship so that his companions, friends and associates should follow his example, then this is good. This benefit which he takes account of may be more excellent and greater than the benefit of keeping it hidden. Therefore Allaah, the Mighty and Majestic, has praised those who spend of their wealth in charity secretly and openly. So whenever performing it secretly is better and more beneficial for the heart, and causes one to be more humble and submissive, and to turn to Allaah more attentively, then they give in secret. But when performing it openly produces benefit for Islaam, due to manifestation of its prescribed practices, and will mean that the people follow this persons example, then they do this openly. The Believer looks to what is most appropriate. So whatever is most appropriate and most beneficial in worship, then it will be what is most complete and most excellent.

فَقَالَ رَسُولُ اللَّهِ صَلَّى اللَّهُ عَلَيْهِ وَسَلَّمَ: " الْإِسْلَامُ أَنْ تَشْهَدَ أَنْ لَا إِلَهَ إِلاَّ اللَّهُ وَأَنَّ مُحَمَّدًا رَسُولُ اللَّهِ ، وَتُقِيمَ الصَّلَاةَ ، وَتُؤْتِيَ الزَّكَاةَ ، وَتَصُوْمَ رَمَضَانَ ، وَتَحُجَّ الْبَيْتَ إِنْ اِسْتَطَعْتَ إِلَيْهِ سَبِيْلاً" قَالَ: صَدَقْتَ ، فَعَجِبْنَا لَهُ يَسْأَلُهُ وَيُصَدِّقُهُ. قَالَ: فَأَخْبِرْنِي عَنِ الْإِيْمَانِ ، قَالَ: "أَنْ تُؤْمِنَ بِاللَّهِ وَمَلَائِكَتِهِ وَكُتُبِهِ وَرُسُلِهِ وَالْيَوْمِ الْآخِرِ ، وَ تُؤْمِنَ بِالقَدَرِ خَيْرِهِ وَشَرِّهِ ، قَالَ: صَدَقْتَ ، قَالَ: فَأَخْبِرْنِي عَنِ الْإِحْسَانِ ، قَالَ: "أَنْ تَعْبُدَ اللَّهَ كَأَنَّكَ تَرَاهُ ، فَإِنْ لَمْ تَكُنْ تَرَاهُ فَإِنَّهُ يَرَاكَ ، قَالَ: فَأَخْبِرْنِي عَنِ السَّاعَةِ ، قَالَ: "مَا الْمَسْؤُوْلُ عَنْهَا بِأَعْلَمَ مِنَ السَّائِلِ ، قَالَ: فَأَخْبِرْنِي عَنْ أَمَارَاتِهَا ، قَالَ: "أَنْ تَلِدَ الْأَمَةُ رَبَّتَهَا ، وَأَنْ تَرَى الْحُفَاةَ الْعُرَاةَ الْعَالَةَ رِعَاءَ الشَّاءِ يَتَطَاوَلُوْنَ فِي الْبُنْيَانِ" قَالَ: فَمَضَى فَلَبِثْنَا مَلِيًّا فَقَالَ: "يَا عُمَرُ أَتَدْرِي مَنِ السَّائِلُ"؟ قُلْتُ: اللَّهُ وَرَسُولُهُ أَعْلَمُ ، قَالَ: "هَذَا جِبْرِيْلُ أَتَاكُمْ يُعَلِّمُكُمْ أَمْرَ دِيْنِكُمْ" .

So Allaah's Messenger (ﷺ) said: "Islaam is that you testify that none has the right to be worshipped except Allaah, and that Muhammad is the Messenger of Allaah; establish the Prayer; pay the zakaat; fast Ramadaan; and perform pilgrimage (hajj) to the House if you are able to do so." He said: "You have spoken the truth." So we were amazed at him asking him a question and then saying that he had spoken the truth. He said: "Then inform me about eemaan." He said: "It is that you truly believe in Allaah, His angels, His Books, His Messengers, the Last Day; and that you truly believe in pre-decree - its good and its bad." He said: "You have spoken the truth." He said:

"Then inform me about al-ihsaan." He said: "It is that you worship Allaah as if you were seeing Him, and though you do not see Him then He certainly sees you." He said: "Then inform me of the (Last) Hour." He said: "The one who is asked about it knows no better than the one who is asking." He said: "Then inform me about its signs." He said: "That the slave-girl will give birth to her mistress; and that you will see the barefooted, unclothed and destitute shepherds competing in the building of tall buildings." He said: so he left, and we remained for some time, then he (*) asked: "O 'Umar, do you know who the questioner was? I replied: "Allaah and His Messenger know best." He said: "That was Jibreel, he came to you to teach you your Religion (Deen)."*[133]

---

[133] Reported by Muslim (Eng. transl. 1/1-3/no. 1). Most of this *hadeeth* has already been explained in this book, and we have given an explanation of it in *Majmoo'ul-Fataawaa war-Rasaail* (i.e. of Shaykh Ibn 'Uthaymeen) 3/143.

الأَصْلُ الثَّالِثُ:

مَعْرِفَةُ نَبِيِّكُمْ مُحَمَّدٍ ﷺ وَهُوَ مُحَمَّدُ بْنُ عَبْدِ اللَّهِ بْنِ عَبْدِ المُطَّلِبِ بْنِ هَاشِمٍ وَهَاشِمٌ مِنْ قُرَيْشٍ وَقُرَيْشٌ مِنَ العَرَبِ وَالعَرَبُ مِنْ ذُرِّيَّةِ إِسْمَاعِيْلَ بْنِ إِبْرَاهِيْمَ الخَلِيْلِ عَلَيْهِ وَعَلَى نَبِيِّنَا أَفْضَلُ الصَّلَاةِ وَالسَّلَامِ.

THE THIRD PRINCIPLE[134]

Knowledge of your Prophet Muhammad (ﷺ), and he was: Muhammad ibn 'Abdullaah ibn 'Abdul-Muttalib ibn Haashim; and Haashim was from (the tribe of) Quraysh; Quraysh were from the Arabs; and the Arabs have descended from Ismaa'eel, the son of Ibraaheem - the chosen beloved (khaleel) - may the most excellent blessings and peace be upon him and upon our Prophet.

---

134 From the three principles that each person must know and be aware of, are the servants knowledge of his Lord, his Religion, and his Prophet. The servants knowledge of his Lord and his Religion are matters that have preceded. As for knowledge about the Prophet (ﷺ) then it covers five matters:

(i) Knowledge about his lineage: He was the noblest of people in lineage since he was Haashimee, of the Quraysh, and an Arab. He was: Muhammad the son of 'Abdullaah ibn 'Abdul-Muttalib ibn Haashim - to the end of the lineage quoted by the Shaykh, rahimahullaah.

(ii) The age he reached, where he was born, and where he migrated to. So the Shaykh explained this with his saying: "And he reached sixty-three years of age, his land was Makkah, and he migrated to al-Madeenah." So he was born in Makkah and he remained there for fifty-three years. The he migrated to al-Madeenah and remained there for ten years. It was there that he died in the month of Rabee'ul-Awwal in the eleventh year after the Hijrah.

(iii) Knowledge about his life as a Prophet, and this was for a period of twenty three years. Revelation was first given to him at the age of forty, just as one of his reciter's of poetry said: 'So forty years came upon him and then the sunlight of prophethood shone forth from him in the month of Ramadaan.'

(iv) Through what did he become a Prophet and then a Messenger? He was a Prophet (*Nabiyy*) since there came to him the Saying of Allaah, the Most High,

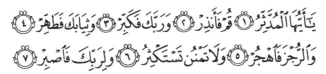

اقْرَأْ بِاسْمِ رَبِّكَ الَّذِي خَلَقَ ۝ خَلَقَ الْإِنسَـٰنَ مِنْ عَلَقٍ ۝ اقْرَأْ وَرَبُّكَ الْأَكْرَمُ ۝ الَّذِي عَلَّمَ بِالْقَلَمِ ۝ عَلَّمَ الْإِنسَـٰنَ مَا لَمْ يَعْلَمْ ۝

"Recite, O Muḥammad, mentioning the name of your Lord who created. He who created mankind from a clot of blood. Recite, O Muḥammad, and your Lord is the Most Generous. He who taught the creation to write and taught them that which they did not know."

[Soorah al-'Alaq (96):1-5]

He (ﷺ) became a Messenger (*Rasool*) when there came to him the Saying of Allaah, the Most High,

يَـٰٓأَيُّهَا الْمُدَّثِّرُ ۝ قُمْ فَأَنذِرْ ۝ وَرَبَّكَ فَكَبِّرْ ۝ وَثِيَابَكَ فَطَهِّرْ ۝ وَالرُّجْزَ فَاهْجُرْ ۝ وَلَا تَمْنُن تَسْتَكْثِرُ ۝ وَلِرَبِّكَ فَاصْبِرْ ۝

"O you (Muḥammad (ﷺ)) wrapped in garments! Arise and warn your people who worship others besides Allaah of Allaah's punishment; and venerate and worship your Lord, making your worship for Him alone; and purify your self, your garment and your deeds; and shun the idols; and do not give anything in order to receive something more in return; and patiently persevere for the sake of your Lord in the face of any harm you encounter."

[Soorah al-Muddaththir (74):1-7]

So he (ﷺ) arose and warned and established what Allaah, the Mighty and Majestic, had commanded him to do.

Then concerning the difference between a Messenger (*Rasool*) and a Prophet

وَلَهُ مِنَ العُمُرِ ثَلَاثٌ وَسِتُّوْنَ سَنَةً مِنْهَا أَرْبَعُوْنَ قَبْلَ النُّبُوَّةِ وَثَلَاثٌ وَعِشْرُوْنَ نَبِيَّا وَرَسُوْلاً ، نُبِّئَ بِاقْرَأْ وَأُرْسِلَ بِالْمُدَّثِّرِ وَبَلَدُهُ مَكَّةُ وَهَاجَرَ إِلَى المَدِيْنَةِ. بَعَثَهُ اللَّهُ بِالنَّذَارَةِ عَنِ الشِّرْكِ وَيَدْعُوْ إِلَى التَّوْحِيْدِ

He lived for sixty-three years: forty years before prophethood, and twenty-three years as a prophet and a messenger. He was sent as a prophet with 'iqra' [i.e. the beginning of *Soorah al-'Alaq*], and as a messenger with [*Soorah*] *Muddaththir*. His land was Makkah and he performed *hijrah* (prescribed migration) to al-Madeenah. Allaah sent him to warn against *shirk* and to call to *tawheed*.135

(*Nabiyy*) the scholars say: A Prophet is one who had a Revealed Way sent to him by Revelation and was not commanded to propagate it, whereas a Messenger is one who had a Revealed way sent down to him by Allaah and was ordered to propagate and act upon it. So every Messenger was a Prophet, but not every Prophet was a Messenger.

(v) What was the message he was sent with, and why was he sent? So he was sent to call to the *tawheed* of Allaah, the Most High, and His Revealed Law - which comprised doing whatever He ordered and avoiding whatever He forbade. He was sent as a mercy to all the creation to bring them out of the oppressive darkness of *shirk* (worship of anything besides Him), *kufr* (unbelief) and ignorance, and to bring them to the light of knowledge, true belief (*eemaan*), and *tawheed* (the pure worship of Allaah alone) - so that they should thereby gain the forgiveness and Pleasure of Allaah, and thus be saved from His punishment and Anger.

135 i.e. to warn them against *shirk*, and to call them to the *tawheed* of Allaah, the Mighty and Majestic, in His Lordship (*ar-Ruboobiyyah*), His right to be worshipped alone (*al-Uloohiyyah*), and His names and attributes (*al-Asmaa was-Sifaat*).

وَالدَّلِيلُ قَوْلُهُ تَعَالَى: ﴿ يَا أَيُّهَا المُدَّثِّرُ قُمْ فَأَنْذِرْ وَرَبَّكَ فَكَبِّرْ
وَثِيَابَكَ فَطَهِّرْ وَالرُّجْزَ فَاهْجُرْ وَلَا تَمْنُنْ تَسْتَكْثِرْ وَلِرَبِّكَ فَاصْبِرْ
﴾ وَمَعْنَى ﴿ قُمْ فَأَنْذِرْ ﴾ يُنْذِرُ عَنِ الشِّرْكِ وَيَدْعُو إِلَى التَّوْحِيدِ ﴿
وَرَبَّكَ فَكَبِّرْ ﴾ أَيْ عَظِّمْهُ بِالتَّوْحِيدِ ﴿ وَثِيَابَكَ فَطَهِّرْ ﴾ أَيْ طَهِّرْ
أَعْمَالَكَ عَنِ الشِّرْكِ ﴿ وَالرُّجْزَ فَاهْجُرْ ﴾ الرُّجْزُ الأَصْنَامُ وَهَجْرُهَا
ـ تَرْكُهَا وَالبَرَاءَةُ مِنْهَا وَأَهْلِهَا. أَخَذَ عَلَى هَذَا عَشَرَ سِنِينَ يَدْعُو
إِلَى التَّوْحِيدِ وَبَعْدَ العَشْرِ عُرِجَ بِهِ إِلَى السَّمَاءِ. وَ فُرِضَتْ عَلَيْهِ
الصَّلَوَاتُ الخَمْسُ وَصَلَّى فِي مَكَّةَ ثَلَاثَ سِنِينَ وَبَعْدَهَا أُمِرَ بِالهِجْرَةِ
إِلَى المَدِينَةِ.

The proof is the Saying of Allaah, the Most High, **"O you (Muhammad(ﷺ) wrapped in garments! Arise and warn your people; and venerate and worship your Lord, and purify your self, your garments and your deeds; and shun the idols; and do not give anything in order to receive something more in return; and patiently persevere for the sake of your Lord in the face of any harm you encounter"** [Soorah al-Mudaththir (74):1-7].

The meaning of **"Arise and warn your people"** is that he was to warn against *shirk* and to call to *tawheed*. **"Venerate and worship your Lord"** means honour and venerate Him with *tawheed*. **"Purify yourself, your garments, and your deeds"** means purify your actions from any *shirk*. **"Shun the idols"**, *ar-rujz* means the idols, and *hajr* of them means shunning them, and freeing and disassociating oneself from them and their people.

He carried out this duty for ten years, calling to *tawheed*,136 and after ten years he was taken up through the heavens [i.e. the *mi'raaj*];137 and the five Prayers were obligated upon him, and he prayed in Makkah for three years,138 and then he was commanded to perform *hijrah* (prescribed migration) to al-Madeenah.139

---

136 Meaning that the Prophet (ﷺ) remained for ten years calling to the *tawheed* of Allaah, the Mighty and Majestic, and for the people to single Him out with all of their worship.

137 *al-'Urooj* - which means ascent, as occurs in the Saying of Allaah, the Most High,

"The Angels and Jibreel ascend (*ta'ruj*) to Allaah."

[Soorah al-Ma'aarij (70):4]

The Night Ascension (*Mi'raaj*) was one of the very great blessings bestowed by Allaah upon the Prophet (ﷺ) in particular, before he migrated from Makkah. So whilst he was sleeping in the detached part of the Ka'bah (*al-Hijr*) someone came to him and cut open his body between his throat and his lower abdomen. Then he took out his heart and filled it up with wisdom and *eemaan* in preparation for what was about to occur with him. Then a white animal - named *al-Buraaq* - smaller than a mule and bigger than a donkey was brought to him. Its pace was the distance the eye could see. So he (ﷺ) mounted it and he was escorted by Jibreel - The Trustworthy. So he came to Jerusalem and prayed along with the prophets, leading all of the prophets and messengers in the Prayer, with them praying behind him. This manifested the pre-eminence of Allaah's Messenger (ﷺ) and his nobility and that he is the *imaam* to be followed. Then Jibreel ascended with him to the lowest heaven and requested entry. So it was said: "Who is there?": He said: "Jibreel." It was said: "And who is with you?" He said: "Muhammad." He said: "Has he been called?" He said: "Yes." It was said: "Welcome to him, what an excellent visitor it is who has come." So entry was granted to him, and he found therein Aadam. So Jibreel said: "This is your forefather Aadam, so greet him with *salaam*." So he greeted him thus and he responded to him with *salaam* and said:

203

"Welcome to the righteous son and the righteous prophet." So on Aadam's right were the spirits of those who will attain salvation and on his left were the spirits of those who will go to destruction, from his descendants. So when he looked to the right he was pleased and laughed, and when he looked to his left he wept. Then Jibreel ascended with him to the second heaven and requested entry. So he found therein Yahyaa and 'Eesaa, *'alayhimus-salaam*, and they are maternal cousins - each of them being the son of the others maternal aunt. So Jibreel said: "This is Yahyaa and 'Eesaa, so greet them with the greeting of *salaam*. So he greeted them with *salaam*, and they replied with this greeting of *salaam* and said: "Welcome to the righteous brother, and the righteous Prophet." Then Jibreel ascended with him to the third heaven, and requested entry. So he found therein Yoosuf, *'alayhis-salaam, and Jibree*l said: "This is Yoosuf so greet him with *salaam*," so he greeted him with *salaam*, so he responded to him with this greeting and said: "Welcome to the righteous brother and the righteous Prophet." Then Jibreel ascended with him to the fourth heaven and requested entry. He found therein Idrees (ﷺ), so Jibreel said: "This is Idrees, so greet him with *salaam.* " So he greeted him with *salaam*, and he replied to him with *salaam* and said: "Welcome to the righteous brother and the righteous Prophet." Then Jibreel ascended with him to the fifth heaven and requested entry. He found therein Haaroon Ibn 'Imraan, the brother of Moosaa(ﷺ), so Jibreel said: "This is Haaroon so greet him with *salaam.* " So he greeted him with *salaam*, and he replied to him with *salaam* and said: "Welcome to the righteous brother and the righteous Prophet." Then Jibreel ascended with him to the sixth heaven and requested entry. He found therein Moosaa (ﷺ), so Jibreel said: "This is Moosaa, greet him with *salaam.* " *So h*e greeted him with *salaam* and he replied to him with the greeting of *salaam* and said: "Welcome to the righteous brother and the righteous Prophet." When he proceeded on Moosaa wept, so it was said: "What causes you to weep?" So he replied: "I weep because a young man was sent as a Messenger after me, and more of his nation than my nation will enter Paradise." So Moosaa's weeping was because of grief for the many virtues missed by his nation, and not out of envy for the nation of Muhammad (ﷺ). Then Jibreel ascended with him to the seventh heaven and requested entry. He found therein Ibraaheem, the chosen beloved of the Most Merciful. So Jibreel said: "This is your forefather Ibraaheem, greet him with *salaam." So he greeted* him with *salaam*, and he replied with *salaam* and said: "Welcome to the righteous son and the righteous Prophet."

Jibreel took Allaah's Messenger (ﷺ) to all of those prophets as an honour for him, and in order to manifest his (ﷺ) nobility and excellence. Also Ibraaheem was seen in the seventh heaven resting with his back against the Oft-Frequented House (al-*Baitul-Ma'moor*) which is such that every day seventy thousand angels enter it to worship and pray, then they leave it and do not return to it. Then on the second day more angles - whose number cannot be enumerated by anyone but Allaah, enter it. Then the Prophet (ﷺ) was raised to the furthest Lote tree (*as-Sidratul-Muntahaa*), and it was covered through Allaah's Command in such splendour and beauty that no one would be able to describe its beauty. Then Allaah made fifty Prayers obligatory upon him (ﷺ) for each day and night. So he was pleased with that and submitted to it. Then he descended until he came to Moosaa, who said: "What did your Lord make obligatory upon your nation?" So he said: "Fifty Prayers in each day and night." He said: "Your nation will not be able to bear that, I have experience of the people before you and struggled hard with Banee Israaeel, so return to your Lord and request that He should make reduction for your nation." The Prophet (ﷺ) said: "So I returned, and ten were reduced from me" and he kept returning to His Lord until the obligation was fixed at five Prayers. Then a call was made: 'I have decreed My obligation, and have reduced the burden on My slaves.'" [Translator: Refer to Sa<u>h</u>ee<u>h</u> al-Bukhaaree, (Eng. transl. vol. 4, pp. 287-290, no. 429) and (vol. 5, pp. 143-148, no. 227)].

Also in this night the Prophet (ﷺ) was entered into Paradise and saw tents of pearl, and saw that its earth was musk, then Allaah's Messenger (ﷺ) descended and returned to Makkah during the period of after-dawn darkness, and he prayed the Dawn (*Sub<u>h</u>*) Prayer.

138 There he prayed the Prayers which now consist of four *rak'ahs* with two *rak'ahs*. Then when he migrated to al-Madeenah the travellers Prayer remained like that, whilst the Prayer of the resident was increased.

139 Allaah, the Mighty and Majestic, ordered His Prophet Mu<u>h</u>ammad (ﷺ) to migrate to al-Madeenah since the people of Makkah prevented him from giving his call. So in the month of *Rabee'ul-Awwal* of the thirteenth year of Messengership the Prophet (ﷺ) reached al-Madeenah. He migrated from Makkah, the land where the Revelation first came down and the most beloved land to Allaah and His Messenger. He left Makkah migrating with the permission of his Lord after

calling the people in Makkah for thirteen years, propagating the Revelation sent to him by his Lord and calling to that upon clear proof. But from most of Quraysh and from their leaders he received nothing but rejection, renunciation, and severe harm at their hands for himself and those who believed in him. Then the matter reached the stage that they were prepared to carry out their treacherous plan to kill the Prophet (ﷺ). Their heads gathered in *Daarun-Nadwah* to consult one another about what should be done with Allaah's Messenger (ﷺ). They saw that his Companions had migrated to al-Madeenah and that he would be sure to join them and thus find the help and the assistance of the *Ansaar* - those who had given their pledge to him that they would defend him just as they would defend their own sons and womenfolk. So if this were to come about, then a great force would have been established against Quraysh. This being the situation the enemy of Allaah Aboo Jahl put forward the idea that each tribe should choose one strong youth, gather them, give each youth a sharpened sword, and that together they should attack Muhammad and strike at him together. In doing so they would be free of him. Furthermore responsibility for shedding his blood would be shared equally amongst the tribes, so that Banoo 'Abd Manaaf - the kinsfolk of the Prophet (ﷺ), would be unable to fight against all of them to exact revenge. Therefore they would have to be pleased with accepting blood-money which could be given to them.

So Allaah informed His Prophet (ﷺ) of what the *mushriks* intended to do, and He granted him permission to migrate to al-Madeenah. Aboo Bakr, *radiyallaahu 'anhu*, had previously prepared to migrate to al-Madeenah, but the Prophet (ﷺ) had told him to wait as he himself hoped for permission to migrate. So Aboo Bakr, *radiyallaahu 'anhu*, remained in order to accompany the Prophet (ﷺ). 'Aai'shah, *radiyallaahu 'anhaa*, said: "So whilst we were in the house of Aboo Bakr at the time of the heat of midday, Allaah's Messenger (ﷺ) came knocking at the door. So Aboo Bakr said: 'May my mother and father be a ransom for him, by Allaah, something serious must have caused him to come at this hour.' So the Prophet (ﷺ) entered, and said to Aboo Bakr: "Cause whoever is with you to leave." So he said: "It is just your family (wife) - may my father and mother be ransom for you." So the Prophet (ﷺ) said: "Permission has been given to me to depart." So Aboo Bakr said: "Am I to accompany you, O Messenger of Allaah?" He replied: "Yes." He said: "O Messenger of Allaah, then take one of these two riding beasts of mine." So the Prophet (ﷺ) said: "With payment." So Allaah's Messenger (ﷺ) departed along with Aboo Bakr, and they remained in a cave of the mountain of Thawr for three nights. 'Abdullaah ibn Abee Bakr who was an intelligent and alert youth used to stay with them during the nights and then return to Makkah towards the end of the night in order to be amongst Quraysh during the daytime. So he would not hear anything spoken about the Prophet (ﷺ) and his companion except that he would remember it, and then when night fell he would go and report it to them. So Quraysh began to search everywhere for the Prophet (ﷺ) and strove to capture him by any means. They even declared that anyone who brought them, or one of them would receive the reward of his blood-wit - of a hundred camels. But Allaah was with them, protecting and guarding them. The Quraysh even stood at the entrance to the cave but did not see the two of them. Aboo Bakr, *radiyallaahu 'anhu*, said: I said to the Prophet (ﷺ) when we were in the cave: "If one of them were to look down towards his feet he would see us." So he replied "Do not be distressed, for Allaah is with us. What do you think, O Aboo Bakr, of two when the third is Allaah." So when the search was relaxed a little the two of them left the cave, after three nights, and headed towards al-Madeenah by the coastal route. So when the people of al-Madeenah, the *Muhaajirs* and the *Ansaar*, heard that Allaah's Messenger (ﷺ) had left Makkah they began to go out every morning to the volcanic lava plain to await the arrival of Allaah's Messenger (ﷺ) and those who accompanied him. So they would only return to their houses when the heat of the sun drove them back. So on the day when Allaah's Messenger (ﷺ) arrived the sun had risen high and the temperature had risen, so the people had returned to their houses. Then a man from the Jews who was on top of one of their forts, looking for something, saw Allaah's Messenger (ﷺ) and his companions coming out of the desert mirage. He could not stop himself from shouting out at the top of his voice: "O Arabs! Here is your great man whom you have been waiting for." So the Muslims rushed to meet Allaah's Messenger (ﷺ), carrying their weapons, both as honour and respect for Allaah's Messenger (ﷺ) and showing that they were ready to fight *jihaad* and to defend him, may Allaah be pleased with them. So they met him on the summit of the lava plain and he turned with them to the right and alighted with Banoo 'Amr ibn 'Awf in Qubaa. He remained amongst them for a few nights and founded the mosque. Then he moved on towards al-Madeenah and the people went along with him, and others joined them on the way. Aboo Bakr, *radiyallaahu 'anhu*, said: "When we arrived in al-Madeenah the people came out into the streets and upon the houses, even the boys and the servants, and they were saying 'Allaah is greater, Allaah's Messenger has come. Allaah is greater Muhammad has come." [Refer to <u>Saheeh al-Bukhaaree</u> (Eng. transl. vol. 5/ 158-167/ no. 245)].

وَالهِجْرَةُ: الاِنْتِقَالُ مِنْ بَلَدِ الشِّرْكِ إِلَى بَلَدِ الإِسْلاَمِ وَالهِجْرَةُ فَرِيْضَةٌ

عَلَى هَذِهِ الأُمَّةِ مِنْ بَلَدِ الشِّرْكِ إِلَى بَلَدِ الإِسْلاَمِ وَهِيَ بَاقِيَةٌ إِلَى أَنْ

تَقُومَ السَّاعَةُ وَالدَّلِيْلُ قَوْلُهُ تَعَالَى:

Hijrah is migrating from the land of *shirk* to the land of Islaam.[140]
Hijrah from the land of *shirk* to the land of Islaam is an obligation
upon this *ummah*[141] and it continues until the Last Hour, and the proof
is the Saying of Allaah, the Most High,

---

140 Al-*Hijrah* in the language is derived from *al-hajr* which means abandonment. As for its meaning in the *Sharee'ah*, then it is as the Shaykh said: "Migrating from the land of *shirk* to the land of Islaam." The land of *shirk* is the land
where the signs manifesting *shirk* are upheld; and the signs manifesting Islaam,
such as the *adhaan*, the Prayer in congregation, the *'Eid* Prayers and the *Jumu'ah*
Prayer, are not commonly and universally established. Not established commonly
and universally to exclude those signs of Islaam that are established restrictedly
such as by the Muslim minorities in the lands of the unbelievers. These lands do
not become the land of Islaam due to the signs of Islaam that the Muslim minorities establish therein. As for the land of Islaam, then it is the land where these
signs are established commonly and universally.

141 It is obligatory upon every Believer to perform *hijrah* who is not able to
manifest his Religion (*Deen*) in the land of the unbelievers. If he is unable to
manifest his Religion then his Islaam will not be complete until he performs *hijrah*.
This is because whatever is essential for the attainment of an obligation is itself
obligatory.

﴿ إِنَّ الَّذِينَ تَوَفَّاهُمُ الْمَلاَئِكَةُ

ظَالِمِي أَنْفُسِهِمْ قَالُوا فِيْمَ كُنْتُمْ قَالُوا كُنَّا مُسْتَضْعَفِينَ فِي الأَرْضِ

قَالُوا أَلَمْ تَكُنْ أَرْضُ اللَّهِ وَاسِعَةً فَتُهَاجِرُوا فِيهَا فَأُولَئِكَ مَأْوَاهُمْ

جَهَنَّمُ وَسَاءَتْ مَصِيرًا إِلاَّ الْمُسْتَضْعَفِينَ مِنَ الرِّجَالِ وَالنِّسَاءِ

وَالْوِلْدَانِ لاَ يَسْتَطِيعُونَ حِيلَةً وَلاَ يَهْتَدُونَ سَبِيلاً فَأُولَئِكَ عَسَى

اللَّهُ أَنْ يَعْفُوَ عَنْهُمْ وَكَانَ اللَّهُ عَفُوًّا غَفُورًا ﴾

"As for those whose souls the angels take in a state of having earned Allaah's Anger, then the angels will say to them: 'In what condition were you regarding your Religion?' They will say: 'We were weakened by the great numbers and strength of the people of *shirk* in our land who prevented us from *eemaan* and from following the Messenger.' They will reply: 'Was not Allaah's earth spacious so that you could leave your land and homes where the people of *shirk* dominate and go to a land where you could worship Allaah alone and follow His Prophet?!' So these people will find their abode in Hell, and what an evil destination that is. Except for the weak ones from the men, women and children who were unable to migrate or find a way to do so. As for such, it may be that Allaah will pardon them, and Allaah is ever One who pardons and forgives the sins of His servants"142 [Soorah an-Nisaa' (4):97-99].

---

142 This *Aayah* contains a proof that those who do not migrate even though they are able to do so will be rebuked by the angels who take their souls, and they will say to them: "Was Allaah's earth not spacious enough for you to migrate therein?!" But as for the weak ones, those unable to migrate - then Allaah has pardoned them due to their inability to migrate, and Allaah does not place a burden on any soul greater than it can bear.

وَقَوْلُهُ تَعَالَى:

﴿ يَاعِبَادِيَ الَّذِينَ آمَنُوا إِنَّ أَرْضِي وَاسِعَةٌ فَإِيَّايَ فَاعْبُدُونِ ﴾ قَالَ
الْبَغَوِيُّ رَحِمَهُ اللَّهُ تَعَالَى: سَبَبُ نُزُولِ هَذِهِ الآيةِ فِي الْمُسْلِمِينَ الَّذِينَ
بِمَكَّةَ لَمْ يُهَاجِرُوا نَادَاهُمُ ا للهُ بِاسْمِ الإِيمَانِ وَالدَّلِيْلُ عَلَى الْهِجْرَةِ
مِنَ السُّنَّةِ قَوْلُهُ ﷺ :" لَا تَنْقَطِعُ الْهِجْرَةُ حَتَّى تَنْقَطِعَ التَّوْبَةُ وَلاَ تَنْقَطِعُ
التَّوْبَةُ حَتَّى تَطْلُعَ الشَّمْسُ مِنْ مَغْرِبِهَا "

Also the Saying of Allaah, the Most High, **"O My servants who believe in Me and My Messenger Muḥammad (ﷺ), indeed My earth is spacious, so flee away from whoever prevents you from obedience to Me, and make your worship and obedience purely and sincerely for Me, and do not obey anyone in disobedience to Me"** [Soorah al-'Ankaboot (29):56]. Al-Baghawee, *raḥimahullaah*, said: "This *Aayah* was sent down with regard to the Muslims who were in Makkah who did not migrate; Allaah addressed them with the title of *eemaan*.[143]

The proof for the *hijrah* found in the *sunnah* is his (ﷺ) saying: *"Hijrah will not be discontinued until repentance is discontinued, and repentance will not be discontinued until the sun rises from its place of setting."*[144]

---

143 What is apparent is that the Shaykh, *raḥimahullaah*, is reporting this quote from al-Baghawee in meaning, if it is the case that he is quoting from his *Tafseer*. This is because what is mentioned with regard to explanation of this *Aayah* is not to be found in al-Baghawee's *Tafseer* with this wording.

144 That will be at the time when acceptance of righteous actions comes to an end. Allaah, the Most High, says,

يَوْمَ يَأْتِي بَعْضُ ءَايَنتِ رَبِّكَ لَا يَنفَعُ نَفْسًا إِيمَنُهَا

لَمْ تَكُنْ ءَامَنَتْ مِن قَبْلُ أَوْ كَسَبَتْ فِي إِيمَنِهَا خَيْرًا

**"On the Day when the sun rises from the west it will not benefit
any unbeliever to then believe, not having believed prior to that;
nor will any righteous action be accepted except from those who
believed and acted righteously beforehand."**

[Soorah al-An'aam (6):158]

Here we shall mention the ruling regarding travelling to the land of unbelief. Travelling to the lands of the unbelievers is not permissible unless three conditions are met:-

(i) That the person has knowledge in order to repel doubts.

(ii) That he is a person adhering to the Religion such that it will prevent him from following desires.

(iii) That he has a need to do so.

If these three conditions are not present, then it is not permissible to travel to the lands of the Unbelievers due to the trials and enticement to evil that it entails or is to be feared. It also would involve wasting of wealth since a person will have to spend a great deal of money upon such journeys.

However if there is a need for that, due to a requirement for medical treatment or to acquire some (technical) knowledge that is not to be found in his own land, and he is a person having knowledge and he adheres to the Religion, as we have described, then there is no harm in that.

But as for travelling to the land of the unbelievers for tourism, then this is not a need. It is possible instead to go to lands of Islaam whose people uphold the manifest signs of Islaam. Furthermore our land [i.e. Saudi Arabia] has become, and all praise is for Allaah, suitable for tourism in some areas, so a person may go there and spend the time of his vacation there.

As for residing in the lands of the unbelievers, then this is something very dangerous for the Muslims Religion, his character, behaviour and manners. We and others have seen many of those who went to reside there being corrupted so that they return in a state different to the state they went in. They returned as shameless folk, and some even as apostates having left and disbelieved in their Religion and in all religions, and we seek Allaah's refuge, to the point that they came to deny the Religion totally and to mock it and its people, the earlier and the later ones. Therefore it is fitting, indeed it is binding that this be avoided and that the aforementioned conditions which prevent one from falling into such destruction are applied.

Residing in the land of unbelief has two fundamental conditions:

(i) That the person's Religion will be safe, such that he has sufficient knowledge and *eemaan,* and strong resolve as will satisfy one that he will remain firm upon his Religion and beware of deviating or being corrupted away from it. He must also have within him enmity and hatred towards the unbelievers and must be far removed from affiliation or love for them. Indeed affiliation and love for them are things that negate *eemaan.* Allaah, the Most High, says,

$$لَّا تَجِدُ قَوْمًا يُؤْمِنُونَ بِاللَّهِ وَالْيَوْمِ الْآخِرِ يُوَآدُّونَ مَنْ حَآدَّ اللَّهَ وَرَسُولَهُ وَلَوْ كَانُوٓاْ ءَابَآءَهُمْ أَوْ أَبْنَآءَهُمْ أَوْ إِخْوَٰنَهُمْ أَوْ عَشِيرَتَهُمْ$$

"You will not find a people who believe in Allaah and the Last Day having love for those who oppose Allaah and His Messenger and contradict Allaah's commands, even if they be their fathers, or their sons, or their brothers or their tribe."

[Soorah al-Mujaadilah (58):22]

بِسْمِ اللَّهِ الرَّحْمَٰنِ الرَّحِيمِ

يَٰٓأَيُّهَا ٱلَّذِينَ ءَامَنُوا۟ لَا تَتَّخِذُوا۟ ٱلْيَهُودَ وَٱلنَّصَٰرَىٰٓ أَوْلِيَآءَ بَعْضُهُمْ أَوْلِيَآءُ بَعْضٍ وَمَن يَتَوَلَّهُم مِّنكُمْ فَإِنَّهُۥ مِنْهُمْ إِنَّ ٱللَّهَ لَا يَهْدِى ٱلْقَوْمَ ٱلظَّٰلِمِينَ ۝ فَتَرَى ٱلَّذِينَ فِى قُلُوبِهِم مَّرَضٌ يُسَٰرِعُونَ فِيهِمْ يَقُولُونَ نَخْشَىٰٓ أَن تُصِيبَنَا دَآئِرَةٌ فَعَسَى ٱللَّهُ أَن يَأْتِىَ بِٱلْفَتْحِ أَوْ أَمْرٍ مِّنْ عِندِهِۦ فَيُصْبِحُوا۟ عَلَىٰ مَآ أَسَرُّوا۟ فِىٓ أَنفُسِهِمْ نَٰدِمِينَ ۝

"O you who believe, do not take the Jews and Christians as friends, protectors and helpers. They are but friends, helpers and protectors of one another. So whoever takes them as such then he is from them, in alliance against Allaah, His Messenger and the Believers. Indeed Allaah will not guide those who ally themselves with the Jews and Christians. So you will see those (hypocrites) who have sickness in their hearts hastening to friendship and alliance with them, saying: we do so for fear that some disaster may befall us from our enemies causing us to need their assistance. So perhaps Allaah will bring about victory or some affair to the benefit of the Believers. Then those hypocrites will come to regret their friendship, love and alliance with the Jews and he Christians that they concealed in their hearts."

[Soorah al-Maa'idah (5):51-52]

It is also confirmed in what is authentic from the Prophet (ﷺ) that: "Whoever *loves a people is from them, and a person is with those whom he loves.*" [Translator: al-Bukhaaree reports in his *Saheeh* from 'Abdullaah ibn Mas'ood, *radiyallaahu 'anhu*, that the Prophet (ﷺ) said: "Every *person will be with those whom he loves.*" (Eng. transl. vol. 8, p. 122, no. 189) and Ahmad reports in part of a longer *hadeeth* from 'Aaishah, *radiyallaahu 'anhaa*, that Allaah's Messenger (ﷺ) said: "...*and a man does not love a people except that Allaah will cause him to be with them.*" (Declared *Saheeh* by Shaykh al-Albaanee in *Saheehul-Jaami'* no. 3021)].

(ii) That he is able to openly manifest his Religion, such that he can establish the outer signs of Islaam without being prevented. So he should not be prevented from establishing the Prayer, nor the *Jumu'ah* Prayer, nor the Congregational Prayers - if others are found such that the Congregational and *Jumu'ah* Prayers can be established. Nor should he be prevented from the *zakaat*, Fasting and *hajj*, and the rest of the rites of Islaam. If he is not able to establish that, then it is not permissible for him to reside there; rather migration from such a place is obligatory.

The author of al-*Mughnee* said (vol. 8, p. 457), whilst mentioning the categories of people with respect to *Hijrah*, said:

> "The first of them is those for whom it is obligatory, and that is the case for one who is able to do it [i.e. migrate] and not able to establish the obligatory duties of his Religion whilst residing amongst the unbelievers. *Hijrah* is obligatory upon him due to the Saying of Allaah, the Most High,

$$\text{إِنَّ ٱلَّذِينَ تَوَفَّىٰهُمُ ٱلْمَلَٰٓئِكَةُ ظَالِمِىٓ أَنفُسِهِمْ قَالُوا۟ فِيمَ كُنتُمْ ۖ قَالُوا۟ كُنَّا مُسْتَضْعَفِينَ فِى ٱلْأَرْضِ ۚ قَالُوٓا۟ أَلَمْ تَكُنْ أَرْضُ ٱللَّهِ وَٰسِعَةً فَتُهَاجِرُوا۟ فِيهَا ۚ فَأُو۟لَٰٓئِكَ مَأْوَىٰهُمْ جَهَنَّمُ ۖ وَسَآءَتْ مَصِيرًا ﴿٩٧﴾}$$

> "**As for those whose souls the angels take in a state of having earned Allaah's Anger, then the angels will say to them: 'In what condition were you regarding you Religion?' They will say: 'We were weakened by the great numbers and strength of the people of *shirk* in our land who prevented us from *eemaan* and from following the Messenger.' They will reply: 'Was not Allaah's earth spacious so that you could leave your land and homes and go to a land where you could worship Allaah alone and follow His Prophet?!' So these people will find their abode in Hell, and what an evil destination that is.**"
>
> [Soorah an-Nisaa (4):97]

214

So this is a severe threat which proves the obligation. Also because it is obligatory to establish the obligations of the Religion for one able to do so. Migration is essential for the obligation and for its completion, and whatever is an essential requirement to perform an obligation is itself an obligation."

Then after these two fundamental conditions are met residing in the land of unbelief falls into different categories:

THE FIRST CATEGORY: That he resides there in order to call to Islaam, and to encourage people to enter into it. This is a type of *jihaad* and is thus *fard kifaayah* [i.e. a communal obligation which if performed by some is no longer obligatory upon the rest] upon those able to carry it out, with the condition that one must be able to establish the call, so that there is no one who will prevent it or prevent the people from responding to it. This is because that call (*ad-Da'wah*) to Islaam is one of the obligations of the Religion, it is the way of the messengers, and the Prophet (ﷺ) commanded that we convey the Message he brought in every place and time. He (ﷺ) said: "Convey *from me even if it be a single Aayah*" [Reported by al-Bukhaaree (Eng. transl. vol. 4, p. 442, no. 667)].

THE SECOND CATEGORY: That he resides there in order to study the condition of the unbelievers and to become aware of their state with regard to the corruption of their beliefs, their false and futile worship, degenerate manners and anarchic behaviour. He does this in order to warn the people against being beguiled by them, and to make the reality of their state clear to those who are attracted to them. This residence is also a type of *jihaad* since it covers warning against unbelief and its people, which comprises an encouragement to Islaam and its guidance. This is because the corruption of unbelief is a proof of the correctness of Islaam. Just as it is said: 'Things are made clear by their opposites.' But this is conditional upon his being able to attain his goal without producing greater harm; if he cannot attain his goal due to his being prevented from revealing what they are upon and from warning against it, then there is no benefit in his residing there. Also if what he intends can be attained, but will also produce some greater evil - for example that they respond by abusing Islaam, and the Messenger of

Islaam, and the scholars of Islaam, then one must withhold from this action due to the Saying of Allaah, the Most High,

"Do not abuse those idols which the *mushriks* invoke so that the *mushriks* then abuse Allaah due to their ignorance of their Lord and vengefully insult without knowledge. Thus do we make the deeds of every nation seem pleasing to it. Then they will be returned to their Lord and He will inform them of the deeds that they used to do, and reward or punish them accordingly."

[Soorah al-An'aam (6):108]

Similar to this is his residing in the land of unbelief in order to be a spy for the Muslims, to become aware of the plots organised against the Muslims, and so warn the Muslims. For this purpose the Prophet (ﷺ) sent Hudhayfah ibn al-Yamaan to the *mushriks* during the battle of the trench (*al-Khandaq*), so that he could find out about their condition.

THE THIRD CATEGORY: Is that he resides there due to the need of a Muslim state, and to maintain diplomatic relations with the state of unbelief, such as the workers in the embassies. The ruling in their regard follows on from the ruling for the purpose for which each of them resides. So the cultural attaché, for example, resides in order to take care of students affairs, and to monitor them, and to encourage them to adhere to the Religion of Islaam and its manners and behaviour. So his residence there brings about great benefit and repels great evil.

THE FOURTH CATEGORY: That he resides there for some personal and permissible need - such as business or medical treatment. Such residence will be permissible in accordance with the need. So the scholars, may Allaah have mercy upon them, stated in their works that it is permissible to enter the lands of the unbelievers for business, and they quote some reports from the Companions, *radiyallaahu 'anhum*, in that regard.

THE FIFTH CATEGORY: That he resides there for studies, and this is of the same class as the previous one, due to a need. However it is more dangerous and more damaging to a person's Religion and character. This is because the students will feel that he is in a position of inferiority with regard to his teacher. This can result in respect for them and satisfaction with their views, opinions and manners so that he imitates them, except for those whom Allaah wills to be protected, and they are few.

Also the student feels a need for his teacher which will lead to love for him and to outward acceptance of the deviation and misguidance that he is upon. Further-more a student will have friends from amongst his fellow students, and will love them and have friendship with them. He will also be influenced by them. Due to the danger of this category it is obligatory that one takes greater care with regard to it than the previous category.

Further conditions are to be attached to it, in addition to the two fundamental conditions. These are:

(i) That the students intellect is very advanced so that he is able to distin-guish between that which benefits and that which harms, and to look to future consequences. But as for sending young students and those with lim-ited intellect, then this is very dangerous for their Religion, character and manners. It is also a source of great danger for their *Ummah* to which they will return and then spread the poison which they received from those un-believers within it. This is something that is witnessed and borne out by reality. Many of those students who are sent return in a different state to that which they went upon. They come back having deviated in their practice of the Religion, in their character and their manners. So this causes such harm to them and their society as is well-known and witnessed. So sending them is just like sending ewes to ravenous dogs.

(ii) That the student should have sufficient knowledge of his Religion as will enable him to distinguish between truth and falsehood; and as will enable him to refute falsehood with the truth, so that he does not become fooled by their falsehood and imagine it to be truth, or that he is confused by it, or unable to rebut it, and so either remains in confusion or follows the falsehood. There occurs in the supplication that is reported: "O Allaah, manifest the truth to me as being the truth, and grant me that I follow it; and manifest falsehood to me as being falsehood, and grant me that I should keep away from it, and do not make it obscure for me so that I should go astray."

(iii) That the students adherence to the Religion is such that it will protect and preserve him from unbelief and wickedness. So one who is weak in his adherence to the Religion will not be safe there, unless Allaah wills; this is due to the strength of the attack against him and the weakness of his defences. The causes of unbelief and wickedness over there are strong, many, and various. So if they assault a place where defences are weak then they will do their work.

(iv) That there is a need for the knowledge that he resides there in order to attain. There must be benefit for the Muslims in what he is learning, and it must be such that its like cannot be found in the educational institutions of their lands. But if it is some superfluous knowledge that is of no benefit to the Muslims, or if it can be studied in the Islamic lands, then it is not permissible to reside in the lands of unbelief to attain it, because of the danger to a persons Religion and character, and due to the pointless waste of large sums of money.

THE SIXTH CATEGORY: That he resides there to take that as a place of residence. this is even more serious and dangerous than what preceded it due to the evils it entails because of complete association with the people of unbelief. Also because he will feel that he belongs to that land, along with whatever that will entail such as love, alliance, and helping to swell the size of the community of unbelievers. Also his family will grow and be educated amongst the unbelievers and will therefore take on some of their manners and customs. They may even follow them in their beliefs and worship. For this reason it is mentioned in the hadeeth from the Prophet (ﷺ) that he said: "Whoever *associates with the Mushrik and resides along with him, then he is like him.*" [Translator: Reported by Aboo Daawood (Eng. transl. vol. 2/p. 782/no. 2781) and declared *hasan* due to a supporting narration by Shaykh al-Albaanee, *hafidhahullaah, Saheehul-Jaami'* (no. 6186) and *Silsilatus-Saheehah* (no. 2330)].

This had*eeth,* even though its chain of narration may be weak, yet what it mentions can be seen to be correct since living along with someone encourages you to conform and be like them. It is reported from Qays ibn Abee Haazim from Jareer ibn 'Abdullaah, *radiyallaahu 'anhu,* that the Prophet (ﷺ) said: "*I am free from responsibility for every Muslim who resides amongst the mushriks.*" They said: "*O Messenger of Allaah, why is that ?*" He said: "*The campfire of each of them should not be (close enough to be) visible to the other.*" [Reported by Aboo Daawood (Eng. transl. vol. 2, p. 730, no. 2639) and at-Tirmidhee, most of its narrators report it as being *mursal* [i.e. as having a missing link between the *Taabi'ee* and the Prophet (ﷺ)] from Qays ibn Abee Haazim from the Prophet (ﷺ). At-Tirmidhee said: "I hear Muhammad (meaning al-Bukhaaree) say: "What is correct is the narration from Qays from the Prophet (ﷺ) is *mursal.*"" [Shaykh al-Albaanee declares it *hasan: Saheehul-Jaami'* (no. 1461), *al-Irwaa* (no. 1207) and *as-Saheehah* (no. 636).] Then how can a believing soul be pleased to live in the land of the unbelievers where the signs of unbelief are displayed openly and where judgement is for other than Allaah and His Messenger. The person who lives there sees all this with his eyes, and hears it, and is pleased with it. Indeed he may affiliate himself to that land, reside in it with his wife and children, and be satisfied with that, just as would be the case with the land of the Muslims. So this is something very dangerous for him and for his family and his children, with respect to their Religion and their manners.

This is the conclusion that we have reached regarding the ruling about residing in the lands of unbelief. We ask Allaah that it be in accordance with the truth and with what is correct.

فَلَمَّا اسْتَقَرَّ بِالمَدِينَةِ أُمِرَ بِبَقِيَّةِ

شَرَائِعِ الإِسْلَامِ مِثْلُ الصَّلَاةِ وَالزَّكَاةِ ، وَالحَجِّ ، وَالجِهَادِ ، وَالأَذَانِ ،

وَالأَمْرِ بِالمَعْرُوفِ وَالنَّهْيِ عَنِ المُنْكَرِ وَغَيْرِ ذَلِكَ مِنْ شَرَائِعِ الإِسْلَامِ

So when he (ﷺ) settled in al-Madeenah he ordered the rest of the prescribed duties of Islaam, such as: the *zakaat*, the Prayer, the *hajj*, *jihaad*, the *adhaan*, and commanding good and forbidding evil, and the rest of the prescribed duties of Islaam.[145]

---

145 The author, *rahimahullaah*, says that when the Prophet (ﷺ) settled in al-Madeenah an-Nabawiyyah (the Prophetic city) he commanded the rest of the pre-scribed duties of Islaam. This was because in Makkah he called to *tawheed* for around ten years, and then the Five Daily Prayers were made obligatory in Makkah. Then he migrated to al-Madeenah before the *zakaat*, fasting and *hajj* and the rest of the prescribed duties were made obligatory. So what is apparent from the words of the author, *rahimahullaah*, is that *zakaat*, in its basis and in its details, was made obligatory in al-Madeenah. However some of the scholars hold that the limits on which it was payable and the amounts that must be given were not pre-scribed in Makkah, but in al-Madeenah. These scholars quote as evidence for this the fact that there are *Aayaat* occurring in *Soorahs* sent down in Makkah which obligate the *zakaat*, such as the Saying of Allaah, the Most High,

وَءَاتُواْ حَقَّهُۥ يَوْمَ حَصَادِهِۦ

"And give what is due from the crops on the day they are har-vested."

[Soorah al-An'aam (6):141]

And the like of the Saying of Allaah, the Most High,

وَٱلَّذِينَ فِىٓ أَمْوَٰلِهِمْ حَقٌّ مَّعْلُومٌ ٢٤ لِّلسَّآئِلِ وَٱلْمَحْرُومِ ٢٥

"And except for those in whose wealth there is a known portion - for the beggar and the destitute."

[Soorah al-Ma'aarij (70):24-25]

أَخَذَ عَلَى هَذَا عَشَرَ سِنِينَ وَبَعْدَهَا تُوُفِّيَ صَلَوَاتُ اللَّهِ وَسَلاَمُهُ عَلَيْهِ

He spent ten years establishing that, after which he passed away, may Allaah extol and send blessings of peace upon him[146]

So whatever the case, then the final settlement of the *zakaat* and the laying down of the amounts on which it was payable, and the amounts to be paid, and who has the right to receive it, then all of this occurred in al-Madeenah. Likewise with regard to the *adhaan* and the *Jumu'ah* Prayer.

What is apparent is that the same was the case with regard to the Congregational Prayers, that they were not obligated as such except in al-Madeenah. This is because the *adhaan* which is the call to the congregation was made obligatory in the second year (after the *hijrah*). As for the *zakaat* and fasting, then they were both made obligatory in the second year after the *hijrah*. As for the *hajj*, then it was not made obligatory until the ninth year, according to the most correct saying of the scholars, after Makkah had become a land of Islaam, having been conquered in the eighth year after the *hijrah*.

Likewise commanding the good and forbidding the evil, and the rest of the manifest duties of Islaam, all of them were made obligatory in al-Madeenah, after the Prophet (ﷺ) settled there and established the state of Islaam there.

146 The Prophet (ﷺ) carried that out for ten years after his migration; then after Allaah had completed the Religion through him, and had perfected His favour upon the Believers, then Allaah chose him to join the highest companionship, that of the prophets, their sincere followers, the martyrs and the righteous folk. So he (ﷺ) became ill at the end of the month of Safar and the beginning of the month of Rabee'ul-Awwal. So he went out to the people with his head bound (with a cloth). He ascended the mimbar, declared the testification of Faith, and the first thing that he said after that was to seek forgiveness for the martyrs who were killed at Uhud. Then he said: "*A servant from the servants of Allaah has been given a choice by Allaah between this world and what is with Him; so he chose that which is with Allaah.*" So Aboo Bakr, *radiyallaahu 'anhu*, understood this and wept, and said: "May my father and mother be a ransom for you, we would pay our fathers our mothers, our children, our selves, and our wealth as a ransom for you." So the Prophet (ﷺ) said: "*Do not be hasty, O Aboo Bakr.*" Then he said: "*The person*

who has favoured me most with his companionship and his wealth is Aboo Bakr, and if I were to take someone as the one particularly beloved friend to me besides my Lord, then I would have taken Aboo Bakr as such. However it is rather the Islamic friendship and love." Then he ordered that Aboo Bakr should lead the people in the Prayer. Then when it was the day of Monday - the twelfth or thirteenth of the month of Rabee'ul-Awwal, of the eleventh year after the *hijrah*, Allaah chose him for His company. So when death came to him he began dipping his hand into some water he had besides him, and wiping his face and saying: *"None has the right to be worshipped except Allaah, indeed death has its agonies."* Then he turned his sight towards the heavens and said: *"O Allaah, amongst the highest companionship."* So he passed away on that day, and the people were greatly distressed and disturbed due to that, and rightly so. Until Aboo Bakr, *radiyallaahu 'anhu*, came and ascended the mimbar and praised and exalted Allaah, and then said: "To proceed, then whoever worshipped Muhammad, then Muhammad has died; and whoever worships Allaah, then Allaah lives and never dies." Then he recited:

وَمَا مُحَمَّدٌ إِلَّا رَسُولٌ قَدْ خَلَتْ مِن قَبْلِهِ ٱلرُّسُلُ أَفَإِيْن مَّاتَ
أَوْ قُتِلَ ٱنقَلَبْتُمْ عَلَىٰٓ أَعْقَٰبِكُمْ

"Muhammad is but a messenger, messengers have passed away before him. So if he dies or is killed will you turn back from you Religion."

[Soorah Aal-'Imraan (3):144]

إِنَّكَ مَيِّتٌ وَإِنَّهُم مَّيِّتُونَ

"O Muhammad (ﷺ), you will soon die and your people, those who deny you and those who believe - will die."

[Soorah az-Zumar (39):30]

So the people wept severely and knew that he had died. So he (ﷺ) was washed in his clothes out of respect for him. Then he was shrouded in three pure white (cotton) sheets, with no robe or turban being used. Then the people prayed over him separately without a single *imaam*. Then he was buried on the night before Wednes-

وَدِينُهُ بَاقٍ ، وَهَذَا دِينُهُ لاَ خَيْرَ إِلاَّ دَلَّ الأُمَّةَ عَلَيْهِ وَلاَ شَرَّ إِلاَّ حَذَّرَهَا

مِنْهُ وَالخَيْرُ الَّذِي دَلَّ عَلَيْهِ: التَّوْحِيدُ وَجَمِيعُ مَا يُحِبُّهُ اللَّهُ وَيَرْضَاهُ ،

وَالشَّرُّ الَّذِي حَذَّرَ مِنْهُ: الشِّرْكُ وَجَمِيعُ مَا يَكْرَهُهُ اللَّهُ وَيَأْبَاهُ ، بَعَثَهُ

اللَّهُ إِلَى النَّاسِ كَافَّةً وَافْتَرَضَ اللَّهُ طَاعَتَهُ عَلَى جَمِيعِ الثَّقَلَيْنِ: الجِنِّ

وَالإِنْسِ وَالدَّلِيْلُ قَوْلُهُ تَعَالَى: ﴿ قُلْ يَا أَيُّهَا النَّاسُ إِنِّي رَسُولُ اللَّهِ

إِلَيْكُمْ جَمِيْعًا ﴾.

and his Religion remains, and this is his Religion: There is no good except that he guided his *ummah* to it, and no evil except that he warned them against it. So the good that he called them to was *at-tawheed*, and all that Allaah loves and is pleased with; and the evil that he warned against was *ash-shirk* and all that Allaah hates and rejects. Allaah sent him as a Messenger to all of the people, and Allaah made it obligatory upon all of the *jinn* and mankind to obey him. The proof is the Saying of Allaah, the Most High, **"Say, O Muhammad, to all of the people: 'I am the Messenger of Allaah to you all'"**[147] [Soorah al-A'raaf (7)158].

---

day - after the pledge of allegiance was completed for the Caliph who came after him. So may the most excellent praise of his Lord and perfect peace be upon him.

[147] This *Aayah* contains a proof that Muhammad (ﷺ) is the Messenger of Allaah to all mankind. Then the continuation of the *Aayah* makes clear that the one who sent him is the Sovereign of the heavens and the earth, in whose Hand is the granting of life and death. Also that He, the One free of all imperfections, is the one who alone has the right to be worshipped, just as He alone is the Lord. Then He, the Perfect and Most High, orders, at the end of the *Aayah*, that we should believe in this unlettered Messenger and Prophet, and that we should follow him, and states this to be a cause of being guided in knowledge and action: both guidance in the sense of being shown the right way, and in the sense of being granted

وَأَكْمَلَ اللَّهُ بِهِ الدِّيْنَ وَالدَّلِيْلُ قَوْلُهُ تَعَالَى: ﴿ الْيَوْمَ أَكْمَلْتُ لَكُمْ دِينَكُمْ وَأَتْمَمْتُ عَلَيْكُمْ نِعْمَتِي وَرَضِيْتُ لَكُمُ الإِسْلاَمَ دِيْنًا ﴾

Through him Allaah completed the Religion, and the proof is the Saying of Allaah, the Most High, **"This day have I completed your Religion for you, and perfected My blessings upon you, and am pleased with Islaam as your Religion"**148 [Soorah al-Maa'idah (5):3].

---

the success to take and remain upon that way. So he (ﷺ) was a Messenger sent for the guidance of all of mankind and *jinn*.

148 Meaning that his (ﷺ) Religion will remain and persist until the Day of Resurrection. Allaah's Messenger (ﷺ) did not die until he had explained to the *Ummah* everything that it would need in all its affairs. Aboo Dharr, *radiyallaahu 'anhu*, said: *"The Prophet (ﷺ) did not leave any bird that spreads its wings in the sky except that he mentioned some knowledge about it to us"* [Reported in the *Musnad* imaam Ahmad (5/152&163)].

Also a man of the *mushriks* said to Salmaan al-Farsee, *radiyallaahu 'anhu*,: "Your Prophet even teaches you about how to go to the toilet!" He replied: "Yes! He forbade us to face the *Qiblah* (direction of Prayer) whilst defecating or urinating, or that we should clean ourselves with less than three stones, or that we should clean ourselves with a piece of animal dung or a bone." [Reported in *Saheeh Muslim* (Eng. transl. vol. 1, p. 160, no. 504)]. So the Prophet (ﷺ) explained all of the Religion through his sayings, his actions, and his tacit approval, either to begin with, or in response to a question; and the greatest of all the affairs which he (ﷺ) made clear is *tawheed*.

Everything which he ordered is something good for the *Ummah*, with regard to the Hereafter and the worldly life, and everything which he forbade is something evil and detrimental for the *Ummah*, with regard to the Hereafter and its worldly life. So anything that some people are ignorant about and which they claim to be

وَالدَّلِيلُ عَلَى مَوْتِهِ ﷺ قَوْلُهُ تَعَالَى: ﴿ إِنَّكَ مَيِّتٌ

وَإِنَّهُم مَّيِّتُونَ ثُمَّ إِنَّكُمْ يَوْمَ الْقِيَامَةِ عِندَ رَبِّكُمْ تَخْتَصِمُونَ ﴾

The proof that he (ﷺ) died is the Saying of Allaah, the Most High,
**"O Muhammad (ﷺ), you will soon die, and your people - those
who deny you and those who believe will die. Then on the Day of
Resurrection you will all dispute before your Lord until everyone
oppressed receives their right from the oppressor, and Judgement
is established between them in truth"**[149] [Soorah az-Zumar (39):30-
31].

---

unnecessary restrictions in the commands and prohibitions, then this claim is due
only to their deficiency in understanding, their lack of patience, and their weakness in their Religion. Rather the general principle is that Allaah has not placed
any hardship upon us in the Religion, and that the whole of the Religion has been
made easy. Allaah, the Most High, says,

يُرِيدُ اللَّهُ بِكُمُ الْيُسْرَ وَلَا يُرِيدُ بِكُمُ الْعُسْرَ

**"Allaah desires ease for you and does not desire hardship for
you."**

[Soorah al-Baqarah (2):185]

وَمَا جَعَلَ عَلَيْكُمْ فِي الدِّينِ مِنْ حَرَجٍ

**"Allaah has not placed you in any situation of inescapable hard-
ship in the Religion."**

[Soorah al-Hajj (22):78]

مَا يُرِيدُ اللَّهُ لِيَجْعَلَ عَلَيْكُم مِّنْ حَرَجٍ

"Allaah does not desire to place you in difficulty."

[Soorah al-Maaidah (5):6]

So all praise and thanks are for Allaah for the completion of His favour and perfection of His Religion.

149 This *Aayah* shows that the Prophet (ﷺ) and those he was sent to will all die,

وَالنَّاسُ إِذَا مَاتُوا يُبْعَثُونَ وَالدَّلِيْلُ قَوْلُهُ تَعَالَى: ﴿ مِنْهَا خَلَقْنَاكُمْ
وَفِيْهَا نُعِيْدُكُمْ وَمِنْهَا نُخْرِجُكُمْ تَارَةً أُخْرَى ﴾

After death the people will be resurrected,[150] and the proof is the Saying of Allaah, the Most High, **"From the earth We created you, O mankind, and to it We shall return you after death, and from it We shall raise you to life yet again"** [Soorah Ṭaa Haa (20):55].

---

and that they will dispute before Allaah on the Day of Resurrection, and that He will judge between them in truth; and Allaah has not made any way for the unbelievers to triumph over the Believers in the Hereafter.

150 The author, *raḥimahullaah*, makes clear in this sentence that after death the people will be resurrected. Allaah, the Mighty and Majestic, will resurrect them to life, after death, in order to reward or punish them. So this is the result of the sending of the Messengers, that a person should therefore act today for the Day of Resurrection. That being the Day whose terrors are described by Allaah, the Perfect and Most High, and to have fear of that Day. Allaah, the Most High, says,

فَكَيْفَ تَتَّقُونَ إِن كَفَرْتُمْ يَوْمًا يَجْعَلُ
ٱلْوِلْدَانَ شِيبًا ﴿١٧﴾ ٱلسَّمَآءُ مُنفَطِرٌ بِهِۦ كَانَ وَعْدُهُۥ مَفْعُولًا ﴿١٨﴾

"Then how if you have disbelieved can you avoid the punishment of a Day whose terrors will cause children to become grey-haired?! The sky will be rent asunder that day; Allaah's promise will be fulfilled."

[Soorah al-Muzzammil (73):17-18]

This sentence indicates the necessity of *eemaan* in the Resurrection, which the Shaykh proves with two *Aayaat*.

وَقَوْلُهُ تَعَالَى :

﴿ وَاللَّهُ أَنْبَتَكُمْ مِنَ الْأَرْضِ نَبَاتًا ثُمَّ يُعِيدُكُمْ فِيهَا وَيُخْرِجُكُمْ
إِخْرَاجًا ﴾ وَبَعْدَ الْبَعْثِ مُحَاسَبُونَ وَمُجْزِيُّونَ بِأَعْمَالِهِمْ

Also the Saying of Allaah, the Most High, **"And Allaah created you from the dust of the earth, then He will cause you to return to being dust within the earth, then He will bring you forth and restore you to life"**[151] [Soorah Noo<u>h</u> (71):17-18].

After the Resurrection the people will be brought to account and will be rewarded or punished for their actions.

---

151   Meaning that **(a)** Aadam, 'alayhis-salaam, was created from dust of the earth; **(b)** Through your burial after death; **(c)** Through the Resurrection on the Day of Resurrection; and **(d)** This *Aayah* fully corresponds with the Saying of Allaah, the Most High,

مِنْهَا

خَلَقْنَاكُمْ وَفِيهَا نُعِيدُكُمْ وَمِنْهَا نُخْرِجُكُمْ تَارَةً أُخْرَىٰ ۝

"From the earth We created you, O mankind, and to it We shall return you after death, and from it We shall raise you to life yet again"

[Soorah <u>T</u>aa Haa (20):55]

The *Aayaat* with this meaning are very many in number. So Allaah, the Mighty and Majestic, has mentioned and repeated affirmation of the Resurrection to life so that the people should have *eemaan* in it, and so that their *eemaan* should increase, and that they should act for that tremendous Day, concerning which we ask Allaah, the free of all imperfections and the Most High, that He makes us from those who act for it, and who are successful in attaining salvation on it.

قَوْلُهُ تَعَالَى: ﴿لِيَجْزِيَ الَّذِينَ أَسَاؤُوا بِمَا عَمِلُوا وَيَجْزِيَ الَّذِينَ أَحْسَنُوا بِالْحُسْنَى﴾

The proof is the Saying of Allaah, the Most High, **"That He may requite those who did evil and disobeyed Him, and punish them in the Fire for what they did; and that He may reward those who did good and were obedient to Him, with what is best (Paradise)"** [Soorah an-Najm (53):3].[152]

---

[152] Meaning that after the Resurrection the people will be brought to account and repaid for their actions - if they were good, then with good; and if evil, then with evil. Allaah, the Exalted and Most High, says,

فَمَن يَعْمَلْ مِثْقَالَ ذَرَّةٍ خَيْرًا يَرَهُ ﴿٧﴾ وَمَن يَعْمَلْ مِثْقَالَ ذَرَّةٍ شَرًّا يَرَهُ ﴿٨﴾

"So whoever does the weight of the tiniest red ant of good shall see the reward of it in the Hereafter; and whoever does evil of the weight of the tiniest red ant shall see its result in the Hereafter."
[Soorah az-Zalzalah (99):7-8]

وَنَضَعُ الْمَوَازِينَ الْقِسْطَ لِيَوْمِ الْقِيَامَةِ فَلَا تُظْلَمُ نَفْسٌ شَيْئًا وَإِن كَانَ مِثْقَالَ حَبَّةٍ مِّنْ خَرْدَلٍ أَتَيْنَا بِهَا وَكَفَى بِنَا حَاسِبِينَ

"And Allaah will set up the Scales of Justice for the people on the Day of Resurrection, so no soul shall be treated unjustly in the least. Even the extent of a mustard-seed shall be brought by Us and recompensed; and Allaah is fully sufficient as a Reckoner."
[Soorah al-Ambiyaa (21):47]

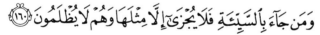

$$\text{مَن جَاءَ بِالْحَسَنَةِ فَلَهُ عَشْرُ أَمْثَالِهَا وَمَن جَاءَ بِالسَّيِّئَةِ فَلَا يُجْزَىٰ إِلَّا مِثْلَهَا وَهُمْ لَا يُظْلَمُونَ ﴿١٦٠﴾}$$

"Whoever meets his Lord on the Day of Resurrection having done a good deed shall have ten times its like in reward, and whoever meets his Lord having done an evil deed, then he will receive only the like of it in recompense, and none shall be treated unjustly by Allaah."

[Soorah al-An'aam (6):160]

A good deed will be rewarded with between ten times its like, up to seven hundred times its like, or many more times - out of Allaah, the Mighty and Majestic's, beneficence and from the bounty He bestows. He, the Majestic and Most High, has bestowed favour by granting that righteous action in the first place, and then has further favoured the person by granting him this huge reward. As for evil actions, then a person who commits a sin does not receive punishment greater than it. Allaah, the Most High, says,

$$\text{وَمَن جَاءَ بِالسَّيِّئَةِ فَلَا يُجْزَىٰ إِلَّا مِثْلَهَا وَهُمْ لَا يُظْلَمُونَ ﴿١٦٠﴾}$$

"And whoever meets his Lord having done an evil deed, then he will receive only the like of it in recompense, and none shall be treated unjustly by Allaah."

[Soorah al-An'aam (6):160]

So this is due to His perfect and complete beneficence and favour. Then the Shaykh mentions as proof for this the Saying of Allaah, the Most High,

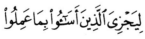

$$\text{لِيَجْزِيَ الَّذِينَ أَسَاءُوا بِمَا عَمِلُوا}$$

"That he may punish those who did evil for what they did."

[Soorah an-Najm (53):31]

He did not say that they would be requited with 'what is most evil', in the same

وَمَنْ كَذَّبَ بِالْبَعْثِ كَفَرَ وَالدَّلِيلُ قَوْلُهُ تَعَالَى:

﴿ زَعَمَ الَّذِينَ كَفَرُوا أَنْ لَنْ يُبْعَثُوا قُلْ بَلَى وَرَبِّي لَتُبْعَثُنَّ ثُمَّ

لَتُنَبَّؤُنَّ بِمَا عَمِلْتُمْ وَذَلِكَ عَلَى اللَّهِ يَسِيرٌ ﴾

Furthermore, whoever denies the Resurrection is an unbeliever, and the proof is the Saying of Allaah, the Most High, **"The unbelievers claim that Allaah will not resurrect them after death. Say to them, O Muḥammad, 'By my Lord you will certainly be resurrected from you graves, and then you will be informed of the deeds which you did in the world. That is easy for Allaah'"**[153] [Soorah at-Taghaabun (64):7].

---

way that He said with regard to the doers of good that they would be rewarded with what is best,

وَيَجْزِيَ الَّذِينَ أَحْسَنُوا بِالْحُسْنَى ﴿٣١﴾

"And that He should reward those who did good with what is best (Paradise)."

[Soorah an-Najm (53):31]

[153] Whoever denies the Resurrection is an unbeliever due to the Saying of Allaah, the Most High,

وَقَالُوا إِنْ هِيَ إِلَّا حَيَاتُنَا الدُّنْيَا وَمَا نَحْنُ

بِمَبْعُوثِينَ ﴿٢٩﴾ وَلَوْ تَرَى إِذْ وُقِفُوا عَلَى رَبِّهِمْ قَالَ أَلَيْسَ هَذَا

بِالْحَقِّ قَالُوا بَلَى وَرَبِّنَا قَالَ فَذُوقُوا الْعَذَابَ بِمَا كُنْتُمْ تَكْفُرُونَ

"The *Mushriks* say: 'There is no resurrection after death, and we will not be restored to life after passing away.' So if you could see, O Mu<u>h</u>ammad, when they stand to be judged by Allaah on the Day of Resurrection and it is said to them: 'Is not this resurrection, that you used to deny, the truth?!' They will say: 'Yes, by Allaah.' So He will say: 'Then taste the punishment for that which you used to deny."

[Soorah al-An'aam (6):29-30]

وَيْلٌ يَوْمَئِذٍ لِّلْمُكَذِّبِينَ ﴿١٠﴾ الَّذِينَ يُكَذِّبُونَ بِيَوْمِ الدِّينِ ﴿١١﴾ وَمَا يُكَذِّبُ بِهِ إِلَّا كُلُّ مُعْتَدٍ أَثِيمٍ ﴿١٢﴾ إِذَا تُتْلَىٰ عَلَيْهِ ءَايَٰتُنَا قَالَ أَسَٰطِيرُ الْأَوَّلِينَ ﴿١٣﴾ كَلَّا بَلْ رَانَ عَلَىٰ قُلُوبِهِم مَّا كَانُوا۟ يَكْسِبُونَ ﴿١٤﴾ كَلَّا إِنَّهُمْ عَن رَّبِّهِمْ يَوْمَئِذٍ لَّمَحْجُوبُونَ ﴿١٥﴾ ثُمَّ إِنَّهُمْ لَصَالُوا۟ الْجَحِيمِ ﴿١٦﴾ ثُمَّ يُقَالُ هَٰذَا الَّذِي كُنتُم بِهِ تُكَذِّبُونَ ﴿١٧﴾

"Woe that Day to the deniers, those who deny the Day of Resurrection: and none deny it except one who transgresses and sins against his Lord in his words and deeds. If Allaah's signs sent down in His Book are recited to him, he says: 'It is just fables written down from the folk of old.' No indeed! Rather the Qur'aan is the Speech of Allaah and His Revelation sent down to His Messenger, and it is just that their hearts are covered and blinded by the blackness of repeated sins and evil deeds. No indeed it is not as those deniers of the Resurrection claim! On that Day they will certainly be prevented from seeing their Lord, then they will enter and be continually roasted in Hell-Fire. Then it will be said to them: This is the punishment that you were told of and which you used to deny,"

[Soorah al-Mutaffifeen (83):10-17]

231

بَل

كَذَّبُوا بِالسَّاعَةِ وَأَعْتَدْنَا لِمَن كَذَّبَ بِالسَّاعَةِ سَعِيرًا ۝

"Rather they disbelieve in the Resurrection and for those who disbelieve in the Resurrection We have prepared a blazing Fire."

[Soorah al-Furqaan (25):11]

وَٱلَّذِينَ كَفَرُوا بِآيَاتِ ٱللَّهِ وَلِقَآئِهِۦ أُوْلَٰٓئِكَ يَئِسُوا مِن رَّحْمَتِى وَأُوْلَٰٓئِكَ لَهُمْ عَذَابٌ أَلِيمٌ ۝

"And those who disbelieve and deny Allaah's signs and deny the meeting with Him on the Day of Resurrection - they will have no hope of My Mercy in the Hereafter, and they will receive an excruciating punishment."

[Soorah al-'Ankaboot (29):23]

The Shaykh, *rahimahullaah*, also quotes as proof the Saying of Allaah, the Most High,

زَعَمَ ٱلَّذِينَ كَفَرُوٓا أَن لَّن يُبْعَثُوا قُلْ بَلَىٰ وَرَبِّى لَتُبْعَثُنَّ ثُمَّ لَتُنَبَّؤُنَّ بِمَا عَمِلْتُمْ وَذَٰلِكَ عَلَى ٱللَّهِ يَسِيرٌ ۝

"The Unbelievers claim that Allaah will not resurrect them after death. Say to them, O Muhammad, by my Lord you will certainly be resurrected from you graves, and then you will be informed of the deeds which you did in the world. That is easy for Allaah."

[Soorah at-Taghaabun (64):7]

As for the convincing proof for those deniers, then it is as follows:

(1) The Resurrection is a matter that is very widely and frequently reported from the prophets and messengers in the Revealed Books, and mentioned in the Revelation sent down, and was accepted by the followers of the messengers. So how can you deny it whilst you accept those reports that reach you from an ancient philosopher, or founder of some ideology or theory, and yet such reports do not reach the level of the former either in strength of the transmission, or in the testimony of reality in its favour?!!

(2) That the Resurrection is a matter whose possibility is witnessed to by the intellect. This is from a number of angles:

(i) Nobody will deny having been created after having been nothing; and that they came newly into existence after not existing. So the One Who created and brought him about after his having been nothing will, without doubt, be able to restore him to existence again. Just as Allaah, the Most High, says

$$وَهُوَ ٱلَّذِى يَبْدَؤُاْ ٱلْخَلْقَ ثُمَّ يُعِيدُهُۥ وَهُوَ أَهْوَنُ عَلَيْهِ$$

"He it is Who originates the creation, then causes it to pass away, then brings them back to life, and that is even easier for Him,"

[Soorah ar-Room (30):27]

$$كَمَا بَدَأْنَآ أَوَّلَ خَلْقٍ نُّعِيدُهُۥ وَعْدًا عَلَيْنَآ إِنَّا كُنَّا فَٰعِلِينَ$$

"We will return the creation on the Day of Resurrection, in the state in which We created them - barefoot, naked and uncircumcised - that is a true promise that We shall certainly fulfil."

[Soorah al-Ambiyaa (21):104]

(ii) Nobody will deny the greatness of the creation of the heavens and the earth due to their huge size and wondrous construction. So it is even more fitting that He who created them both will be fully able to create and then resurrect man. Allaah, the Most High, says,

لَخَلْقُ ٱلسَّمَٰوَٰتِ وَٱلْأَرْضِ أَكْبَرُ مِنْ خَلْقِ ٱلنَّاسِ

"The origination and creation of the heaven and earth is something greater, O people, then the creation of man."

[Soorah Ghaafir (40):57]

أَوَلَمْ يَرَوْاْ أَنَّ ٱللَّهَ ٱلَّذِى خَلَقَ ٱلسَّمَٰوَٰتِ
وَٱلْأَرْضَ وَلَمْ يَعْىَ بِخَلْقِهِنَّ بِقَٰدِرٍ عَلَىٰٓ أَن يُحْـِۧىَ ٱلْمَوْتَىٰ بَلَىٰٓ
إِنَّهُۥ عَلَىٰ كُلِّ شَىْءٍ قَدِيرٌ ۝

"Do those who deny that Allaah will resurrect the dead not know that it is Allaah who created the seven heavens and the earth from nothing, and was not wearied by creating them. Will He not then be fully able to resurrect the dead?! Yes, He is able to, and able to do all things He wills."

[Soorah al-Ahqaaf (46):33]

أَوَلَيْسَ ٱلَّذِى خَلَقَ ٱلسَّمَٰوَٰتِ وَٱلْأَرْضَ
بِقَٰدِرٍ عَلَىٰٓ أَن يَخْلُقَ مِثْلَهُمۚ بَلَىٰ وَهُوَ ٱلْخَلَّٰقُ ٱلْعَلِيمُ ۝
إِنَّمَآ أَمْرُهُۥٓ إِذَآ أَرَادَ شَيْـًٔا أَن يَقُولَ لَهُۥ كُن فَيَكُونُ ۝

"Is not He who created the seven heavens and the earth able to create the like of you from scattered bones after your death?! Say: Yes He is fully able to do that, and He is the One who creates whatever He wills, the One who knows everything about His creation. If Allaah will's to create anything He just says 'Be' and it is."

[Soorah Yaa Seen (36):81-82]

(iii) Everyone with sight can see that the earth becomes barren and its vegetation dies. Then if the rain descends upon it, it becomes fertile and its vegetation is brought to life after having been dead. So the One who is able to give life to the earth after its death is able to resurrect and bring the dead to life. Allaah, the Most High, says,

$$وَمِنْ ءَايَـٰتِهِ أَنَّكَ تَرَى ٱلْأَرْضَ خَـٰشِعَةً فَإِذَآ أَنزَلْنَا عَلَيْهَا ٱلْمَآءَ ٱهْتَزَّتْ وَرَبَتْ إِنَّ ٱلَّذِىٓ أَحْيَاهَا لَمُحْيِ ٱلْمَوْتَىٰٓ إِنَّهُۥ عَلَىٰ كُلِّ شَىْءٍ قَدِيرٌ ﴿٣٩﴾$$

"And from the signs proving Allaah's ability to bring the dead to life is that you see the earth dry and dusty, devoid of plants and crops. Then when Allaah sends down rain upon it the earth swells and puts forth vegetation. Indeed He who brought it to life will certainly bring the dead back to life. Indeed He is fully able to do all things."

[Soorah Fussilat (41):39]

(3) That the matter of the Resurrection is something whose possibility is witnessed to by what is experienced and what occurs - from those cases of the dead being brought back to life, as informed to us by our Lord. So Allaah, the Most High, has mentioned five examples of that in *Soorah al-Baqarah*. From them is His Saying,

$$أَوْ كَٱلَّذِى مَرَّ عَلَىٰ قَرْيَةٍ وَهِىَ خَاوِيَةٌ عَلَىٰ عُرُوشِهَا قَالَ أَنَّىٰ يُحْىِۦ هَـٰذِهِ ٱللَّهُ بَعْدَ مَوْتِهَا فَأَمَاتَهُ ٱللَّهُ مِائَةَ عَامٍ ثُمَّ بَعَثَهُۥ قَالَ كَمْ لَبِثْتَ قَالَ لَبِثْتُ يَوْمًا أَوْ بَعْضَ يَوْمٍ قَالَ بَل لَّبِثْتَ مِائَةَ عَامٍ فَٱنظُرْ إِلَىٰ طَعَامِكَ وَشَرَابِكَ لَمْ يَتَسَنَّهْ وَٱنظُرْ إِلَىٰ حِمَارِكَ وَلِنَجْعَلَكَ ءَايَةً لِّلنَّاسِ وَٱنظُرْ إِلَى ٱلْعِظَامِ كَيْفَ نُنشِزُهَا ثُمَّ نَكْسُوهَا لَحْمًا فَلَمَّا تَبَيَّنَ لَهُۥ قَالَ أَعْلَمُ أَنَّ ٱللَّهَ عَلَىٰ كُلِّ شَىْءٍ قَدِيرٌ ﴿٢٥٩﴾$$

235

"Or did you not consider, O Muḥammad, the one who passed by a town and it was desolate and in ruins. He said: 'How will Allaah give life to this after its death?' So Allaah caused him to die for a hundred years, then raised him to life again. He said to him: 'How long have you remained dead?' He said: 'I have remained for a day, or rather part of a day.' He said: 'Rather you have remained dead for a hundred years. So look at your food and drink - they have not become spoiled through the years; and look at your donkey, how Allaah gives life to it while you are looking on. Thus We have made you a sign for the people, proving the Resurrection. Look at the bones: how We bring them together and then clothe them with flesh. So when this was clearly shown to him he said: I have certain knowledge that Allaah is fully able to do all things."

[Soorah al-Baqarah (2):259]

(4) That wisdom demands that there be a Resurrection after death so that each soul should receive the reward that it has earned for its deeds. If this were not the case, then the creation of the people would be something pointless and worthless and without any wisdom. If this were the case, then there would be no difference in this life between mankind and the animals. Allaah, the Most High, says,

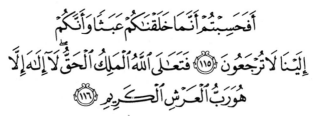

"Do you think that We have created you idly and for no purpose, and that you will not be returned to life after you deaths in order to be requited for what you did in your worldly life?! High is Allaah, the True King, above what they attribute to Him. None has the right to be worshipped but Him, the Lord of the magnificent Throne."

[Soorah al-Mu'minoon (23):115-116]

إِنَّ ٱلسَّاعَةَ ءَاتِيَةٌ
أَكَادُ أُخْفِيهَا لِتُجْزَىٰ كُلُّ نَفْسٍ بِمَا تَسْعَىٰ ﴿١٥﴾

"Indeed the Final Hour is certainly coming, which I keep hidden from all except Myself, in order to reward each soul in accordance with its good or its evil deeds."

[Soorah Taa Haa (20):15]

وَأَقْسَمُوا بِٱللَّهِ جَهْدَ أَيْمَٰنِهِمْ لَا يَبْعَثُ ٱللَّهُ مَن يَمُوتُ بَلَىٰ
وَعْدًا عَلَيْهِ حَقًّا وَلَٰكِنَّ أَكْثَرَ ٱلنَّاسِ لَا يَعْلَمُونَ ﴿٣٨﴾
لِيُبَيِّنَ لَهُمُ ٱلَّذِى يَخْتَلِفُونَ فِيهِ وَلِيَعْلَمَ ٱلَّذِينَ كَفَرُوا أَنَّهُمْ
كَانُوا كَٰذِبِينَ ﴿٣٩﴾ إِنَّمَا قَوْلُنَا لِشَىْءٍ إِذَا أَرَدْنَٰهُ أَن نَّقُولَ
لَهُۥ كُن فَيَكُونُ ﴿٤٠﴾

"Those *mushriks* of Quraysh swear by Allaah with their strongest oaths that Allaah will not resurrect anyone who dies. Rather Allaah will resurrect him to life, this is a true promise that Allaah has made and will certainly be done, yet most of the people do not know. In order that He may manifest to them the truth of that which they disputed about, and that the unbelievers should know that they are the liars. If We wish to create anything then We just say: 'Be' and it is."

[Soorah an-Naml (16):38-40]

زَعَمَ ٱلَّذِينَ كَفَرُوا أَن لَّن يُبْعَثُوا قُلْ بَلَىٰ وَرَبِّى
لَتُبْعَثُنَّ ثُمَّ لَتُنَبَّؤُنَّ بِمَا عَمِلْتُمْ وَذَٰلِكَ عَلَى ٱللَّهِ يَسِيرٌ ﴿٧﴾

$$\text{لَتُنَبَّؤُنَّ بِمَا عَمِلْتُمْ وَذَلِكَ عَلَى اللهِ يَسِيرٌ ۞ وَأَرْسَلَ اللهُ جَمِيعَ}$$

$$\text{الرُّسُلِ مُبَشِّرِينَ وَمُنْذِرِينَ وَالدَّلِيْلُ قَوْلُهُ تَعَالَى: ﴿ رُسُلاً مُبَشِّرِينَ}$$

$$\text{وَمُنْذِرِينَ لِئَلاَّ يَكُونَ لِلنَّاسِ عَلَى اللَّهِ حُجَّةٌ بَعْدَ الرُّسُلِ ﴾}$$

Allaah sent all of the messengers as bringers of good tidings and as warners, and the proof is the Saying of Allaah, the Most High, **"Messengers who were sent with the good news of Allaah's reward for those who obey Allaah and believe in His messengers, and as warner's of Allaah's punishment for those who disobey Allaah and disbelieve in His messengers: so that those who disbelieve in Allaah and worship others besides Him may have no excuse to avoid punishment after the sending of the messengers"**[154] [Soorah an-Nisaa' (4):165].

"The unbelievers claim that Allaah will not resurrect them after death. Say to them O Mu<u>h</u>ammad, by my Lord you will certainly be resurrected from your graves - and then you will be informed of the deeds which you did in the world. That is easy for Allaah."

[Soorah at-Taghaabun (64):7]

If these great proofs are made clear to the deniers of the Resurrection and they then persist in their denial, then it means that they are just haughty and obstinate deniers; and the transgressors will soon come to know their destinations.

[154] The author, may Allaah the Most High have mercy upon him, makes clear that Allaah sent all of the messengers as bringers of good tidings and warner's, as Allaah, the Most High, says,

$$\text{رُّسُلاً مُّبَشِّرِينَ وَمُنذِرِينَ}$$

"Messengers who were sent with the good news of Allaah's reward for those who obey Allaah and believe in His messengers, and as warner's of Allaah's punishment for those who disobey Allaah and disbelieve in His messengers."

[Soorah an-Nisaa (4):165]

They gave glad tidings of Paradise for those who obeyed them, and they warned those who opposed them of the Fire. So the sending of the messengers had very great and wise reasons, from the most important of which - indeed the most important of which - was so that the proof should be established upon the people; so that no excuse remained for them before Allaah after the sending of the messengers, just as Allaah, the Most High, says,

$$لِئَلَّا يَكُونَ لِلنَّاسِ عَلَى اللَّهِ حُجَّةٌ بَعْدَ الرُّسُلِ$$

"So that those who disbelieve in Allaah and worship others besides Him may have no excuse to avoid punishment after the sending of the messengers."

[Soorah an-Nisaa (4):165]

Also from this wisdom is that it is from the completion of Allaah's blessing upon His servants. This is because no matter how fine human intellect is it cannot, on its own reach the details of that which it is obligatory to affirm for Allaah, with regard to the rights that are particular to Allaah, the Most High. Nor can it reach knowledge of those perfect attributes that are to be affirmed for Allaah, the Most High, nor knowledge of His perfect names. Therefore Allaah sent the Messengers, *'alayhimus-salaam*, as bringers of glad tidings and warner's; and with them He sent the Book, in truth, so that they should judge between the people regarding that which they differed about.

So the greatest affair that the messengers, from the first of them: Muhammad (ﷺ), called to was *tawheed*, just as Allaah, the Most High, says,

$$وَلَقَدْ بَعَثْنَا فِي كُلِّ أُمَّةٍ رَسُولًا أَنِ اعْبُدُوا اللَّهَ وَاجْتَنِبُوا الطَّاغُوتَ$$

"We sent a messenger to every nation ordering them that they should worship Allaah alone, obey Him and make their worship purely for Him, and that they should shun everything worshipped besides Allaah."

[Soorah an-Nahl (16):36]

239

وَأَوَّلُهُمْ

نُوحٌ عَلَيْهِ السَّلَامُ وَآخِرُهُمْ مُحَمَّدٌ ﷺ وَالدَّلِيلُ عَلَى أَنَّ أَوَّلَهُمْ نُوحٌ

عَلَيْهِ السَّلَامُ قَوْلُهُ تَعَالَى: ﴿ إِنَّا أَوْحَيْنَا إِلَيْكَ كَمَا أَوْحَيْنَا إِلَى نُوحٍ

وَالنَّبِيِّينَ مِنْ بَعْدِهِ ﴾

The first of them was Noo<u>h</u>, *'alayhis-salaam*, and the last of them was Mu<u>h</u>ammad(ﷺ); and the proof that the first of them was Noo<u>h</u>, *'alayhis-salaam*, is the Saying of Allaah, the Most High, **"We have sent you, O Mu<u>h</u>ammad, as a Messenger with Revelation, just as We sent Revelation to Noo<u>h</u> and the Messengers after him"**[155] [Soorah an-Nisaa' (4):163].

وَمَا أَرْسَلْنَا مِن قَبْلِكَ مِن رَّسُولٍ إِلَّا نُوحِى إِلَيْهِ أَنَّهُ لَا إِلَٰهَ إِلَّا أَنَا۠ فَٱعْبُدُونِ ۝

"We did not send any messenger before you, O Mu<u>h</u>ammad, except that We revealed to him that none has the right to be worshipped except Allaah, so make all of your worship purely for Him."

[Soorah al-Ambiyaa (21):25]

[155] *Shaykh-ul-Islaam* Mu<u>h</u>ammad ibn 'Abdul-Wahhaab, *rahimahullaah*, makes clear that the first of the messengers was Noo<u>h</u>, *'alayhis-salaam*, and then he quotes as proof for that the Saying of Allaah, the Most High,

إِنَّا أَوْحَيْنَا إِلَيْكَ كَمَا أَوْحَيْنَا إِلَى نُوحٍ وَٱلنَّبِيِّـۧنَ مِنۢ بَعْدِهِ

"We have sent you, O Mu<u>h</u>ammad, as a Messenger with Revelation, just as We sent Revelation to Noo<u>h</u> and the Messengers after him."

[Soorah an-Nisaa (4):163]

240

وَكُلُّ أُمَّةٍ بَعَثَ اللَّهُ إِلَيْهَا رَسُولاً مِنْ نُوحٍ إِلَى

مُحَمَّدٍ يَأْمُرُهُمْ بِعِبَادَةِ اللَّهِ وَحْدَهُ وَيَنْهَاهُمْ عَنْ عِبَادَةِ الطَّاغُوتِ

وَالدَّلِيلُ قَوْلُهُ تَعَالَى: ﴿ وَلَقَدْ بَعَثْنَا فِي كُلِّ أُمَّةٍ رَسُولاً أَنِ اعْبُدُوا

اللَّهَ وَاجْتَنِبُوا الطَّاغُوتَ ﴾

Allaah sent a Messenger to every nation, from Noo**h** until Mu**h**ammad, commanding them to worship Allaah alone, and forbidding them from the worship of *at-taaghoot* [i.e. everything that is worshipped besides Allaah], and the proof is the Saying of Allaah, the Most High, **"We sent a Messenger to every nation ordering them that they should worship Allaah alone, obey Him and make their worship purely for Him, and that they should shun everything worshipped besides Allaah"**[156] [Soorah an-Na**h**l (16):36].

Furthermore it is established in the *Sa**h**eeh*, in the *hadeeth* of the intercession: *"That the people will come to Noo**h** and say to him: 'You are the first messenger whom Allaah sent to the people of the earth'"* [al-Bukhaaree (Eng. transl. vol.6, p.198-202, no.236); and Muslim (Eng. transl. vol.1, pp.125-126, no. 373)].

There was no Messenger (*Rasool*) before Noo**h**. We therefore know the error of those historians who say that Idrees, *'alayhis-salaam* came before Noo**h**. Rather what is apparent is that Idrees was from the Prophets of Banee Israaeel. And the last and final Prophet was Mu**h**ammad (ﷺ), as Allaah, the Most High, says,

مَّا كَانَ مُحَمَّدٌ أَبَا أَحَدٍ مِّن رِّجَالِكُمْ وَلَـٰكِن

رَّسُولَ ٱللَّهِ وَخَاتَمَ ٱلنَّبِيِّـۧنَ وَكَانَ ٱللَّهُ بِكُلِّ شَىْءٍ عَلِيمًا ﴿٤٠﴾

"Muh**ammad is not the father of any of your menfolk, but he is the Messenger of Allaah and the final Prophet; and Allaah knows everything that you do or say."**

[Soorah al-A**h**zaab (33):40]

There is no Prophet after him, so anyone who claims prophethood after him is a liar and an unbeliever (*kaafir*) who has apostasised from Islaam.

وَافْتَرَضَ اللَّهُ عَلَى جَمِيعِ الْعِبَادِ الْكُفْرَ

بِالطَّاغُوتِ وَالإِيمَانَ بِاللَّهِ قَالَ ابْنُ الْقَيِّمِ رَحِمَهُ اللَّهُ تَعَالَى: الطَّاغُوتُ

مَا تَجَاوَزَ بِهِ الْعَبْدُ حَدَّهُ مِنْ مَعْبُودٍ أَوْ مَتْبُوعٍ أَوْ مُطَاعٍ

Allaah made it obligatory upon all of the servants to reject and disbelieve in *at-taaghoot*, and to have *eemaan* in Allaah. Ibnul-Qayyim, *rahimahullaah*, said: "*At-taaghoot* is anyone regarding whom the servant goes beyond the due bounds, whether it is someone worshipped, obeyed, or followed."[157]

---

156 Meaning that Allaah sent a Messenger to every nation, calling them to the worship of Allaah alone, and forbidding them from *shirk*, and the proof is the Saying of Allaah, the Most High,

وَإِن مِّنْ أُمَّةٍ إِلَّا خَلَا فِيهَا نَذِيرٌ ﴿٢٤﴾

"And there was no nation except that We sent a warner to them, warning of Our punishment for those who disbelieve."
[Soorah Faatir (35):24]

وَلَقَدْ بَعَثْنَا فِي كُلِّ أُمَّةٍ رَّسُولًا أَنِ اعْبُدُوا اللَّهَ وَاجْتَنِبُوا الطَّاغُوتَ

"We sent a messenger to every nation ordering them that they should worship Allaah alone, obey Him and make their worship purely for Him, and that they should shun everything worshipped besides Allaah."
[Soorah an-Nahl (16):36]

157 Means by this is that *tawheed* will not be established except by worshipping Allaah alone, attributing no share of worship to any besides Him, and by shunning *at-taaghoot*. This is something which Allaah has made obligatory upon the servants. The word *taaghoot* is derived from *tughyaan*, and *tughyaan* means to go

beyond the bounds, as occurs in the Saying of Allaah, the Most High,

$$إِنَّا لَمَّا طَغَا ٱلْمَآءُ حَمَلْنَكُمْ فِى ٱلْجَارِيَةِ$$

"When the water of the flood rose beyond the normal bounds (_taghaa_) We carried you in the Ark."

[Soorah al-Haaqqah (69):11]

Then the best explanation of the usage of the term in the Religion is what Ibnul-Qayyim, _rahimahullaah_, mentions, that _at-taaghoot_ is "Anyone, regarding whom the servant goes beyond the due bounds, whether it is someone worshipped, obeyed or followed." What he means by "someone worshipped, obeyed or followed" is other than the righteous and pious people. As for the righteous folk, then they are not _taaghoots_ even if the evil doers coming after their deaths began to direct worship to them, or if they are followed or obeyed by the people. But the idols which are worshipped besides Allaah are _taaghoots_; and the evil scholars - that is: those who call to misguidance and unbelief, or call to innovation, or to making lawful that which Allaah has forbidden, or forbidding that which Allaah has made lawful, and those who present it as being acceptable - to those in authority - that they should abandon the _Sharee'ah_ of Islaam in favour of systems introduced from outside that are contrary to the system of the Religion of Islaam; then they are _Taaghoots_ since they have gone beyond their bounds. This is because the scholars limit is that he should be one who follows that which the Prophet (ﷺ) came with, because the scholars are truly the inheritors of the prophets. They inherit from them, with regard to their _Ummah_, in knowledge, action, manners, in their call, and in teaching. So if they go beyond this limit and began to present it as acceptable to the rulers that they can move away from the _Sharee'ah_ of Islaam in favour of the like of these systems, then they are _taaghoots_. They have gone beyond what it was binding upon them to restrict themselves to, that they should follow the _Sharee'ah_.

As for his, _rahimahullaah_, saying: "or one obeyed", then what is meant by that is those rulers who are obeyed due to that being required by the _Sharee'ah_, or due to something decreed necessitating that. So the _Sharee'ah_ requires that rulers be obeyed if they command that which is not contrary to the command of Allaah and

His Messenger. In this condition the description of *taaghoot* does not apply to them, and the people should hear and obey them. Obedience to those in authority in this situation, with this condition, is obedience to Allaah, the Mighty and Majestic. So because of this when we carry out what the ruler has ordered, from those matters in which he must be obeyed, we should bear in mind that we are therefore worshipping Allaah, the Most High, through this act and drawing closer to Him through this obedience. Thus our carrying this matter out will be something that draws us closer to Allaah, the Mighty and Majestic. It is fitting that we are conscious of this due to the Saying of Allaah, the Most High,

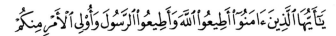

"O you who believe, obey Allaah, and obey the Messenger, and those of you in authority."

[Soorah an-Nisaa (4):59]

As for obedience to rulers due to necessity and something decreed, then if the rulers are strong in their authority then the people will obey them due to the strength of authority they possess, even if they are not motivated to do so by *eemaan*. So it is the case that obedience to the ruler should be due to the motivation of *eemaan*, this is beneficial obedience. This is the obedience that will benefit the ruler and the people also. But obedience may come about because of the rulers authority and strength such that the people fear him and are intimidated by him due to the punishment he metes out to those who oppose him.

Therefore we say that the peoples situations with regard to their rulers vary:
(i) That the motivation of *eemaan* is strong, and the rulers authority is strong - then this is the most complete and highest situation.
(ii) That the motivation of *eemaan* is weak, and the rulers authority is weak - then this is the lowest state and the one most dangerous for the society. It is a danger for the rulers and the ruled since in such a condition there will be anarchy in thoughts, manners and actions.
(iii) That the motivation of *eemaan* is weak, but the rulers authority is strong - then this is a middle level, since if the rulers authority is strong then it will be better for the nation with regard to what is manifest. But if the rulers authority in this case diminishes, then it will result in corruption and evil within that nation.

وَالطَّوَاغِيْتُ كَثِيْرَةٌ وَرُؤُوسُهُمْ خَمْسَةٌ: إِبْلِيْسُ لَعَنَهُ اللَّهُ

The *taaghoot* are many, and their heads are five:158

(i) Iblees - may Allaah's curse be upon him;159

(iv) That the motivation of *eemaan* is strong and the rulers authority is weak. Then the apparent state of this nation will be weaker than the third case, however the peoples connection and obedience to their Lord will be more complete and higher than in the former case.

158 Meaning: Their leaders and those who are blindly followed by them.

159 Iblees is the outcast and accursed Satan to whom Allaah said

وَإِنَّ عَلَيْكَ لَعْنَتِيٓ إِلَىٰ يَوْمِ ٱلدِّينِ ۝

"And My curse is upon you till the Day of Resurrection."

[Soorah Saad (38):78]

Iblees was with the angels, in their company, and performing their actions. Then when he was commanded to prostate to Aadam the foulness, disdain and haughty pride within him was manifested, and he refused, became haughty and became from the unbelievers. So he was cast out from the Mercy of Allaah, the Mighty and Majestic. Allaah, the Most High, says,

وَإِذْ قُلْنَا لِلْمَلَٰٓئِكَةِ ٱسْجُدُواْ

لِءَادَمَ فَسَجَدُوٓاْ إِلَّآ إِبْلِيسَ أَبَىٰ وَٱسْتَكْبَرَ وَكَانَ مِنَ ٱلْكَٰفِرِينَ

"And when We said to the angels: 'Prostrate to Aadam,' they prostrated, but not Iblees - he refused and was proud and was then one of the unbelievers."

[Soorah al-Baqarah (2):34]

245

وَمَنْ عُبِدَ وَهُوَ رَاضٍ،

وَمَنْ دَعَا النَّاسَ إِلَى عِبَادَةِ نَفْسِهِ

وَمَنِ ادَّعَى شَيْئاً مِنْ عِلْمِ الْغَيْبِ

(ii) whoever is worshipped and is pleased with that;[160]

(iii) whoever calls the people to the worship of himself;[161]

(iv) whoever claims to possess anything from the knowledge of the affairs of the hidden and unseen (*al-Ghayb*);[162]

---

[160] Meaning: that he is worshipped besides Allaah, and he is pleased that he should be worshipped besides Allaah, then he is one of the heads of the *taaghoots*, and Allaah's refuge is sought from that, and it is the same whether he is worshipped in his lifetime or after his death, if he dies whilst having been pleased with that.

[161] Meaning: whoever calls the people to worship him, even if they do not do so. He is one of the heads of the *taaghoots* whether the people respond to his call or not.

[162] *al-Ghayb* is whatever is hidden and unseen by man, and is of two types: that which exists at present, and that which lies in the future. What is hidden and unseen in the present is a relative matter: something may be known to one person and unknown to another. But the hidden and unseen of the future is something absolute and not known to anyone except Allaah alone, or to a messenger granted such knowledge by Allaah. So whoever claims such knowledge is an unbeliever, for he has denied what Allaah, the Mighty and Majestic, and His Messenger said. Allaah, the Most High, says,

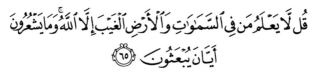

"Say: O Muḥammad, None in the heavens or the earth knows the hidden and unseen, only Allaah knows that, and they do not know when they will be resurrected."

[Soorah an-Naml (27):65]

So since Allaah, the Mighty and Majestic, has commanded His Prophet (ﷺ), to announce to all, that none in the heavens or the earth know the hidden and unseen, and that Allaah alone knows that, then whoever claims knowledge of the hidden and unseen has rejected what Allaah, the Mighty and Majestic, and His Messenger said.

We furthermore say to such people: How is it possible that you know the hidden and unseen when the Prophet (ﷺ) did not know the hidden and unseen?! Are you more noble and excellent or the Messenger (ﷺ)?! So if they say: 'We are more noble and excellent than the Messenger' - then they are unbelievers due to this saying; and if they say: 'He is more noble and excellent,' then we say; Then why was the hidden and unseen concealed from him when you know it?! And Allaah, the Mighty and Majestic, says concerning Himself,

عَـٰلِمُ ٱلۡغَيۡبِ فَلَا
يُظۡهِرُ عَلَىٰ غَيۡبِهِۦٓ أَحَدًا ۝ إِلَّا مَنِ ٱرۡتَضَىٰ مِن رَّسُولٍ فَإِنَّهُۥ
يَسۡلُكُ مِنۢ بَيۡنِ يَدَيۡهِ وَمِنۡ خَلۡفِهِۦ رَصَدًا ۝

"The Knower of the hidden and the unseen, and he does not reveal anything from the hidden and unseen to anyone except to one He has chosen as a Messenger, and He sends angels in front and behind to guard that."

[Soorah al-Jinn (72):26-27]

So this is a second *Aayah* proving the unbelief of anyone who claims knowledge of the hidden and the unseen.

Also Allaah, the Most High, commanded His Prophet (ﷺ) to proclaim,

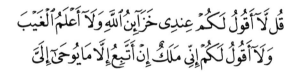

247

وَمَنْ حَكَمَ بِغَيْرِ مَا أَنْزَلَ اللَّهُ:

(v) and whoever judges by other than what Allaah sent down.[163]

"Say, O Mu<u>h</u>ammad: I do not say that I possess the treasures of the heavens and the earth, nor do I say to you that I know the hidden and the unseen, nor do I say to you that I am an angel. I only follow that which Allaah reveals to me."

[Soorah al-An'aam (6):50]

[163] Judging by that which Allaah, the Most High, sent down is from the *tawheed* of Lordship (*ar-Ruboobiyyah*) since it is applying the Judgement of Allaah, which pertains to His Lordship, and His complete sovereignty and authority. Therefore Allaah, the Most High, calls those who are followed upon other than what Allaah, the Most High sent down 'lords' for their followers, so He, the Most Perfect, says,

اتَّخَذُواْ أَحْبَارَهُمْ وَرُهْبَانَهُمْ أَرْبَابًا مِّن دُونِ اللَّهِ وَالْمَسِيحَ ابْنَ مَرْيَمَ وَمَا أُمِرُوٓا إِلَّا لِيَعْبُدُوٓا إِلَٰهًا وَٰحِدًا لَّآ إِلَٰهَ إِلَّا هُوَ سُبْحَٰنَهُۥ عَمَّا يُشْرِكُونَ ﴿٣١﴾

"They have taken their learned men and their Rabbis as Lords besides Allaah, and also the Messiah, the son of Mary. But they were not commanded except to worship Allaah alone. None has the right to be worshipped except Him. How free and far removed is Allaah from the partners they associate with Him."

[Soorah at-Tawbah (9):31]

So Allaah, the Most High, calls those who are followed 'lords' since they are taken as legislators along with Allaah, the Most High, and He called those who followed them their worshippers/devotees due to their having submitted to them and obeyed them in contradiction to the Judgement of Allaah, the Perfect and Most High.

'Adiyy ibn Haatim said to Allaah's Messenger (ﷺ) that they did not worship them, to which the Prophet (ﷺ) said: *Indeed, they used to prohibit lawful things for them, and make lawful that which is forbidden for them, and they followed them - so that is their worship of them.* [Translator: Reported by Aḥmad and at-Tirmidhee and declared *ḥasan* by Shaykh al-Albaanee in Saheeḥ Sunanit-Tirmidhee (no. 2471)].

If you understand this, then know that whoever does not judge by what Allaah sent down, and he desires that judgement should be referred to other than Allaah and His Messenger, then there are *Aayaat* denying *eemaan* for him and *Aayaat* declaring his unbelief, transgression and evildoing. So with regard to the first category:

(i) The Saying of Allaah, the Most High,

أَلَمْ تَرَ إِلَى ٱلَّذِينَ يَزْعُمُونَ أَنَّهُمْ ءَامَنُوا بِمَآ أُنزِلَ إِلَيْكَ وَمَآ أُنزِلَ مِن قَبْلِكَ يُرِيدُونَ أَن يَتَحَاكَمُوٓا إِلَى ٱلطَّٰغُوتِ وَقَدْ أُمِرُوٓا أَن يَكْفُرُوا بِهِۦ وَيُرِيدُ ٱلشَّيْطَٰنُ أَن يُضِلَّهُمْ ضَلَٰلًۢا بَعِيدًا ﴿٦٠﴾ وَإِذَا قِيلَ لَهُمْ تَعَالَوْا إِلَىٰ مَآ أَنزَلَ ٱللَّهُ وَإِلَى ٱلرَّسُولِ رَأَيْتَ ٱلْمُنَٰفِقِينَ يَصُدُّونَ عَنكَ صُدُودًا ﴿٦١﴾ فَكَيْفَ إِذَآ أَصَٰبَتْهُم مُّصِيبَةٌۢ بِمَا قَدَّمَتْ أَيْدِيهِمْ ثُمَّ جَآءُوكَ يَحْلِفُونَ بِٱللَّهِ إِنْ أَرَدْنَآ إِلَّآ إِحْسَٰنًا وَتَوْفِيقًا ﴿٦٢﴾ أُولَٰٓئِكَ ٱلَّذِينَ يَعْلَمُ ٱللَّهُ مَا فِى قُلُوبِهِمْ فَأَعْرِضْ عَنْهُمْ وَعِظْهُمْ وَقُل لَّهُمْ فِىٓ أَنفُسِهِمْ قَوْلًۢا بَلِيغًا ﴿٦٣﴾ وَمَآ أَرْسَلْنَا مِن رَّسُولٍ إِلَّا

لِيُطَاعَ بِإِذۡنِ ٱللَّهِ ۚ وَلَوۡ أَنَّهُمۡ إِذ ظَّلَمُوٓاْ أَنفُسَهُمۡ جَآءُوكَ فَٱسۡتَغۡفَرُواْ ٱللَّهَ وَٱسۡتَغۡفَرَ لَهُمُ ٱلرَّسُولُ لَوَجَدُواْ ٱللَّهَ تَوَّابࣰا رَّحِيمࣰا ۝ فَلَا وَرَبِّكَ لَا يُؤۡمِنُونَ حَتَّىٰ يُحَكِّمُوكَ فِيمَا شَجَرَ بَيۡنَهُمۡ ثُمَّ لَا يَجِدُواْ فِىٓ أَنفُسِهِمۡ حَرَجࣰا مِّمَّا قَضَيۡتَ وَيُسَلِّمُواْ تَسۡلِيمࣰا ۝

"Do you not consider, O Muḥammad, those who claim that they believe in the Book sent down to you and in the Revealed Books sent down before you; those who wish to refer for judgement to *at-ṭaaghoot* [i.e. to other than the Book of Allaah and the *Sunnah* of His Messenger] whilst they were commanded to reject that, and Satan wishes to lead them far astray from the truth. When it is said to them: 'Come to the judgement Allaah has sent down in His Book and the judgement of His Messenger' you see the hypocrites turn away haughty. So how is it then that if some calamity comes upon them due to the sins they have committed they come to you swearing false oaths by Allaah that all they intended was reconciliation and to attain what was good. Allaah knows what is in the hearts of those hypocrites. So turn aside from them and do not punish them, but warn them and cause them to fear Allaah's punishment, and admonish them sternly and privately. And We have not sent any Messenger, O Muḥammad, except that We made it obligatory upon his people to obey him - by Allaah's leave. And if those hypocrites, when they had wronged themselves by earning the great sin of going to other than the Book of Allaah and the *Sunnah* of His Messenger for judgement and of turning away from the Book and the *Sunnah*, had only come to you, O Muḥammad (ﷺ), repentant and had asked Allaah to pardon them, and the Messenger had asked for them to be pardoned, then they would have found that Allaah pardoned and had mercy upon them. But no, by your Lord, none will be Believers until they make you, O Muḥammad (ﷺ), the judge in all matters of dispute between them, then they do not find any resistance in themselves to your judgement, and they fully submit to it outwardly and inwardly."

[Soorah an-Nisaa (4):60-65]

250

So Allaah, the Most High, described those claimants to *eemaan* who were hypocrites with a number of characteristics:

(i) That they desire that judgement should be sought from *at-taaghoot* - and that is everything that is contrary to the Judgement of Allaah, the Most High, and His Messenger (ﷺ) because whatever is contrary to the Judgement of Allaah and His Messenger is a transgression beyond the bound, and is an offence against the Judgement of Him to Whom Judgement belongs and to Whom all affairs return, and that is Allaah. Allaah, the Most High, says,

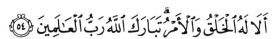

"Indeed all creation and the command are for Him; exalted is Allaah, the Lord of all creation."

[Soorah al-A'raaf (7):54]

(ii) That when they are called to that which Allaah sent down, and to the ...ssenger, they refuse and turn away.

(iii) That when a calamity comes upon them due to the evil they have committed, and it may be that their action has been uncovered, then they come swearing that they only intended good and reconciliation - like the case of those who reject the ruling of Islaam these days and judge by laws contrary to them, claiming that this is something good and in accordance with the modern age.

He, the Most Perfect, warned those claimants to *eemaan* who have these characteristics that He knows what is in their hearts and whatever they conceal, with regard to affairs that are contrary to their Lords.

Then He commanded His Prophet to cause them to fear, and to admonish them sternly in private. The he made clear that the wisdom in sending a messenger is that he should be obeyed and followed; him and not someone else from the people - no matter how strong their thinking and how far-reaching their understanding. Then He, the Most High, swore by His Lordship of His Messenger, that being the most particular and special part of His Lordship, and which contains an indication of the correctness of his (ﷺ) Messengership, He swore by this an emphatic oath that *eemaan* will not be correct except along with three matters:

(1) That judgement in every disagreement be referred back to Allaah's Messenger (ﷺ).

(2) That the hearts welcome and accept his judgement, and that no resistance or dislike is found in their souls towards it.

(3) That there is full submission and acceptance of his judgement, and that it is applied without slackness and without distorting it at all.

(ii) As for the second category, then such as the Saying of Allaah, the Most High,

وَمَن لَّمْ يَحْكُم بِمَآ أَنزَلَ ٱللَّهُ فَأُوْلَٰٓئِكَ هُمُ ٱلْكَٰفِرُونَ

"And whoever does not judge by what Allaah has sent down, then they are the ones guilty of unbelief."

[Soorah al-Maa'idah (5):44]

وَمَن لَّمْ يَحْكُم بِمَآ أَنزَلَ ٱللَّهُ فَأُوْلَٰٓئِكَ هُمُ ٱلظَّٰلِمُونَ

"And whoever does not judge by what Allaah has sent down, then they are the transgressors."

[Soorah al-Maa'idah (5):45]

وَمَن لَّمْ يَحْكُم بِمَآ أَنزَلَ ٱللَّهُ فَأُوْلَٰٓئِكَ هُمُ ٱلْفَٰسِقُونَ

"And whoever does not judge by what Allaah has sent down, then they are the disobedient."

[Soorah al-Maa'idah (5):47]

So are these three descriptions to apply to a single person all at once? Meaning: Is it the case that everyone who does not judge by what Allaah has sent down is one guilty of unbelief, and is a transgressor, and is a disobedient evildoer, since Allaah, the Most High, has described the unbelievers with transgression and disobedience (elsewhere in the Qur'aan), so He, the Most High, says,

$$وَٱلْكَٰفِرُونَ هُمُ ٱلظَّٰلِمُونَ ﴿٢٥٤﴾$$

"And the unbelievers they are the wrongdoers/oppressors."

[Soorah al-Baqarah (2):254]

$$إِنَّهُمْ كَفَرُوا۟ بِٱللَّهِ وَرَسُولِهِۦ وَمَاتُوا۟ وَهُمْ فَٰسِقُونَ$$

"They (the hypocrites) have rejected the *tawheed* of Allaah and the Messengership of His Messenger and have died outside Islaam as evildoers, disobeying the commands and prohibitions of Allaah."

[Soorah at-Tawbah (9):84]

So every Unbeliever is therefore a transgressor/oppressor, and disobedient evildoer.

Or is it that these characteristics are such that each applies to a separate class of person, applying it in accordance with the reason that lead him to leave judging by that which Allaah sent down? This is more correct in my view, and Allaah knows best.

Whoever does not judge by that which Allaah has sent down, whilst mocking or belittling it, or whilst believing that something other than it is better and more beneficial for the creation, or is like it, then he is an unbeliever who has left the Religion. From these are those who lay down systems of law contrary to the Islamic system of laws - in order for that to be a way of life for the people to proceed upon. They do not lay down such systems that contradict the Islamic Sharee'ah except due to their belief that they are better and more beneficial for the creation. This is because it is known necessarily by the intellect and by inborn nature that man does not turn away from one whole way of life to another that is contrary to it unless he believes that the one he turns to is more excellent, and that the one he leaves is deficient. But whoever does not judge by that which Allaah has sent down, but he does not mock it, or belittle it, nor does he believe that something else is better and more beneficial for him, or the like of it, then he is a transgressor and is not an unbeliever. The level of his transgression will vary according to the judgement given and how it was reached.

As for one who does not judge by that which Allaah sent down, but he does not mock or belittle Allaah's judgement, nor does he believe that something other than it is better and more beneficial for the creation, or is like it. Rather he judges by other than it due to bias towards the one in whose favour he passes judgement, or due to having been bribed, or due to other worldly motives - then this is a disobedient sinner and is not an unbeliever. The level of his sin will be in accordance with the judgement given and how it was reached.

Shaykh-ul-Islaam Ibn Taymiyyah, *rahimahullaah*, said, concerning those who took their learned men and their Rabbis as Lords besides Allaah, that they are of two sorts:

(1) Those who knew that they had changed the Religion of Allaah, and yet they followed them upon that distortion; and they believed in the permissibility of forbidden things, and in the forbiddence of things made lawful by Allaah - due to their following their heads, even though they knew that they had gone against the Religion of the Messengers, then this is unbelief and it is declared to be *shirk* by Allaah and His Messenger.

(2) That their belief and their faith in the allowance of forbidden things, and in the prohibition of lawful things - these are the words reported from him - is confirmed, but they just obeyed them in disobedience to Allaah just as the Muslim may commit sins, but whilst believing them to be sins. So they carry the ruling of their like from the people of sin.

There is a distinction between those matters that are counted as a general and universal law, and a particular case about which a judge gives judgement by other than that which Allaah sent down. This is because matters that are considered general and universal laws are not covered by the previous classification. Rather it is from the first category only because this person who is laying down a system of laws contrary to Islaam only lays it down due to his belief that it is better than Islaam and more beneficial for the servants - as has already been indicated.

This affair, i.e. the matter of judging by other than that which Allaah sent down is a very great affair which has become a trial for the rulers of this time. A person should not be hasty in passing judgement upon them with that which they do not deserve, until the truth becomes clear to him, because it is a very dangerous mat-

وَالدَّلِيْلُ قَوْلُهُ تَعَالَى : ﴿ لَا إِكْرَاهَ فِي الدِّينِ

قَدْ تَبَيَّنَ الرُّشْدُ مِنَ الغَيِّ فَمَنْ يَكْفُرْ بِالطَّاغُوتِ وَيُؤْمِنْ بِاللَّهِ فَقَدِ

اسْتَمْسَكَ بِالْعُرْوَةِ الوُثْقَى ﴾

The proof[164] is the Saying of Allaah, the Most High, **"No one is to be compelled to enter the Religion,[165] true guidance has been made clear and distinct from falsehood. So whoever rejects** *at-taaghoot* **(all that is worshipped besides Allaah) - and truly believes and worships Allaah alone,[166] then he has grasped the firmest handhold that will never break"[167]** [Soorah al-Baqarah (2):256]

---

ter, and we ask Allaah, the Most High - to rectify for the Muslims those in authority over them and their advisors. It is also upon a person to whom Allaah has given knowledge that he makes the matter clear to those rulers in order that the proof is established upon them and the truth is clear, and in order that those who go to destruction do so having had the affair made clear to them, and that those who live may do so upon clear proof. One should not belittle himself and so fail to make it clear, nor should he fear any person in that regard for indeed might and honour are for Allaah, and for His Messenger and the Believers.

164 i.e. the obligation of judging by that which Allaah sent down, and for rejecting *at-Taaghoot*.

165 There is to be no compulsion upon people to enter the Religion since its proofs and clear signs are manifest, therefore Allaah says after this,

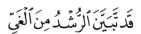

"True guidance has been made clear and distinct from falsehood."
[Soorah al-Baqarah (2):256]

Since true guidance has been made clear and distinct from falsehood, then sincere souls must choose and prefer true guidance to error.

وَهَذَا مَعْنَى لَا إِلَهَ إِلَّا اللَّهُ. وَفِي

الْحَدِيثِ: " رَأْسُ الْأَمْرِ الْإِسْلَامُ وَعَمُودُهُ الصَّلَاةُ وَذِرْوَةُ سَنَامِهِ

الْجِهَادُ فِي سَبِيلِ اللَّهِ

and this is the meaning of *laa ilaaha illallaah* (None has the right to be worshipped except Allaah).

And in the *hadeeth*: *The head of the affair is al-Islaam,*[168] *and its supporting pillar is the Prayer,*[169] *and its highest part is jihaad in Allaah's cause.*[170], [171]

---

166 Allaah, the Mighty and Majestic - mentioned rejection of *at-taaghoot* before mentioning *eemaan* in Allaah because in order for anything to be fully complete everything that stands in its way and prevents it must be removed before establishing it.

167 That is he firmly and fully clings to it, and the firmest handhold is Islaam; and consider how Allaah, the Mighty and Majestic, says: *qadistamsaaka* "**has grasped**" and He did not just say: *tamassaka* "**he has caught hold of**" because *al-istimsaak* "**firmly grasping**" is stronger than *at-tamassuk* "holding on to", since a person may be holding on to something but has not firmly grasped it.

168 What the author, *rahimahullaah ta'aalaa*, intends is to use this *hadeeth* to prove that everything has a head, and the head of the affair that Muhammad (ﷺ) came with is *al-Islaam*.

169 That is because it cannot stand without it, therefore upon the most correct saying one who abandons the Prayer is an unbeliever and is not within Islaam.

170 That is its highest and most perfect part is *jihaad* fought in Allaah's cause. This is because when a person has rectified himself he tries to rectify others by *jihaad* in Allaah's cause in order for Islaam to be established and so that Allaah's Word is the Highest. Whoever fights in order that Allaah's Word is the highest, then he is fighting in Allaah's cause, and it is the highest part since through it Islaam is given ascendancy over everything else.

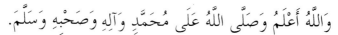

وَاللَّهُ أَعْلَمُ وَصَلَّى اللَّهُ عَلَى مُحَمَّدٍ وَآلِهِ وَصَحْبِهِ وَسَلَّمَ.

And Allaah knows best, and may Allaah extol and send blessings of peace upon Muhammad, his true followers and his Companions.[172]

---

171 Translator: Reported by Ahmad, at-Tirmidhee, and Ibn Maajah, and declared *Saheeh* by Shaykh Muhammad Naasiruddeen al-Albaanee, *hafidhahullaah*, in *Saheeh Sunanit-Tirmidhee* (no. 2110).

172 *Shaykhul-Islaam* Muhammad ibn 'Abdul-Wahhaab, *rahimahullaah*, closes his treatise by referring knowledge back to Allaah, the Mighty and Majestic, and by supplicating that Allaah extol and send blessings of peace upon His Prophet Muhammad (ﷺ).

So with this 'The Three Principles' and that which pertains to it is completed, so we ask Allaah, the Most High, that He grant the best reward to its author, and that He grants us a share of the reward for it, and that He gathers us and him in the final domain where He bestows honour, indeed He is the Generous, the Beneficent Bestower and all praise is for Allaah, Lord of all creation and may Allaah extol and send blessings of peace upon our Prophet Muhammad.

Glossary

Aayah (pl. Aayaat): a Sign of Allaah; a verse of the Qur'aan.

Aayaat: See *Aayah*.

'Abd: worshipper.

Aboo (Abee, Abaa): father of; used as a means of identification.

Adhaan: call to Prayer.

'Alayhis-salaam: "may Allaah protect and preserve him." It is said after the name of a Prophet of Allaah or after the name of an angel.

Ahaadeeth: See *Hadeeth*.

Ansaar: "Helpers"; the Muslims of Madeenah who supported the Muslims who migrated from Makkah.

'Aqeedah: that which binds or that which is rooted in the heart; the principles and details of belief.

'Arsh: Throne.

Barzakh: lit. barrier; the life between the life of this world and the Hereafter (i.e. the period in the grave).

Companions (Ar. *Sahaabah*): the Muslims who saw the Prophet (ﷺ) and died upon Islaam.

Da'eef: weak; unauthentic (narration).

Da'eef Jiddan: very weak; unauthentic (narration).

Da'wah: invitation; call to Allaah.

Deen: way of life prescribed by Allaah i.e. Islaam.

Du'aa: invocation; supplication.

'Eed: a day of festival for the Muslims, there are two *'eeds* every year, one marking the end of Ramadaan and the other in the month of Dhul-Hijjah.

Eemaan: faith; to affirm all that was revealed to the Messenger (ﷺ), affirming with the heart, testifying with the tongue and acting with the limbs. The actions of the limbs are from the completeness of *eemaan*. Faith increases with obedience to Allaah and decreases with disobedience.

Fard Kifaayah: collective obligation - if fulfilled by a part of the community then the rest are not obliged to fulfil it.

Fataawa: see *fatwa*.

Fatwa (pl. Fataawa): religious verdict.

Fiqh: the understanding and application of the *Sharee'ah* from its sources.

Fitrah: the natural disposition that one is born upon..

Hadeeth (pl. Ahaadeeth): narration concerning the utterances of the Prophet (ﷺ), his actions or an attribute of his.

Hafidhahullaah: "may Allaah protect him." Usually said after the name of a scholar who is still alive.

Hajj: Pilgrimage to Makkah.

Halaal: permitted under the *Sharee'ah*.

Haraam: prohibited under the *Sharee'ah*.

Hasan: fine; term used for an authentic *hadeeth*, which does not reach the higher category of *saheeh*.

Hijrah: the migration of the Prophet (ﷺ) from Makkah to al-Madeenah; migration of the Muslims from the land of the disbelievers to the lands of the Muslims.

'Ibaadah: worship; worship of Allaah.

Ibn: son of; used as a means of identification.

Ijmaa': consensus.

'Ilm: knowledge.

Imaam: leader; leader in *salaah*, knowledge or *fiqh*; leader of a state.

Isnaad: the chain of narrators linking the collector of the saying to the person quoted.

Istiwaa: ascending; the ascending of Allaah above the throne.

Jannah: Paradise.

Jihaad: striving and fighting to make the Word of Allaah supreme.

Jinn: a creation of Allaah created from smokeless fire.

Jumu'ah: Friday.

Kaafir (pl. Kuffaar): a rejector of Islaam i.e. a disbeliever.

Khutbah: sermon.

Kufr: disbelief.

Masaajid: see *masjid.*

Masjid (pl. Masaajid): mosque.

Mimbar: pulpit.

Muhaajir (pl. Muhaajiroon/Muhaajireen): One who migrates from the lands of the disbelievers to the land of the Muslims for the sake of Allaah.

Muhaajireen: see *muhaajir.*

Muhaajiroon: see *muhaajir.*

Mushrik: one who worships others along with Allaah or ascribes one or more of Allaah's attributes to other than Him; one who commits *shirk.*

Niyyah: intention.

Qiblah: the direction the Muslims face during prayer (i.e. towards Makkah).

Radiyallaahu 'anhu/'anhaa/'anhum/'anhumaa: may Allaah be pleased with him/her/them/both of them.

Rahimahullaah/Rahimahumullaah: may Allaah bestow His mercy upon him/them.

Ramadaan: the ninth month of the Islamic calendar, in which the Muslims fast.

Saheeh: correct; an authentic narration.

Salaat: prescribed prayer (e.g. the five obligatory prayers); prayers upon the Prophet (ﷺ).

Salaf: predecessors; the early Muslims; the Muslims of the first three generations: the *Companions*, the *Successors* and their successors.

Salafee: one who ascribes himself to the *salaf* and follows in their way.

Shahaadah: to bear witness (that none has the right to be worshipped except Allaah and Muḥammad (ﷺ) is His Messenger); Martyrdom.

Shaykh: scholar.

Shaytaan: Satan.

Sharee'ah: the Divine code of Law.

Shirk: associating partners with Allaah; compromising any aspect of *tawḥeed*.

Soorah: a Chapter of the Qur'aan.

Sunnah: in its broadest sense, the entire *Deen* which the Prophet (ﷺ) came with and taught, i.e. all matters of belief, rulings, manners and actions which were conveyed by the *Companions*. It also includes those matters which the Prophet (ﷺ) established by his sayings, actions and tacit approval - as opposed to *bid'ah* (innovation).

sunnah: an action of the Prophet (ﷺ).

Ṭaaghoot: one who goes beyond the limits (set by Allaah); one who is worshipped besides Allaah and is pleased with it.

Tafseer: explanation of the Qur'aan.

Taqwaa: *"taqwaa* is acting in obedience to Allaah, hoping for His mercy upon light from Him and *taqwaa* is leaving acts of disobedience, out of fear of Him, upon light from Him."

Ṭawaaf: circling the Ka'bah seven times as an act of worship (many ignorant people have begun to circle graves and other such places, this is completely forbidden, being a flagrant violation of the Qur'aan and the Sunnah).

Tawḥeed: Allaah is the only Lord of creation, He alone, is their provider and sustainer, Allaah has Names and Attributes that none of the creation share and Allaah is to be singled out for worship, alone. *Tawḥeed* is maintaining the Oneness of Allaah in all the above mentioned categories. Islaam makes a clear distinction between the Creator and the created.

Umm: mother of; used as a means of identification.

Ummah: "nation"; the Muslims as a group.

'Umrah: the lesser pilgrimage (to Makkah).

Uṣool: the fundamentals.

Waleemah: the wedding feast.

Wudoo': the ablution (ritual washing) that is performed before the Prayer and certain other acts of worship.

Zakaat: charity that is obligatory on anyone who has wealth over and above a certain limit over which a year has passed.